Men and Masculinities

For my daughter, Eleanor,
who no doubt will come to
understand men much better than I

MEN AND MASCULINITIES

KEY THEMES AND NEW DIRECTIONS

STEPHEN M. WHITEHEAD

Polity

First published in 2002 by Polity Press in association with Blackwell Publishers Ltd

Editorial office:
Polity Press
65 Bridge Street
Cambridge CB2 1UR, UK

Marketing and production:
Blackwell Publishers Ltd
108 Cowley Road
Oxford OX4 1JF, UK

Published in the USA by
Blackwell Publishers Inc.
350 Main Street
Malden, MA 02148, USA

A catalogue record for this book is available from the British Library.

Library of Congress Cataloging-in-Publication Data

Whitehead, Stephen (Stephen M.).
  Men and masculinities : key themes and new directions / Stephen M. Whitehead.
    p.   cm.
Includes bibliographical references and index.
  ISBN 0-7456-2466-9 (alk. paper) – ISBN 0-7456-2467-7 (pbk. : alk. paper)
  1. Men.   2. Masculinity.   3. Men – Identity.   I. Title.
HQ1090 .W475 2002
305.31–dc21

2001003767

Typeset in 10.5 on 12.5 pt Sabon
by SNP Best-set Typesetter Ltd., Hong Kong
Printed in Great Britain by MPG Books Ltd, Bodmin, Cornwall

This book is printed on acid-free paper.

Contents

Acknowledgements

No literary project is ever the product of a single person, and this book is no exception. I am very pleased to acknowledge numerous friends, colleagues and family, all of whom supported me and offered guidance at various stages in the writing of this work. The moment when the book started to really take shape in my mind was during my first telephone conversation with Sophie Ahmad, then of Polity. Thereafter, she proved to be the most supportive editor any writer could wish for. As the book moved towards completion I came into contact with numerous Polity personnel, all of whom, without exception, were a pleasure to work with. In particular, I would like to thank Sandra Byatt, Jenny Liddiard, Frances Maher, Pam Thomas, John Thompson, Carolyn Twigg and Ali Wyke.

There are numerous pitfalls lying in wait for men writing critically on masculinity. However, although I have on many occasions fallen into such holes, I acknowledge my debt to Jeff Hearn and Sheila Scraton, both of whom, from early on in my academic writing, provided me with invaluable guidance on researching men and writing about gender.

One of the pleasures of academic writing and being part of the wider academic community is the opportunity to share ideas and thoughts with like-minded individuals, people also struggling with often obscure concepts and ideas. I have been fortunate to share such intellectual journeys with a number of friends and acquaintances. However, I would particularly like to acknowledge the value of the discussions I have had with Randa Alestawanie, Frank Barrett, Mike Dent, Valerie Fournier, Becky Francis, Roy Moodley, David Morgan, Martin Parker, Craig Prichard, Aiden Rankin, Julia Rouse, Sarah Rutherford, Diane Seymoor and Farzana Shain, all of whom, in slightly different ways, have influenced my understanding of social and gender processes.

At some point in the writing of an academic text it becomes necessary to expose the work to a wider critical audience. This can be quite a threatening moment. So I am particularly indebted to Becky Francis, Roy Moodley and Julia Rouse for assisting me over this hurdle by reading and commenting on several chapters as they came to completion. Also, I would like to thank the two anonymous academics who reviewed the first draft of this book. Their comments and observations were very positive, as well as being most useful in indicating some important gaps in the original manuscript.

Although I write about the public and the private in a critical fashion, as a man I am certainly not immune from the temptation to compartmentalize these spheres. Nor, indeed, to channel all my energies into one (the public) at the expense of the other (the private). The person who has most carried the consequences of this dividing is Deborah Kerfoot. I am grateful to her for persevering with me as I have done it, while at the same time providing me with invaluable intellectual support and stimulation.

Finally, I acknowledge the support of Keele University for allowing me the study leave during which this work was completed.

Introduction

All the selfish propensities, the self-worship, the unjust self-preference, which exist among mankind, have their source and root in, and derive their principal nourishment from, the present constitution of the relationship between men and women. Think what it is to a boy, to grow up to manhood in the belief that without any merit or exertion of his own . . . his is by right the superior of all and every one of an entire half of the human race.

John Stuart Mill, *On Liberty and the Subjection of Women*

Every philosophy conceals another philosophy; every opinion is also a hiding-place, every word a mask.

Friedrich W. Nietzsche, *Beyond Good and Evil*

It is not possible to critically engage with men and masculinities without recognizing two factors influencing the lives of every person on this planet. First, the relationship between women and men is not now nor ever has been, in most societies, an equitable one. Second, whatever is spoken of, by and about men, hides other agendas, other philosophies. There are no core truths to men. Once these understandings are established and acknowledged then it is far easier to move on to the harder part, which is to understand how so many males come to believe in their innate superiority over women.

This book provides some routes through the conundrum that is 'man'. As such, it is part of a rapidly growing international study of men and masculinities, now recognized as the *sociology of masculinity*. The depth and breadth of this sociology is staggering. In writing this book I have tried to address, in some detail, all key aspects of this sociology and more besides. This has produced over 700 references. Not all directly relate to masculinities, but enough do to indicate the sheer volume of writings now available on men.

In describing this book as a comprehensive examination of the sociology of masculinity, signalling key themes and new directions in this field, it is necessary, then, to acknowledge its incompleteness. For as I have been putting together each chapter, I have been painfully aware of the gaps, the absences, the unacknowledged writings rapidly coming through from numerous cultural and social sites. Yet to have attempted to include every possible aspect, every key work, would have resulted in a book three times the size and possibly never to be completed.

However, despite its attempt at comprehensiveness, what this book does not concern itself with, other than critically, is 'men's studies'. By that I mean those more populist writings that either portray men as needing to reject feminism (if they are, that is, to 'find themselves'), or ignore feminist theories altogether in their research on men. These issues are discussed in various chapters, especially chapter 2, but long before then the reader will have acquired a sense of my political affiliations in respect of feminism. For I write this book as a profeminist, in the process explicitly aligning the content with feminist agendas. This is not to say that I am in any way superior or substantively different to those men who are not profeminist. Far from it. Like most people, my personal practices are not always, or inevitably, compatible with my political affiliations. Nevertheless, one of the aims of this book is to connect feminist theories with the sociology of masculinity in such a way that it makes attempts at appropriation of this field by non-feminists almost impossible.

Why is this important? Well, as this book clearly reveals, gender remains highly politicized. Consequently, to write of men in a critical or questioning sense is to be inevitably aligned with a larger desire for gender equality – feminism. Such scholarship recognizes that men, for the most part, remain the privileged gender category so succinctly named by John Stuart Mill nearly one-and-a-half centuries ago. While much progress has been made towards gender equity, especially in Western countries, a lot remains to be done. To be sure, feminist thinking is having an enormous influence on the subjectivities of millions of women, and a lot of men. But anyone who believes that a few decades of feminist thought and action is about to overturn centuries of ingrained prejudice, stereotype and discrimination against women is not living in the real world. Certainly, any talk of a post-feminist era is decidedly premature. Perhaps we will move to such an age sometime during this millennium. If so, we will know its appearance by one assessment: that is, the question will be asked to what extent women are valued, worldwide; not just as sexual objects, domestic labour, or less costly industrial labour, but as individuals exercising power across the public and private spheres. If the answer is, from every country and cultural site, 'equal to men', then we will have postfeminism. One does not need to read this book to know that we are a long way from that scenario.

Yet, while it seems to me self-evident that women's rights remain severely limited and constrained by masculinist cultures and maleist attitudes, the idea that men are the ones in crisis has become a popular notion across the Western world. In chapter 2 I explore this phenomenon in some detail. But I would make the point here that we should be wary of talking up a crisis of masculinity. The reasons for this are complex, but they come down to understanding that men are not a predictable, homogenous group, needing to control women and others in order to 'be masculine'; a natural state that, if knocked back, inevitably results in some sort of profound sense of rejection and existential crisis for males. Men are much more complicated than that. First, we should recognize the multiple ways of being a man and the multiple masculinities now available to men in this, the postmodern, age.[1] There can be no prevailing, singular masculinity in crisis. Second, the crisis of masculinity thesis can be used by some to inform a backlash against feminism and women's interests. One outcome of such antifeminist feeling is that it stops many men from coming to recognize that perhaps their traditional, blinkered ways of seeing the world are no longer tenable. Third, although this book argues for seeing men as a political gender category, I also recognize that men, as individuals, are riven with contesting pressures and variables, particularly in respect of class, culture, ethnicity, economics, education, nationhood and sexuality. Finally, men (particularly white, heterosexual, Anglo-Saxon men) control, directly or indirectly, most of the world's resources, capital, media, political parties and corporations. It is difficult to imagine this group in crisis. Though the idea of a crisis can, paradoxically, be quite attractive for such men. For it posits them as victims, thus offering them a new form of validation and identity – as wounded and now under threat.

In fact, a crisis of masculinity (if there could be such a thing) that challenged dominant ways of being male, resulting in men ceasing to behave violently and abusively towards women, children, other men, animals, the earth itself, would be very welcome. However, unfortunately, that particular crisis of masculinity is less visible and barely talked of.

In explicitly associating the sociology of masculinity with feminist scholarship, this book is countering another common discourse at large in the Western world: that feminism is no longer relevant to women's lives. As the writings in this volume reveal, the death of feminism has been much exaggerated. Indeed, feminism, both as scholarship and as a way of looking at and being in the world, is very much alive and kicking. As I undertook the research for this book I was particularly struck by the growth of feminist literature, and associated new feminisms, emerging from the so-called Third World. There are clear indications that it will be in these countries and across these cultures that we will see the fourth wave of feminism coming to prominence in the twenty-first century. This process, one nigh inevitable I suspect, will issue a direct challenge to traditional gender attitudes and dominant masculinities, and do so in ways never before witnessed. Not surprisingly, there are already signs that some groups of men will resist this process, either through recourse to fundamentalist dogma and/or more direct means.

It is realistic to assume, then, that there will always be a need for feminists and feminisms. To believe differently would be to deny that so long as women and men exist there will be personal–political issues between these two gender categories. To be sure, these issues will be culturally specific, and worked out in everyday life in very different, contrasting ways by individuals. However, despite differences across national borders and ethnic groups, the desire for gender justice is of (increasing) concern to millions of women, whatever their race, class or creed.

In the midst of all these fascinating contemporary and future shifts sits masculinity: those practices and ways of being that serve to validate the masculine subject's sense of itself as male/boy/man. But what, precisely, is masculinity? How do we measure it? Can we measure it? Can some men have more of it than others? How does it correlate to class, ethnicity, sexuality? Where does it come from? Can one lose it? How does one know if one has it? As a man, how do I know when I'm performing it? Is it constant, unchanging?

These are compelling questions, of interest not just to sociologists, psychologists, anthropologists and the like, but also to individuals in all societies and cultures. We may never find complete 'answers' to these questions, and, certainly, while this book offers numerous insights into men, it does not seek to suggest the matter is closed. Far from it. The more we delve into men and masculinities, the more is revealed of the complex dynamics of difference, subjectivity, power and identity, weaving their way across the social web. These processes are never fixed and never settled. They are under constant revision, negotiation and movement; in which case the idea that a core masculinity lies deep in men's inner biological state, to be rendered unto the social through men's natural propensities, is just not tenable. Men, and the masculinities they exhibit, are often strange, always variable and inevitably amorphous. Yet men and masculinities are also symbiotically entwined, in so much as they coexist in a political landscape that assumes a natural gender order to things. This order is largely concealed, but also exposed, through discourse – how we speak, think and act as individuals. It is trying to understand these connections – between the illusory character of masculinities, the material consequences of men's practices and the influence of culture/environment on this process – that is at the heart of the sociology of masculinity.

The turn of the millennium appears to be a particularly appropriate moment to cast a critical eye on men. For there are social movements and transformations taking place, beyond the control of any individual or group, that are shaking up gender relations and turning the spotlight on males in ways unimaginable just a few decades ago. This is not to suggest that men have previously been invisible. On the contrary, men, as a gender group, are omnipresent across the social world. Are not men the very centre, the core, the drive, the universal 'mankind'? Certainly, many men have been prone to seeing themselves as such. But is being at the 'centre' the same as being 'visible'? No, for, paradoxically, being at the centre can serve to hide, obfuscate, confuse, obscure. Often we do not see, through any critical lens, that which is most obvious. And this is where feminism comes in. For it is through feminist scholarship that men have been brought, often reluctantly, into the critical gaze. In this respect, men have nowhere to hide now. There are no overarching ideologies or dominant discourses into which men can retreat, claiming the need to find their mythical masculine self. To be sure, many men claim this, but many more look upon such pronouncements with incredulity.

While there were profound political and individual transformations taking place in women's lives throughout the twentieth century, they were not noticed by most men. Men were too engrossed in performing the masculine discourses handed down to them by their fathers and others. They were too focused on making their mark in the public sphere, at the expense of the private. They were too seduced by the media-inspired imagery of men and masculinity, part of a larger gender code idealizing manhood. They were too busy building their particular empires, conquering and controlling others. In short, we were all too busy being men to see that women were moving on.

I am not suggesting that all this constitutes a male crisis, though there are changes afoot around men. It is beyond the scope of this book to suggest where such changes may lead, for there are both positive and negative indicators. It is positive that a larger, feminist-inspired debate has opened up about men and their practices. Yet it is depressing that male violence, men's desire for control of self and others, remains a deep signifier of masculinity for many males. What is for sure is that notions of masculinity are increasingly multiple, rendering traditional forms of being male, if not redundant, certainly marginal. But, as this book argues, men adapt, though do not expect them to stop being men as they do so. And that is the paradox: how to be men, but to be different men; is this possible? It is into this fascinating if confusing gender vortex that this book plunges.

FURTHER READING

Connell, R. W. (1995) *Masculinities*. Cambridge: Polity.

Edley, N. and Wetherall, M. (1995) *Men in Perspective: Practice, Power and Identity*. London: Prentice Hall/Harvester Wheatsheaf.

Kimmel, M. S. (2000) *The Gendered Society*. Oxford: Oxford University Press.

Mac an Ghaill, M. (ed.) (1996) *Understanding Masculinities*. Buckingham: Open University Press.

Renzetti, C. M. and Curran, D. J. (1999) *Women, Men, and Society*. Boston: Allyn and Bacon.

Whitehead, S. M. and Barrett, F. J. (eds) (2001) *The Masculinities Reader*. Cambridge: Polity.

1
Masculinity – Illusion or Reality?

In what might be termed the 'everyday world', those behaviours of males that are violent, dysfunctional and oppressive are frequently excused or explained away as 'natural' masculine behaviour, being understood in common-sense terms as fixed and, thus, as an inevitable aspect of social 'reality'. A key aim of feminism is to critique and destabilize such notions, the ultimate intention being to challenge those practices and beliefs that contribute to sustaining men's power (Charles and Hughes-Freeland, 1996). Likewise, central to the sociology of masculinity is a desire to name, examine, understand and hopefully change those practices of men that hinder or confront the possibility of gender equity (Connell, 1987; Hearn, 1992; Kimmel, 2000). In this respect there is, an important personal–political dimension to such study, for as an arm of feminist scholarship the critical study of men and masculinities cannot, indeed should not, claim 'neutrality' (Canaan and Griffin, 1990). However, as this book will explore, a number of tensions then arise for critical gender theorists, one of which occurs in the attempt to reconcile or straddle the nature–nurture dualism. The dilemma is in how far to go in seeing women and men as biologically inspired gender categories, albeit with material and epistemological differences, or in deconstructing the terms 'men' and 'women' from any biological or essential basis – in so doing possibly losing the sense of men as a political grouping with particular power effects (for discussion, see Assiter, 1996; Ramazanoglu, 1993; also Segal, 1997, 1999). In short, how much of masculinity is (cultural) illusion, and how much is (material) reality?

Any critical study of men and masculinity invariably comes back to this relationship between the amorphous character of masculinity and those behaviours of males considered problematic or dysfunctional. In examining the issue, this chapter will open with a discussion of the debates surrounding the biological basis of masculinity. Following a brief examination of the historical variability of dominant social understandings of masculinity, the chapter will consider some of the earliest theoretical influences on the sociology of masculinity, particularly those emerging out of sex role theories and psychoanalytic scholarship, specifically the writings of Freud and Jung. These areas of study have long been influential across feminist and profeminist scholarship, especially so in respect of second-wave feminist theories. While there were few studies critically examining men's practices and experiences prior to the late 1970s, the 1980s was a very significant period for the emergent sociology of masculinity. For it was during this decade that the political and theoretical framework was laid that was to inform much of the future research. However, while many of the writings on men during this period attempted to deconstruct masculinities from any given biological basis, much of the ensuing theory often unproblematically located men and women as unitary identities. In critiquing this perspective, the chapter will emphasize the multiplicity of masculinities, while also recognizing that men's behaviours have a material (often violent) and political actuality, though not one based in biology.

Men's nature, men's history

Natural men?

There is little that is more subject to heated speculation, myth, ideology and misinterpretation, by 'experts' and others, than the debates surrounding nature, nurture and the so-called natural behaviours of women and men. One does not have to look too closely at the fabric of the social web to see that common-sense understandings of natural gender difference play a central role in maintaining power differentials, accessing material wealth, limiting/enabling lifestyle choices, and, probably most importantly, structuring language itself. For example, merely talking about women and men as distinct entities contributes to maintaining the nature–nurture dualism underpinning our understanding of 'reality' and our individual place within it (Petersen, 1998). Gender stereotypes are rooted in dualisms such as passive/assertive, strong/weak, irrational/rational, gentle/forceful, emotional/distant (Archer and Lloyd, 1985; Edley and Wetherall, 1995) and, as such, form a significant part of our everyday language and understanding. Without wishing to discount the importance of class, ethnicity, race and cultural capital, our sex/gender identity is probably most central to how we see ourselves and how others see us: it transcends all cultural boundaries, is not limited by access to wealth or education and is, other than via the surgical and legal processes of gender reassignment, unchangeable.[1] Yet despite the importance of sex/gender in configuring social and individual experiences, little critical analysis was undertaken on this subject until feminists themselves brought it to the fore in the middle part of the last century. In one respect, this absence of critical enquiry is hardly surprising given that men dominated much of the knowledge production in Western societies up until the latter part of the twentieth century. As feminists and profeminist men have noted, there is little obvious motivation for men to critique themselves either as individuals or as a gender group (for discussion, see Hall, 1990; Hearn, 1994; Heath, 1987). It was this relative absence of women in the production of knowledge that enabled malestream discourse to become so prominent and powerful (O'Brien, 1983).

In developing the sociology of masculinity, critical gender theorists have been forced, then, to confront many powerful myths. These include the notion that gender is destiny; the belief that men are natural knowledge holders; the understanding that women are marginal to 'his'story; and the idea that a traditional gender dichotomy is a natural state and contributes to a 'healthy' society. Such ideologies and myths are rarely absent from any society or any culture (Gilmore, 1990; Hess and Ferree, 1987; Ortner and Whitehead, 1981), and at any one time individuals and institutions will be reproducing such myths, often without being fully aware of doing so. Beyond the world of critical gender theory, research purporting to 'prove' a fundamental biological basis to sex and gender differentials continues apace, attracting much media interest (for example, Pinker, 1998; Wright, 1995). One attraction of such research, for the

layperson at least, is that it seems to speak to a readily understand-
able, accessible and common-sense version of an otherwise highly
complex reality. Consequently, the media quickly pick up on such
accounts without, however, the desire or capacity to critically deconstruct the notions being presented as 'truths'. Examples of such reductionist thinking in terms of gender differences are numerous, but are
especially apparent in the works of sociobiologists, evolutionary psychologists and some geneticists. In recent decades, researchers into
the biological basis of gender have attempted to prove sex differences
in brain functioning (Moir and Jessell, 1989); suggest that all sexual
behaviour can be reduced to a 'sperm war' (Baker, 1996); posit
people as 'robots' programmed to perpetuate genes (Dawkins, 1976);
explain male violence in terms of an 'aggressive gene' (Monaghan and
Glickman, 1992); suggest that feminism 'denies female nature'
(Brand, 1996); and provide an evolutionary 'explanation' for rape
(Palmer and Thornhill, 2000) and male infidelity (Wright, 1995). In
a reversal of the biology-as-destiny thesis, some evolutionary
psychologists argue for understanding human psychology as unitary,
universal and fixed not in nature, but in deeply inscribed cultural,
gendered behaviours and attitudes rooted in the Pleistocene; an
inevitable 'human psychological architecture' (Tooby and Cosmides,
1992: 48).

In short, according to these and similar studies, the 'key to masculinity' (and femininity) (Lahn and Jegalian, 1999) lies either in our
genetic/hormonal make-up or in prehistory. Either way, whichever
perspective one chooses, the fundamental premise is the same: our
gender (and race, IQ, psychology and so on) is fixed, universal,
inevitable and, thus, beyond our control. Yet despite the continuing
proliferation of Darwinian-inspired research and populist writing
contributing to the misperception that 'women are from Venus, and
men from Mars' (*pace* Gray, 1999), the evidence for biologically
grounded sex/gender differences is neither convincing nor conclusive,
nor even coherent (see for discussion Bateson and Martin, 2000;
Clare, 2000; Edley and Wetherall, 1995; Henriques et al., 1984; Hess
and Ferree, 1987; Rogers, 2000; Rose and Rose, 2000a; Segal, 1999).
As Rogers (herself a neuroscientist) observes, even hormones, the
usual suspects in any nature–nurture debate, are not unaffected by
environment factors. Similarly, Clare discusses in some detail the
ambiguous relationship of testosterone to male aggression, noting
that while numerous studies 'show a *correlation* between levels of

aggression and levels of testosterone, there is more than one explanation for such a correlation' (2000: 22; original emphasis). This leads to the question of how to explain aggression in individuals with very little testosterone, such as prepubertal boys? As Marilyn Strathern argues, a baby/child is simultaneously biological and social, it is not simply one or the other (Rose, 2000: 119). Women and men have a biological dimension to their sense of reality and formation of subjectivity; not least, as is discussed in chapter 6, through their experience of being *embodied* agents/actors in the social world. But biology is not destiny, and to take it as such is to slip into dangerous assumptions about human potential. As Hilary and Steven Rose put it:

> For evolutionary psychologists, everything – from men's propensity to rape to our alleged preference for grassy scenery – derives from our mythical origin in the African savannah. In its prioritising of explanations of, for instance, rape as a device for sexually unsuccessful men to propagate their genes, it is completely unable to explain why most men do not rape. . . . We argue that the theory's all-embracing soundbites are for the most part not just mistaken, but culturally pernicious [not least because] these new fundamentalists assert that their view of human nature should inform the making of social and public policy. (Rose and Rose, 2000b)

As the Human Genome Project[2] reveals, the approximately 30,000 genes that make up the human being are insufficient to account for the complexity and diversity of human life. Moreover, the relatively small number of genes we each have may be biologically fixed, but their expression as social action is subject to environmental conditions and external contingencies. The individual is neither passive in the face of his/her genetic make-up, nor, indeed, simply an empty vessel to be filled with ideological material. To suggest otherwise borders on the arrogant, and is at best a blinkered view of human diversity and potential. As Rose and Rose suggest, biologically reductive explanations not only tend to reflect conservative values and forces; they assume that what appears 'real' in terms of human behaviour is what ought to be. This ideological stance produces a form of (gendered) knowledge that is itself then co-opted as 'evidence' for social policy. The reductionists purport to objectively examine the world, but do so from a gender-blind perspective that takes the status quo at a single point in time as given (also Rogers, 2000). The idea that behaviour cannot alter as a consequence of environmental changes is clearly a misreading of human past and a foreclosing of human possibilities. Such a perspective is untenable in the light of the rapidity and skill with which humans have colonized every corner of the world, are on the verge of colonizing other worlds and yet continue to act in diverse, unpredictable, and often illogical and irrational ways. There are no set patterns of predictable, biologically given human behaviours from which we can assume certainty, though I accept that attempts to construct these can be a 'comfort blanket' when faced with human irrationality.

Whether it be altruism, aggression, alliance or accommodation, the human subject acts in ways that are not, in every instance, reducible to either survivalism or an instrumental pursuit of power. A key aim of this book is to argue that cultural environments are not 'out there', somehow existing external to the individual, but are (in)formed by individual subjects, though not necessarily in cognitive fashion. In the very moment that individual action impacts on the social, so a cultural environment is created – local and temporary as it might be. It is this (discursive) moment that is, I suggest, key to understanding something of the complexities of gender relations – and of men and masculinities.

One way of appreciating the continued attraction many have towards simplistic explanations for gender differentials is to recognize that the sheer unpredictability and uncertainty that surrounds us makes 'readily available answers' to complex questions highly seductive. Every culture, through each generation, seems to be inevitably required to develop new responses to the changing and inherently insecure environment in which it is situated; a constant reworking of 'reality' that is no less apparent in Western[3] countries at the turn of the millennium. Indeed, it can be argued that the psychological and existential impact of the millennium has itself significantly contributed to the sense of movement and discord that many commentators note to be pronounced at the end of the twentieth century (for example, Fukuyama, 1997; also, Castells, 1998; Bauman, 1997). An important characteristic of the millennium *Zeitgeist* is the sense that gender relations are undergoing some important and profound reshaping by forces that are only partly understood. One result of such movement is the increased attention being given to the concept of masculinity and, not least, to men's own sense of being men

(Faludi, 1999). It is an interesting time, then, to be a sociologist – of either gender. For not only is sociological enquiry being undertaken during a period of intense change, sociologists themselves are also implicated in these discursive transformations. As some feminist scholars have noted, there is no individual who stands outside of the social dynamics that she/he purports to analyse and comment on (Stanley and Wise, 1993; also Game, 1991). Recognizing this raises interesting issues surrounding research methodology, particularly for feminists and profeminist men, and these issues will be explored in more depth in the following chapter. However, in terms of attempting to locate current social movement in a wider context, while reminding oneself of the fact that change is the only constant in the social, much use can be gained by a focus on the historical. Thus in addressing the questions surrounding masculinity as biology and destiny, a glance at the changing nature of the language and cultural representations informing 'men' can be enlightening.

Masculinities in history

While the term 'masculinity' has achieved a remarkable pre-eminence across the cultural landscape, it has been in use only since the mid-eighteenth century, originating out of the Latin word *masculinus* (see Petersen, 1998). By contrast, the terms 'manly' and 'manliness' were part of everyday vocabulary during Victorian and Edwardian periods. Newsome (1961), for example, describes the relationship that 'being manly' had to notions of godliness and Christian virtue during the nineteenth century and early 1900s. Such exhibitions of manliness, which were clearly defined in terms of class and social standing, might come in the form of 'straightforwardness, manly simplicity, openness and transparent honesty', all somehow combined with a stoical endurance and intellectual energy (ibid., 1961: 195). Or, influenced by the 'muscular Christian' school of Charles Kingsley and Thomas Hughes, manliness in the Victorian and Edwardian eras was to be more openly 'not feminine', and more directly associated with physical strength, muscularity, physical trial, denial (of luxury) and 'endurance in the face of death and torment' (Newsome, 1961: 198). Although by the end of the nineteenth century an idealized version of masculinity – encompassing physicality, virility, morality and civility – had emerged to some prominence (see Mosse, 1996), there was no one clear and absolute definition of what being a man meant. As today, the notion of manliness was always open to conscription by those with wider, possibly ideological, agendas – for example, politicians, church leaders, the military. Nevertheless, there is a sense that a century or so ago manliness was perceived as less fluid, less amenable to individual interpretation, and, importantly, something to be openly strived for and welcomed as an achievement of male maturity (Roper and Tosh, 1991).

These Victorian and Edwardian views of 'the male' are not only class and culture specific; they also sit in marked contrast to dominant gender perspectives of even earlier times. For example, the aristocratic Renaissance man of the sixteenth century – the class that 'set the pace and standards of that century' (Armitage, 1977: 48) – was typified by King Henry VIII himself. Here was a man, the very 'symbol of English nationhood' (ibid.: 49), ruthless and at times brutal, who also displayed an overtly emotional side. He danced, played instruments, sang and composed, and like many men of that period, was apparently not averse to displaying his deeper emotions and feelings. Man as a complex combination of emotional, sentimental, foppish beau and militaristic aggressor reached an apex in the subsequent Elizabethan age, when it was fashionable for males to dress in extravagant, diverse and outlandish garments, eclipsing women in their 'sartorial splendour' (ibid.: 50). Such displays, which served to connect manliness with an emotive exhibitionism and hedonism, became less fashionable, if not reversed, in Europe under the class-based puritanical surveillances of the late seventeenth and eighteenth centuries (Mosse, 1996). As Kingsley Kent describes it:

> ... [this] aristocratic, rakish vision of masculinity would [come to] prove incompatible with the values and outlook of a fast-growing bourgeoisie. Their greater confidence in their social position, and their predominance in the life of the nation as a consequence of vast economic expansion, would render them capable of insisting on and imposing a *reform of manners on men and women that dramatically transformed the way men and women looked, behaved, thought, and interacted in the eighteenth century.* (1999: 30; my emphasis)

It is possible, then, to look back on the various terms and descriptions being used in earlier periods to describe 'a man' and see something of the malleability of masculinity. Far from being a naturally given attribute, masculinity/manliness is revealed as historically variable and subject to change within and across social groupings. Moreover, as many scholars note (for example, Mangan and Walvin, 1987; Newsome, 1961; Roper and Tosh, 1991; Sinha, 1999), there are evident ideological and political struggles connected to the metamorphosis undertaken by the concept of manliness, particularly during the Victorian and Edwardian eras. For example, notions of 'neo-Spartan virility, hardness and endurance' (Mangan and Walvin, 1987: 1) can be traced back to the needs of the British Empire during the late 1880s and leading up to the First World War (see also Dawson, 1991). Similarly, connecting manliness to intellectual endeavour and educational achievement (Newsome, 1961), industrialism and the Protestant work ethic (Morgan, 1992; Roper, 1994), Victorian middle-class paternalism (Mangan, 1981; Mosse, 1996; Tosh, 1991), Christian virtue (Mangan and Walvin, 1987; Walker, 1991) and 'fixed' definitions of race and nationhood (Carby, 1998; Kingsley Kent, 1999; Rutherford, 1997) signals a warning to all gender theorists that notions of 'men and masculinity' are always likely to remain, to some extent, idealized products, representative of both the social conditions of the time and dominant ideological or discursive 'truths'.

To emphasize the variability of masculinity it is only necessary to briefly consider which practices, imagery and symbols best represent 'manhood' at the turn of the millennium: from the 'gym queens' to suited politicians, from Boy George to Arnold Schwarzenegger, from the ageing leathered 'biker' to the ageing hippy 'drop-out', from the gun-toting male LA (or Manchester) gang member to the male nurse, from Rupert Murdoch to the black 'rapper', from 'Masters of the Universe' (*pace* Wolfe, 1987) to the male charity worker, from the Muslim cleric to the atheist househusband, from Mike Tyson to Danny Glover, indeed, from profeminist man to the Christian 'promise keepers' – each is 'real' in its local cultural setting, yet none is able to capture, in any absolute sense, modern masculinity. One important reason for this, as this book suggests, is that no such thing as 'modern masculinity' exists, certainly not in any fixed or predetermined form and as a definite standard for all males to follow. To be sure, there are numerous media-inspired images of 'masculine perfection' (Pope, Phillips and Olivardia, 2000), but for most men such images remain plastic and, thus, distant. As was suggested in the introduction, it is now more appropriate to talk of postmodern masculinities, a term that allows us to recognize the influence globalization is having upon ways of being a man, while also highlighting the contingency of masculinities and differences between men in terms of class, race, ethnicity, sexuality and so on (for discussion, see Gutterman, 2001).

It is evident that without a historical perspective as a point of reference, masculinity might appear as some constant, solid entity, embedded not only in the social network but in a deeper 'truer' reality. Yet while recognizing the fluidity of masculinity, the question remains as to what extent masculinity is simply a by-product of social and cultural change. For the issue of (male) power can never be removed from the debates surrounding masculinity. Despite the historical evidence revealing the fluidity of descriptions such as manliness, manly and masculinity, the material actualities that surround gender differentials remain depressingly constant. Of course, as is discussed in chapter 3, power can be understood in numerous ways, and one of these is in terms of social and cultural pressure to conform to, for example, gender-appropriate behaviour. And it was this rather limited perspective of power with which the earliest critical studies of men and masculinity attempted to grapple. In so doing, not surprisingly, they tended to draw on and be influenced by the dominant academic theories of the time, which during the 1950s was, most notably, Parsonian structural functionalism. Without engaging from a critical perspective, or indeed, a historical one, the enquirer might be tempted to fall into the trap of seeing masculinity, as many Victorians and Edwardians did, as biologically given: unassailable, singular, discrete and containing natural models of best practice. As has been discussed, at the end of the twentieth century such notions are increasingly untenable, and not only in Western societies, for one advantage of global media and research is that they expose something of the diversity of masculine representations worldwide (see for discussion Cornwall and Lindisfarne, 1994; Craig, 1992; Gilmore, 1990; Mirande, 1997; Nixon, 1997; Sweetman, 1997). As will now be discussed, for critical gender theorists the process of engagement with and subsequent disengagement from functionalist perspectives took place through the 1950s and 1960s, when it became increasingly apparent in America and other countries that male socialization, far from being a 'natural' process towards a 'good model', was fraught with tensions, disruptions and oversimplifications.

Functionalism and the male sex role

Gender and functionalism

Talcott Parsons was one of the most prominent sociologists of the 1950s, and his concept of 'functionalism' became a key tool in 'understanding' how the social web maintained some sense of order, equilibrium and consensus despite ever-present potential conflicts over, for example, material resources (Parsons, 1951). Parsons placed great emphasis on the processes of 'socialization', particularly in respect of the family as a 'factory' for the production of 'stable adult personalities' (Parsons and Bales, 1955; Parsons, 1969). Central to this concept were the roles of men and women, seen by functionalists as naturally different but complementary. Parsons argued that inequality of power between women and men was a natural phenomenon, one that arose as a consequence of necessary social stratification. The divisions of labour and resources, which are manifest across the public and private spheres, are understood, in functionalist terms, to result from the collective goals and identities of various groups. For society to remain effective and orderly, there is a functional prerequisite that dictates that the allocation of tasks and roles must go to those most suited to execute them (see also Davis and Moore, 1967). Thus the surgeon (stereotypically rational, reasoned, unemotional and distant) must be male, while the nurse (stereotypically caring, compassionate, maternal and emotive) must be female. At a wider level it becomes seen as natural for men to be breadwinners and women to be homemakers. Functionalism did not invent the gendered dichotomy; it did, however, attempt to justify and explain the inequalities that arise from it by presenting them as naturally occurring phenomena and, thus, necessary for the smooth operation of the social system.

The idea that women and men function as socialized beings at some subliminal but essentially biological level for the wider benefit of an 'ordered society' is, for many, a compelling and seductive notion. It engages with a view of society as fundamentally harmonious, conflict being minimalized so long as individuals come to 'learn the normative standards of society' (Lee and Newby, 1984). This perspective is reinforced by Durkheim (1957, 1961), another prominent sociologist to connect social order with human nature. He argues that socialization is the means by which the greater needs of society are transmitted through generations. Social stability occurs in the 'collective conscience' of common belief systems. Social obligation, and the coercive properties of moral codes, have a compelling impact on the personalities and behaviours of individuals, the result being integrated social units. At this point, the relationship between functionalism and role theory becomes quite apparent. However, unlike functionalism, which has experienced a significant decline since the 1960s, role theory continues to exert a powerful influence across both sociology and psychology, influencing a variety of perspectives – for example, symbolic interactionism (Blumer, 1969), Marxism (Dahrendorf, 1973) and social interactionism (Goffman, 1970; Hargreaves, 1967).

Role theorists argue that people are compelled to perform culturally prescribed roles for the benefit of both society and themselves (Komarovsky, 1950; Linton, 1945; Mead, 1934). In so doing, individuals are seen to be engaged in a theatrical-like performance, one that requires them to learn lines, assimilate behaviours and display appropriate social behaviours in a multitude of settings. As actors on the (social) stage (Goffman, 1959) women and men benefit from the sense of belonging that accrues from the recognition that their role performance triggers membership of a given collective. Conversely, for individuals to act in ways that undermine the social – being 'antisocial' – brings forth approbation and various forms of censure. This process of socialization acts as a conveyor, (re)producing 'ideal' models of behaviour and transmitting dominant stereotypes. When such perspectives are allied with the gender dichotomy and notions of biological difference, then what emerges is a variation of role theory – sex role theory.

Perspectives on sex/gender roles

As a by-product of functionalism and role theory, sex role theory emerged to prominence in the early 1950s, in part spurred on by the impact of the social and economic transformations being felt throughout the Western world. These social shifts were seen by many, especially in America, to have profound consequences for men, particularly in respect of changing patterns of work, the increase in divorce and unemployment, and the demise of traditional industries.

Thus, sex role theory was enlisted to give some insights into, and make sense of, the changing roles of men and women and the new expressions of masculinity being acted out and 'forced on' men following social changes arising at the end of the Second World War (Pleck, 1976). Prior to the 1950s little had been written about men and masculinity, at least in a questioning or critical sense. This started to change as, first, feminist thinking developed, inspired particularly by Simone de Beauvoir's classic text (1973, [1953]), and, second, the first stages of the 'disorganization' of capitalism (Lash and Urry, 1987) began to be felt across the industrialized world. What had hitherto been understood as positive, fixed and concrete – masculinity – quickly took on the appearance of being a problem. In one of the earliest articles on the subject, Hacker (1957) argued that male socialization had become fraught with uncertainty as men were increasingly expected to show more feminine traits, such as emotional expression, while maintaining their 'natural' instrumental functions. Similarly, Hartley (1959) described the pressures and tensions surrounding the male socialization of boys; absent fathers; the rejection of the feminine; and the limitations of dominant models of masculinity. Far from being a natural, functionalistic process, the acquisition of 'appropriate' models and codes of gender behaviour began to be seen as fundamentally damaging for both females and males. Moreover, the recognition slowly dawned that gender socialization was not a pregiven and predictable process. The possibility, indeed the likelihood, of change within gender roles and expectations was apparent.

In a matter of just a few years from the late 1960s men and male culture came under critical scrutiny in a way seldom witnessed prior to this. Pleck (1976, 1981), David and Brannon (1976), Fein (1978) and Fasteau (1974) were just a few of the writers openly questioning the 'hostile, devouring (male) culture in which men must adopt an aggressive stance toward the world in order to survive' (Pleck, 1976: 262). Influenced by a burgeoning feminist critique of patriarchy and dominant patterns of gender socialization (see Tong, 1993), men writers began to publish numerous critiques of the 'male sex role identity paradigm' (Pleck, 1981). The inflexibility of the gender stereotypes underpinning sex roles was also heavily critiqued, with Brannon (1976) arguing that the male sex role basically consisted of four core models,[4] and Pleck and Sawyer (1974) managing to reduce this cluster to just two: 'stay cool' and 'get ahead'. A fundamental argument in the critique of the male sex role was the cost to men which the ideology of a dominant but dysfunctional masculinity elicited, particularly in terms of fractured relationships, damaged health and inflexibility. As Pleck describes it: 'masculinity ideology directly creates trauma in male socialization' (1995: 20).

In contrast to the notion that the acquisition of dominant models of masculinity is somehow a natural and harmonious experience, contributing to the sum of social equilibrium and personal well-being, the male sex role began to be seen as a burden, a trial from which boys, especially, should be spared. This particular critical perspective on dominant masculinities has remained pretty much intact throughout the past few decades, with numerous writers claiming that masculinity does not come without a price, but that it carries costs for both men and women (Levant and Pollack, 1995; for discussion, see Messner, 1992). Indeed, Pleck (1995) has revisited the literature on gender role theory in order to 'update' and strengthen the 'male gender role strain paradigm'.

Despite itself being locked into the essentialist notion that men and women are fundamentally complementary, just so long as men forsake 'traditional roles' for 'modern' ones (Pleck, 1976), role research did begin to lay the ground for questioning a singular, unchanging masculinity, one that all males, given the 'right circumstances', would naturally aspire to and achieve. For it became apparent that not only were sex role models under constant pressure to change, but that as role models underwent transformation, so would associated behaviours. Not surprisingly, as Connell (1995) notes, sex role research became an attractive tool for those with political agendas. For it became assumed that if the behaviours of young people were subject to the impact of, for example, peer pressure, the media and other external influences, then new more 'positive' role models could be set up via, for example, educational processes.

Despite the increasing evidence that women and men were neither passive recipients of socialization processes, nor unitary and reciprocal entities, sex role theory and notions of 'male role strain' continued to play a central role in gender research. This was the case certainly through until the late 1970s, when researchers such as Robert J. Stoller[5] and Sandra Bem[6] produced influential research on 'core gender identity' that threw new light on gender assimilation. Consequently, within the imminent sociology of masculinity the first substantive critiques of gender role theory did not emerge until the mid- to late 1980s. Informed in the main by second-wave feminism and theories of patriarchy (for discussion, see Tong, 1993; Humm, 1992), scholars such as Carrigan, Connell and Lee (1985), Brod (1987), Kaufman (1987), Kimmel (1987a), Hearn (1987), Tolson (1977), Connell (1987) and Brittan (1989) argued for a new trajectory in the critical study of men. In their emphasis on the social constructionist dynamics of masculinity, these and other feminist and profeminist writers drew attention to the absence of any theory of male power in gender role perspectives, a point that writers such as Pleck (1995) have subsequently acknowledged. Moreover, they noted that sex/gender role theory was erected on a biological determinism, where 'roles are added to biology to give us gender' (Brittan, 1989: 21). As Connell (1987) acknowledges, despite being fundamentally illusory, the idea of a dominant gender role does appear to offer a ready means by which to connect apparent social order with the formation of personality, thus straddling the often incompatible disciplines of sociology and psychology. What it cannot do, however, is provide an explanation for differences between women and men, particularly in respect of power. Nor can gender role theory account for what would otherwise be seen as 'deviant behaviour' in those who do not conform to dominant gender stereotypes. Certainly, the concept of 'gender role strain' indicates that socialization processes are neither uniform nor unproblematic for men. But, nevertheless, gender role theory cannot account for differences within the lived experiences of individuals, nor can it explain the underlying motivations behind the 'socializer' (Connell, 1987). As Connell stresses, how do those left marginal in sex/gender role research, for example, gay men and women and black people, 'fit' into this perspective?

In the final analysis role theory fails to adequately develop an understanding of femininity and masculinity as multiple in expression, invested with power and, as was discussed earlier, historically variable. As this book seeks to emphasize, far from being unitary grounded categories, male and female reveal themselves as ambivalent arenas, dynamic, unpredictable and in a constant state of change. However, the criticisms directed at role theory are also applicable to social constructionism. In drawing primarily on second-wave feminism's developing critique of men's power, second-wave sociology of masculinity can be seen to have failed to adequately develop a theory of masculinity as identity work, beyond, that is, the notion of men 'learning gender scripts appropriate to our culture' (Kimmel and Messner, 1989: 10). In recognizing this hitherto absence of a substantive theoretical exploration of the identity dimensions to men and masculinity, a number of writers have turned their attention to psychoanalytical perspectives. However, as will now be discussed, this combination of (pro)feminist social constructionism and psychoanalysis is also not without its tensions.

Psychoanalytical perspectives

Freud

Sex role theory found some resonance with research being undertaken into sex, sexuality and gender by psychoanalysts. This is particularly so in respect of notions of an 'authentic' or 'real' self. For example, if we live our lives as 'actors' on the social 'stage' (Goffman, 1959), then what is the underpinning self that adopts these roles? Where is this inner self located and what are its origins? (How) might this 'core personality' be 'civilized' or, indeed, 'damaged' through immersion in the social world? It is these and related questions that psychoanalysts primarily seek to address, if not answer; in the process they open up the Pandora's box of human sexuality and the unconscious.

The 'founding father' (*sic*) of pyschoanalytic theory is Sigmund Freud. His numerous studies into the unconscious state, begun in the late 1800s, have influenced virtually every aspect of social science and to some degree continue to do so. Beyond academia, Freudian terminology has become commonplace, with terms such as 'penis envy', 'Freudian slip' and 'Oedipus complex' coming to signify what many see to be the darker, more profound side to the human condition. Like that of other influential thinkers (for example, Nietzsche and Foucault), Freud's work is notoriously elusive and difficult to pigeonhole, not least because his theories shifted and changed over the course of his life. Consequently, any direct critique of Freudian theory has something of the 'straw man' about it – it depends on one's perspective and interpretation, and also on the particular theories under discussion (Frosh, 1994; Rowley and Grosz, 1990). As is discussed below, feminists, particularly, have found Freud's work to be both liberating (from male dominance) and oppressive (contributing to malestream accounts of 'normality') (for elaboration, see Buhle, 1998). Any critical examination of Freudian theory, or indeed psychoanalysis itself, needs, then, to be interpreted with one eye on the fluidity of the concepts under discussion.

Central to Freudian theory is the idea that children go through stages of sexual maturation, the 'successful' outcome of which is their assimilation into the 'civilized' world of adulthood (Freud, 1953, 1968). The underlying assumption is that children are not born with a social and cultural identity, but that this comes to be formed as a direct consequence of their contact with others, in particular parents. As infants, boys and girls are neither naturally heterosexual nor homosexual; rather, they are in a stage of 'polymorphous perversity' and open to numerous forms of sensual gratification (Freud, 1953). As infants come to recognize their biological sex, mainly through observing parents, so this generalized sexual instinct or drive comes to be shaped and influenced by their identification with their biologically common parent. This process is not one without tension or conflict. Indeed, it requires the child to suppress otherwise natural desires in order to be accepted into the 'real' world of adults (see Frosh, 1994). The early stages of childhood were described by Freud as the 'oral' and 'anal' stages, during which the parents and infant vie for control. Ultimately, the 'normal' child will emerge out of these stages having learnt to give up some bodily pleasures in return for more authority and independence. The next stage, from around three years, sees the onset of specific gender development. This period, the 'phallic' or 'Oedipal' stage, is, according to Freud, the key stage wherein masculine and feminine traits are established. The child discovers the pleasures of the genitals, but because of their different biological make-up (i.e., the boy has a penis and the girl does not), boys and girls resolve the complexities of this phase quite differently. For boys, their first erotic choice is their mother – their primary nurturer. In wanting to possess her he must, however, also symbolically 'reject' or 'kill' his father, who he sees as a rival for her attention. The fear the boy then has is one of castration by his father should he act on his desires for his mother. In learning to suppress his mother love, the boy comes to 'be a male', partly through learning to submit himself to the authority of the father. His 'normal' heterosexuality is, then, transferred to the female as 'Other' (Beauvoir, 1973). Woman subsequently comes to occupy a fraught dualist identification/rejection within his subconscious: that of 'whore/Madonna' (see Edley and Wetherall, 1995; also Rutherford, 1992). Thus adult masculinity requires the male both to identify with males and to remain intensely competitive with them, particularly for the attention of females. This positive, indeed 'maleist', view of masculinity is one that sees males as the natural, superior sex. Females, by contrast, are, according to Freud, constantly obsessed by their lack of penis, creating resentment of their mother for having failed to provide one. Girls' desire for their father is desire for a penis. As this 'love object' cannot be resolved, it requires a (penis) substitute. Natural femininity can be achieved by girls turning into women who want babies, a process of development that offers women a new 'love object' (Freud, 1953).

First-wave feminism, which was substantiated from the mid-1950s and through to the early 1970s, saw writers such as Shulamith Firestone (1970), Betty Friedan (1974) and Kate Millett (1970) denounce what they saw as Freud's misogynism, manifest in his notion that masculinity is a secure and stable property, superior to femininity and, thus, women, whom he positioned as unstable and overly emotional. Millett challenged his assumption that women's physicality (mainly their 'lack' of penis) not only results in an essentially different subjectivity to men, but creates different 'ethical norms' (Millett, 1970); women's 'super-ego' being seen by Freud as largely a product of their heightened emotionality, lack of rationality and greater disposition towards disobedience (of authority). Feminist critics of Freudian theory argued that women's position in the world was less to do with their 'penis envy' and more to do with the social construction of femininity, a patriarchal condition that Freud failed to acknowledge (Firestone, 1970) and, moreover, a condition he contributed to as a malestream theoretician (O'Brien, 1983). This feminist critique was supported by psychoanalytical research of the time which noted that it was extremely rare for women to be sexual 'perverts'; it was men who were more likely to engage in necrophilia, exhibitionism, coprophilia and voyeurism (Edley and Wetherall, 1995).

Freudian theory strikes an uneasy 'balance' between the biological and the social. On one hand there is his emphasis on biological sex as a fundamental determinant of 'normal' gender behaviour; the penis, or lack of it, being seen as the starting point of gender construction. Yet Freud's understanding of 'normal sexuality' is itself not grounded in 'objective' scientific research, but is clearly an outcome of his own cultural and gendered assumptions, reflecting dominant Western thought of the early twentieth century (Friedan, 1974). Freud appears to equate 'normal' human psychology with male development; women and femininity being a deviation from this 'norm' (Segal, 1997). While he did not write directly about masculinity, Freud presents 'normal' male development and subjectivity as a complex process of denial, contradiction and suppression of feelings and inner emotions. That which is required to be denied or repressed is 'weakness', homosexuality and those 'awkward things' (such as women) which 'lie hidden in the repressed unconscious' (Winnicott, 1986, quoted in Segal, 1997: 72). Yet despite the constant presence of ambivalence and fragility, Freud did view male maturation as less problematic than female maturation, with men and masculinity being presented as central to the continued operation of society. In this respect, Freud's perspectives are very close to Parsonian functionalism in so much as they rest on gendered dualisms of public/private, rational/irrational, order/disorder. Freudian theory starts from the premise that there is a 'natural' (thus biological) state of affairs, in which 'primitive' sexual desires (manifest only by infants and 'perverts') are, in the main, controlled and ultimately subsumed under civilizing pressures, all for the common good. Yet as feminists have since pointed out, 'over 50 million have died at the hands of psychiatrically normal males since 1900' (Miles, 1992: 15). However, as is discussed below, despite these criticisms, Freudian theory can also be interpreted as an attempt to explain the socially constructed character of sexuality and gender, thus providing a form of critical gender theory, a point not lost on many feminist and profeminist writers.

Jung

Freud's work has, arguably, had more impact on gender theory than that of any other single psychoanalyst, and his theories are regularly referred to in contemporary literature on the subject. However, the work of one of Freud's most famous disciples, Carl Jung, is of equal significance for the sociology of masculinity, particularly in respect of his notion of gender balance. Freud had always emphasized that women and men have both masculine and feminine traits as part of their inner self. However, Freud saw these gendered dualisms as the outcomes of childhood to adulthood psychic construction, a process fraught and contradictory certainly, but, nevertheless, with a final state that is stable and balanced for most people. Jung spotted the ambiguity in this theory, notably that masculinity somehow, for men, unconsciously prevails over feminine 'instincts'. Jung questioned the extent and ease with which the masculinity/femininity tension might be resolved for males. The basis of Jung's reasoning was that masculinity and femininity were 'rooted in the timeless truths about the human psyche' (Connell, 1994: 21) and in notions of a public self (the *persona*) and a private self (the *anima*). This dualism was itself gendered in so much as Jung saw the 'natural' expression of these different selves as gendered archetypes, representing, for example, men's inner and outer psyches, a condition that, far from being easily 'resolvable', often leads to 'unnatural repressions'.

> No man is so entirely masculine that he has nothing feminine in him. The fact is, rather, that very masculine men have – carefully guarded and hidden – a very soft emotional life, often incorrectly described as 'feminine'. A man counts it a virtue to repress his feminine traits as much as possible, just as a woman, at least *until recently*, considered it unbecoming to be 'mannish'. The repression of feminine traits and inclinations clearly causes these contrasexual demands to accumulate in the unconscious. (Jung, 1928/1953, quoted in Connell, 1994: 20; my emphasis)

At the heart of Jung's thesis are the issues of social order, functionalism and gender-appropriate roles discussed earlier. And again, as was highlighted above, the temptation to slip into essentialist, or mythological-inspired, notions proves too much for the theorist. In the above quote Jung reveals his concern at the social shifts he perceives as taking place within Western societies, that is the tendency for 'modern' women to adopt 'mannish' traits. For Jung, such a trend appears to have an element of disorder about it, for it signals that the feminine is being dominated by the masculine, when what is needed is for 'modern men' to 'carefully guard' their feminine side. As will be discussed in chapter 2, it is a notion that has had a profound impact in certain areas of 'men's studies', in particular in the mythopoetic men's movements (see, for example, Bly, 1990). Jung stresses that all men have a feminine essence within them, which can, he argues, be reached and 'healed' through therapy, through talking to one's anima. What remains vital is that the masculine prevails as the dominant persona of men, with the feminine repressed, to varying degrees, as a consequence. The alternative, as Jung saw it, was for men and their masculinity to be subordinated to women and femininity. Similarly, for women to become 'mannish' signalled a similar imbalance in their gender psyche.

The lack of any clinical study to underpin his theories pushed Jung into searching for archetypal figures in mythology and world religions in order to 'prove' his thesis. Jung needed 'evidence' of gender archetypes, seen to exist somehow at the core of the social world, to make his point that such archetypes come to accumulate in the collective and individual unconscious. Basically, as Connell (1994) notes, Jung's thesis is an early attempt at a theory of masculinity, but one founded in a given system and constitution of gender. Rather than question the very idea of an essential, inner self – an archetypal being – Jung attempts to present the concepts of masculinity and femininity as rooted in some 'timeless truths'. One outcome of such reasoning is that femininity and masculinity become seen as so fixed and given that no change is possible. All that can alter is the balance between these two conditions. Contemporary Jungian theorists have taken this notion to a certain logical, but I would suggest flawed, conclusion by arguing that modern feminism is, for example, *'tilting the balance too far the other way* and suppressing the masculine' (Connell, 1994: 22; original emphasis). A contemporary example of such thinking is given by Guggenbuhl (1997), who suggests that one means by which a 'natural polarization' of women and men can be achieved is, in Jungian terms, for women and men to lead more separate lives and to inhabit different 'retreat zones', territories where men can 'get back in touch with their masculine qualities'.

Connell's long-term study of Jungian theory in the context of the sociology of masculinity is probably the most thorough and comprehensive of its type (see also Connell, 1987, 1994, 1995).[7] Of particular interest is the way in which Connell traces the connections between Jungian theory and the more recent antifeminist backlash as represented by the 'men's mythopoetic movement'. As Connell puts it, '[Jungian theory] is enthusiastically received in the North American 'men's movement' as an explanation for men's troubles with feminist women' (1994: 22). Such an approach is exemplified in Robert Bly's *Iron John* (1990), which is little more than a plea for modern men to 'heal their grief' and renounce contemporary images of adult manhood in favour of a mythological 'Wild Man'; an Arthurian warrior figure, connected with the earth and an inner mysticism. As this book reveals, despite a proliferation of theories deconstructing such notions, myths of masculinity and accompanying 'truths' remain firmly implicated in the politics of gender.

Moving from first- to second-wave (pro)feminism

Despite the many critiques, not all feminist scholars felt affronted by psychoanalytic theories. Indeed, many saw Freud's ideas as highly liberating for women. The first wave of feminist theorizing had largely been concerned with issues of equality and equity; laying stress on men and women being equal in ability, while pointing out that women were being denied their potential by traditional relationships, male-dominated work environments and patriarchal settings. Liberal feminism, typified by the work of, for example, Betty Friedan (1974), was seen by many to be a call for gender equality, while, however, accepting some aspects of gender difference as given and, in functionalist terms, complementary. In part inspired by the social, educational and economic changes occurring in Western societies from the 1960s onwards, liberal feminism seemed to capture the sense that many women had of being able to 'have it all', emulating men's power in the public sphere and exercising their maternal instincts, while also remaining, fundamentally, 'feminine'. The challenge to men in such theorizing was to make space for women, particularly in work and organizations (Kanter, 1977), whilst, as legislators, introducing and enacting laws that enabled women to become assimilated, on equal terms, into (masculine) work cultures and environments. Similarly, Marxist feminists, who consider women's oppression to be a direct consequence of capitalism's system of exploitative power relations, place emphasis on improving women's experiences as workers and on women receiving practical recognition of the economic value of their housework (Barrett, 1980; MacKinnon, 1982). In calling for fundamental changes in the system of production, Marxist feminists, like liberal feminists, imply that gender equality can be achieved, but without men, as individuals and as a gender group, necessarily having to change.

In laying the 'blame' for women's oppression at the doors of, respectively, legislative injustices and the capitalist system, many feminists consider, however, that liberal and Marxist feminisms fail to adequately challenge the everyday practices of men themselves (Humm, 1992). Again, the tension that arises for feminists in attempting to straddle the nature–nurture dualism is evident, for the implication in much of first-wave feminism is that gender differences, while unjust, have to be negotiated alongside an implicit acceptance of the inherent biological factors that construct women and men as different. The next question of course is, 'How can men (and women) change if their behaviour is biologically given?' Freudian theory appeared to offer a way through this particular conundrum by positing male and female behaviour as a 'natural' outcome only in respect of particular social experiences, notably family relationships. Represented in particular by the writings of Nancy Chodorow (1978) and Dorothy Dinnerstein (1976), feminist psychoanalytic theorists then argued that women's social and economic condition is a direct consequence of men's practices, an example being their absence from the processes of parenting:

> It is central to my argument that our sexual arrangements are part of a wider human malaise. By 'sexual arrangements', I mean the division of responsibility, opportunity, and privilege that prevails between male and female humans, and the patterns of psychological interdependence that are implicit in this division. The specific nature of such arrangements varies, often dramatically, under varying societal conditions. Their general nature, however, stems from a core fact that has so far been universal: the fact of primary female responsibility for the care of infants and young children. (Dinnerstein, 1976: 4)

Both Chodorow and Dinnerstein reject any biological assumptions that posit women as destined by nature to be mothers. Furthermore, they also reject any social determinism that suggests that women are conditioned to be mothers. Drawing on Freud's Oedipal theory, Chodorow, for example, traces the contrasting psychosexual development of boys and girls and the points of separation and symbiosis that, she argues, occur during their maturing and changing relationship with their mother and father. An important and, for feminists, significant outcome of the sexual and familial division of labour is that 'women's mothering produces asymmetries in the relational experiences of girls and boys', one outcome of which is that 'the basic feminine sense of self is connected to the world, the basic masculine sense of self is separate' (Chodorow, 1978: 283).

In their respective accounts of how sexuality and gender are constructed in favour of male dominance through the gendered processes of mothering, second-wave feminists, particularly psychoanalytic feminists such as Chodorow and Dinnerstein (also Miller, 1978; Mitchell, 1976) opened up a new critique in the study of men. Whilst some feminists have pointed out that aspects of female biology may lead daughters to identify more with their mothers than fathers (Rossi, 1977), the point remains that the sexual and familial division of labour works to men's material benefit. Equally importantly, this cultural arrangement cannot be divorced from a public and private divide; organizational practices (for example, equal opportunities policies, (un)paid paternity leave); the continued imbalance in women's wages when compared with men's; and the exploitative and oppressive conditions that directly result for many women in their attempt to manage multiple roles across both the public and private spheres (Franks, 1999). In short, while much of first-wave feminism championed 'women's rights', second-wave feminism began to challenge the 'cultural arrangements', male power and maleist assumptions increasingly recognized as sustaining gender injustice.

Feminist psychoanalytic theory also gave credence and substance to the idea that women's sense of being female, while a 'reality', was one born of a particular gendered subjectivity created out of their lived experiences as women (for example, see Lennon and Whitford, 1994). This understanding of a feminine subjectivity offers some potential for developing in a political context by exploring (and potentially changing) the gendered power relationships that serve to influence if not determine the 'gender order' (Connell, 1995) within which women's and men's subjectivities are constructed. Not only that, but once gender politics is connected with female subjectivity, particularly through epistemological formations, then the ground is laid for a 'women's standpoint' perspective (Harding, 1991; Smith, 1988). In developing such a perspective, writers such as Harding and Smith (also Gilligan, 1982; hooks, 1984) suggest that women's ways of knowing and being are not only different, but can be celebrated as interpretively and epistemologically privileged in a masculinist world (for discussion, see Assiter, 1996; Holmwood, 1995; Lennon, 1995; Whitehead, 2001b).

Feminist utilizations of Freudian theory have been employed to good effect within second-wave sociology of masculinity, particularly that work which has sought to connect men's power and the problematic behaviour of men with theories of male identity. Prominent examples of such studies include Connell (1994, 1995), who traces the progression of Freudian theories through the work of, amongst others, Alfred Adler, to highlight both the complexity of masculinities and the compelling yet oppressive character of dominant cultural notions of heterosexuality; Craib (1987), who draws on Freudian theory to emphasize the centrality of gender to identity, and of masculinity to male dominance (also MacInnes, 1998); Middleton (1992), who explores Freud's 'Rat Man' essay as a study wherein both Freud and his patient 'Rat Man' are seen as duly implicated in the formation and enaction of a particular vehement form of masculine symbiosis – traumatic, defensive, violent and fantastical; and Rutherford (1992), who uses various psychoanalytic theories to explore mother–son relationships, men's violence and the repressed dimensions of masculine performance.

Whatever the possibilities of integrating Freudian and Jungian perspectives within gender theory and the sociology of masculinity – possibilities that are certainly not exhausted (for discussion, see Buhle, 1998) – they are, however, ultimately in tension with a notion of masculinity as variable and fluid but, importantly, politically implicated. Thus, while appearing to subvert gender and sexual difference, it can be argued that Freud and Jung merely serve to reinforce the difference. Frosh, for example, in one of the most detailed studies of masculinity and psychoanalysis, acknowledges the many 'masculinist assumptions [that are] endemic to psychoanalytic theory' (1994: 13) and inevitably corrupt the possibility of employing most forms of such theory in any neutral or objective fashion. Probably the most telling critique of both Freud and Jung is, then, the combination of the misogynistic thinking that pervades their work and their reliance on gender dualisms of, for example, rational/irrational, framed within a notion of an inner and outer (masculine/feminine) self. In short, the psychoanalytical theories of Freud and Jung rely on a gender(ed) reductionism that is partly concealed behind a complex and polymorphous analysis. Whilst being pliant, and, thus, susceptible to often quite opposing understandings, interpretations and utilizations, the theories of Freud and Jung remain problematic for critical gender theorists. Nevertheless, despite these reservations, I would argue that opportunities do exist for employing certain psychoanalytical concepts within both a critical and deconstructive context, and these are discussed in respect of masculinity and identity in chapter 7.

Multiplicity, materiality – and illusion

Multiple masculinities

While the works of, for example, Parsons, Freud and Jung offer diverse, sometimes compelling, interpretations, they commonly draw on an understanding of masculinity and femininity as rooted in timeless 'truths', often connected to some deeper, almost spiritual, mythology. As such, these scholars and their works remain firmly rooted in malestream thinking. However, as has been discussed, the influence of these writers on the developing sociology of masculinity has to be recognized. In serving to strengthen the notion of men and women as unitary identities – problematic only in respect of the individual's ability to assimilate, act or represent dominant social and cultural gender codes and symbols – functionalism, gender role theory and Freudian and Jungian theories speak to the dualism that underpins what Connell (1987) terms the 'gender order'. Despite this inherent weakness, such theories have contributed, often indirectly, to both feminist and profeminist scholarship, not least because the categorical assumptions that inform gender dualisms have a political resonance for many critical gender theorists. Assiter (1996), for example, makes a strong case for maintaining the gender dualism in order to focus attention on women's uniqueness as an 'epistemic community', a grouping formed by their universal experiences (as women) in a gendered political class (also Stanley, 1997).

Despite the argument for seeing women and men as political categories – and this is discussed in more detail in chapter 2 – it remains the case that any notion of fixed or final gender roles or definitions is implausible. Similarly, it is no longer tenable, given recognition of the multiplicity, historicity and dynamism of gender representations, to talk of masculinity in the singular. Rather, we can see that masculinities are plural and multiple; they differ over space, time and context, are rooted only in the cultural and social moment, and are, thus, inevitably entwined with other powerful and influential variables such as sexuality, class, age and ethnicity. Yet in purporting to speak of the practices, behaviours and attitudes of males – boys and men – masculinities are very powerful, for they have ideological or discursive elements that appear to embed given 'truths'; the same 'truths', as we have seen, that scholars such as Parsons, Freud and Jung found so seductive and elementary to their thinking, and to which many psychoanalysts and sociologists are still drawn (see, for example, Clare, 2000).

At the level of, for example, biology, the brain or genetics, masculinity does not exist; it is mere illusion. Masculinity is not a product or an entity that can be grasped by hand or discovered under the most powerful microscope. No amount of cultural representation can make masculinities biologically real (Threadgold and Cranny-Francis, 1990). Any sense of masculinity's embeddedment in men's 'inner selves' comes only from fictional and superficial accounts of what a 'man' is. Yet there is also the fact that masculinity, while in this sense illusory, remains fixed by one important consideration, that is, it exists in relation to femininity. Indeed so long as the notion of femininit(y)ies exist so will masculinit(y)ies (Brittan, 1989). It is a dualism that remains fundamental to Western societies and beyond (Petersen, 1998). Consequently, despite being basically illusory, masculinity is not so ephemeral as to be dislocated from the social web; it is not a free-floating entity that inhabits men's subjectivity in some ad hoc or randomly happenstance manner. On the contrary, masculinities are implicated in the everyday practices of men – and women. In this respect, Freud and Jung were quite correct to centralize gender and sexuality in the everyday lives of females and males. However, their use of the masculine/feminine dialectic was not one that was gender critical. Both theorists, as with Parsons and sex role theoreticians, assume the presence of some underpinning gender essence at work on the subjectivities of women and men. In so doing, they not only reify that which has no biological basis; they clearly fail to recognize the issues of power and politics at work in this dualism. As Brittan observes: 'How men behave will depend upon the existing social relations of gender. By this I mean the way in which men and women confront each other ideologically and *politically*' (1989: 3; my emphasis).

The materiality of men's violences

Whether gender politics, as with all power plays, is acted out, resisted and/or engaged through ideologies or discourses (or both) is a matter of some debate (for discussion, see Purvis and Hunt, 1993), a point that is explored in more detail in chapter 3. However, what is clear is that there is a material actuality to masculinities, frequently underpinned by violence or its threat (Archer, 1994; Bowker, 1998; Dobash et al., 2000; Hatty, 2000; Hearn, 1998b; Miles, 1992). As Bowker puts it, violence represents the 'dark side of masculine role performance' with 90 per cent of violence being perpetrated by men (1998: xiii). It is important, then, to recognize that masculinities are not necessarily benign, but are directly implicated in those practices of men that are oppressive, destructive and violent. Directly arising from this recognition, research into men's violences has developed into a key field within the sociology of masculinity. Yet as Jeff Hearn (1998b) notes, the study remains problematic, not least because of the diverse range of such research, encompassing disciplines such as criminology, history, social policy, education, sociology, pyschology and cultural studies. Similarly, in highlighting the materiality of men's violence it is important to recognize both the plurality of its expression and its often unseen character. For example, research by Edwards (1989) and Dobash and Dobash (1992) signals the violent character of home and family life for many women and children. As Edwards puts it: 'The safest place for men is the home, the home is, by contrast, the least safest place for women (1989: 214, quoted in Hearn, 1998b: 4). Men's violences towards those women to whom they are in close relationship is endemic across many societies, and yet it is frequently codified through everyday cultural practices and legal systems, thus rendering such behaviours 'invisible' other than to sustained critical (usually feminist) enquiry. An important element in feminist and pro-feminist research into men's violences is, then, to prise open those hitherto dark sides of men's behaviour and associated masculinities that are oppressive and violent in their construction and expression, in the process naming and focusing on 'the problem of men as the major *doers* of violence to women, children, each other' (Hearn, 1998b: 5; original emphasis). A further aim is to illuminate the interconnections not only between masculinities and men's violences, but between different forms of men's violences. For example, men's association with violence extends beyond the private sphere into the public one, coming to characterize the organization and control of weapons and means of violence (see Barrett, 1996, 2001 for examples); the control of state-sponsored violence (for example, the police); violence by corporations; and violence undertaken by organized criminal gangs (see Bowker, 1998; Newburn and Stanko, 1994). Within the public sphere there is also the random violence, sexual or otherwise, perpetrated by individual men and groups of men on strangers, be they women, children or other men. This latter aspect of men's violences is particularly corrosive to the well-being, security and comfort of those who are, or perceive themselves to be, at risk from such aggression. For it should be recognized that, whether it be in the public or private spheres, the constant threat of violence is, itself, an aggression, a form of violation of human dignity. In short, to recognize the extent and range of men's violences is to face the depressing and disturbing realization that men's propensity for cruelty and violence is probably the biggest cause of misery in the world.

Within the sociology of masculinity, and feminist scholarship generally, there is a paramount need to expose and examine not only the singular violence undertaken by individual men within both the public and private realms, but also the cultural condition of violence itself. Suzanne Hatty discusses the example of serial killing (a crime invariably perpetrated by white males), which, she argues, is marked out as a 'cultural formation', rooted beyond individual psyches and into the core of societal values. Hatty argues that such values sustain and validate the conditions under which men may be violent to women, children and other men.

> Today, serial killing can be regarded as a cultural formation typical of the late twentieth century. As such, it is emblematic of the motifs of machine culture: the mass-produced images, the multiple representations and simulations, and the retreat of the ideals of humanism. The insertion of graphic violence at the heart of society and its replication in numerous visual forms provides the optimum context for the generation of the 'logic of killing for pleasure' (Seltzer, 1998: 7). (Hatty, 2000: 197)

Hatty is stressing that men's violences are neither simply nor usefully compartmentalized as either legitimate or illegitimate, for they are frequently acted out and performed in a wider cultural theatre wherein what it means to be a man is inextricably connected to the perceived ability and opportunity to (re)act violently towards others. Such violent acts should not be seen solely as an aberration by psychologically damaged males. There is a deeper root to men's violences. Or, to put it another way, the root of men's violences is anchored as much in social and cultural values as in individual pathology (see Archer, 1994). Obvious examples of the connection between individual violence and masculine culture would be acts of violence, sexual or otherwise, by men while they are supposedly carrying out 'legitimate' functions and activities for the state or other organizations (for example, as members of the armed forces, educators, carers, sports coaches, prison warders, policemen). These men are, in the main, entrusted with the means and opportunity for violence by virtue of their jurisdiction over others, but they subsequently abuse this freedom by either transgressing the boundaries laid down for appropriate physical response, or by undertaking planned, routine acts of violence on those under their care and administration. The violence undertaken by men in such positions frequently exposes the deeper culture of violence at the heart of the organizational setting (see Bowker, 1998 for examples). Such organizations, for example a care home, may not be self-evidently masculinist in orientation, but they may have a deeper-rooted value system that serves to legitimize violence and abuse and/or hides its practice.

In summarizing the challenges facing feminists in coming to explicate, understand and challenge men's violences, Jeff Hearn raises a number of key questions:

> To put this rather bluntly, to focus on men and men's violence to women unsettles, makes problematic, the way men are, not just in the doing of particular actions of violence, but also more generally. It raises question marks against men's behaviour in general. For example, how is it possible that men can be violent to women, perhaps over many years, and this can be part of a socially accepted way of being a man? How does violence relate to the social construction of different forms of masculinity in school, in sport, in work, in the media? What is the link between violence and dominant forms of masculinities? What is the connection between men and violence, men's violence? In raising these questions, two major themes need to be stressed: power and control; and the taking apart of what is usually taken for granted. (1998b: 6)

As Hearn goes on to recognize, although central to the continued well-being of women and children – and other men – none of the issues and questions surrounding men's violences are reducible to simple biological, genetic or deterministic solutions. There is a social dimension to men's violences that pervades most cultures. Therefore, following Hatty (2000), I would argue that a particularly persuasive and insidious discourse of violence is at large in this new millennium, be it articulated through the media, social and state organizations, 'machine culture' or the practices of individual men. It is a discourse that is particularly powerful in that it serves to legitimize male violence as voyeuristic entertainment and through forms of state security. This discourse is not simply one of verbal communication, but also, fundamentally, a set of practices, attitudes and belief systems that render men's violences as 'normal' and, thus, inevitable. Consequently, men's violences have assumed the status of a cultural arrangement across most societies, in as much as the matter of violence itself, if examined at all, is invariably done through a gender invisible lens. For example, while politicians and policy makers may seek to reduce the levels of violence in society, they invariably fail to subject to critical scrutiny the masculinist culture that feeds and validates the violent practices of men. In this respect, the work of feminists and profeminists is of particular importance in that it not only serves to highlight the connections between men and violence, but it keeps these connections in the public eye. Feminism makes explicit the materiality of gender differentials. The political categories of man and woman are not confined to intellectual discourse but played out in the subways, in organizations, on the sports terraces and on the streets at night, by men, often violently. When you wake at 3.00 a.m. having caught the sound of movement downstairs, it is not usually a woman you fear wielding gun or knife.

Men's violences, of whatever dimension, can be seen, then, as important and influential material actualities directly arising from those dominant discourses that serve to reify men as 'masculine beings' (see also chapter 7). In short, if we are to have some understanding of otherwise inexplicable acts of violence by men, whether it be serial killing, sexual assault, rape, child abuse, mass violence, random violence or torture, then we must recognize that dominant forms and codes of masculinity serve to legitimize, to some degree, that which is, arguably, the major social problem of our time.

Material actualities - a global perspective

As a critical focus on men's violences reveals, masculinities may be fundamentally illusory, but the consequences of men's practices and gender myths - and the underpinning belief in the supremacy of men contained in, for example, some religions, organizational sites, work practices, political systems, cultures and divisions of labour - has a very real material/physical consequence. These material dimensions are complex, often being concealed behind notions of 'tradition' if not plain ignorance and stereotype. For example, biological reproduction may, at first sight, appear to be the province of women (as carriers of the unborn child and as, predominantly, midwives). Yet, as Hearn (1987) argues, there is a social organization to conception, pregnancy, birth and childrearing that is not gender neutral but invested in relations of male control and power (see also Shorter, 1984). Similarly, in the public sphere, the fact of whether you are a man or a women will have a direct bearing on your chances of becoming, for example, a company director, politician, surgeon, senior manager, army officer, detective, professional athlete, priest, judge, high-ranking civil servant, economist, professor and so on (EC, 1998; EOC, 1999, 2000; IoM, 1998). Moreover, the limited number of women who do achieve their career aspiration in many of the above jobs can expect to be paid significantly less than men for the equivalent work (ONS, 1998, 2000; Reskin and Padavic, 1994). Indeed, recent research undertaken in the UK on behalf of the government reveals that most women, regardless of their experience and qualifications, will suffer a 'female forfeit' in terms of lower lifetime earnings than men (Cabinet Office, 2000; EOC, 2000). Also, if you are a woman in paid employment you are more likely than a man to be in temporary, non-unionized, part-time, low-skilled, lower-paid work (Ginn et al., 1996; Hakim, 1996; Pilcher, 1999). As a woman, you are more likely than a man to be holding down two jobs, and, if a parent, to be doing this while engaged in multiple roles across both the public and private spheres (Franks, 1999; Hochshild, 1989; Rubery, 1998). If you are a union member, it is likely that union will be male-dominated and masculinist in its expression of solidarity (Cockburn, 1991; Creese, 1999; Mann, 1992). As an employee, a woman is more likely to suffer sexual harassment than a man (Hearn et al., 1989), and, as a single parent, a woman is more vulnerable to poverty than a man single parent (Creighton, 1999; Halford, Savage and Witz, 1997; Irwin, 1999).

In sum, material advantage, autonomy and opportunity remain gendered, despite the notion of a postfeminist era and more than a century of Western feminist discourse (see also Singh, 1998). And if this is the case in Western societies, where feminism has been largely sourced and energized and women's aspirations publicized and politicized, the situation is even more marked in other parts of the world. The material inequalities that arise from gender politics and dominant understandings of masculinity are explicit, unapologetic and deeply embedded in the social relations and nationalisms of most African, Middle Eastern, Asian, Caribbean and South American countries (see, for example, Alumnajjed, 1998; Fisher, 1993; Green, 1999; Hensman, 1992; Karam, 1998; Sweetman, 1997). Perhaps it has become too easy for many, men especially, to look at the absolute increasing material prosperity of the advantaged 40 per cent in the West (Hutton, 1996), to make a connection with women's heightened visibility in employment, the media industry, politics and education, and to conclude that previous gender inequities have been 'resolved'. Such notions require to be put into a global perspective. From Afghanistan to China, from Kuwait to Brazil, from Turkey to Thailand, from Sudan to Pakistan, women's rights, and women's opportunities for security, education, financial well-being and political power – indeed, many of women's most important life choices – remain significantly constrained by the attitudes and practices of men. Some fifty years after the Universal Declaration of Human Rights, male discrimination and violence remain everyday realities for millions of women: 80 per cent of the victims in male-led wars are not men but women and children; and the vast majority of the one billion people unable to read or write are women (Amnesty International, 1998a). In countries such as China and India traditional attitudes place a higher value on the male than the female, with female infanticide being the grim reality of such ideas.[8] Yet, despite experiencing this severe material and physical oppression, to be a woman seeking equal rights with men is, in many countries, to risk at the very least social marginalization, if not imprisonment or worse (see Abdo, 2000; Afshar, 1998; Green, 1999; Hensman, 1992; also Amnesty International, 1998b, 2000).

However, it is evident that often the only difference between Western societies and many other countries is that, in the West, feminism at least has a public voice and some political presence, though the extent and degree to which such progress translates to equality in practice and material change is, as discussed above, much contested and less evident (Burke, 2000; Godenzi, 1999). Moreover, in recognizing what progress has been made in the West for women's rights, one should not assume that women's political and social enfranchisement in other countries is dependent on Western societies or Western feminisms. Indeed, many women fighting for equality in so-called Third World countries reject Western feminism in favour of indigenous alternatives that allow for their particular religious or cultural positions (see for discussion Mohanty, Russo and Louides, 1991). As recent research has shown, although they may reject the label feminism, many women from developing countries are evolving a feminist consciousness to the extent that women's rights has become a powerful momentum within even the most reactionary cultural spaces, and in so doing they are creating localized resistances to patriarchal conditions (Afshar, 1998; Alumnajjed, 1998; Fisher, 1993; Green, 1999; Karam, 1998; Paya, 2000). Such movements and resistances are not confined to developing countries but are also apparent in those spaces in the UK and other Western societies where the changing aspirations of ethnic minority women (for example, Muslim) meet male intransigence and resistance (see, for example, Shain, 2000). Indeed, one can speculate, as does Anthony Giddens, that contemporary expressions of religious fundamentalism are, in part, an 'attempt (by men) to stall the gender revolution' (2000: 27) – though in saying this it is necessary to recognize that for Islamic feminists and Muslim feminists the very term 'religious fundamentalism' is imbued with imperialist assumptions and fails to capture the cultural, political and religious alliances that exist across and between groups of women and men (for discussion, see Karam, 1998).

Conclusion

In exploring the question 'masculinity – illusion or reality?', this chapter has charted some of the transformations and trajectories in the developing sociology of masculinity, doing so from a perspective that draws on a historical recognition of the shifting representations of manliness and masculinity and on the contemporary diversity and fluidity of what it means to be a man. In the same way that feminist scholarship has moved through first, second and now third waves of academic critique and investigation, so is the developing sociology of masculinity. The first wave was represented by those writings that drew attention to the problematic dimensions of masculinity as a culturally privileged or idealized form of male behaviour. The work of Pleck (1981) was particularly significant at this stage, for it provided the basis of a theory of masculinity that challenged the notion of masculinity as functional and socially stable. Importantly, Pleck and others drew attention to the ambiguities and discontinuities in any male socialization processes, describing this as 'male gender role strain' (see also Levant and Pollack, 1995).

The absence of any theory of power in sex/gender role theory was, however, a primary concern of those theorists who contributed to the second-wave sociology of masculinity. Largely influenced by second-wave feminism, writers such as Connell (1987a), Kimmel (1987a), Hearn (1987) and Brittan (1989) made important contributions to our understanding of gender power relations by developing pro-feminist social constructionist understandings of men and masculinities. Recognizing that such theoretical perspectives, while illuminating of hegemonic processes, provide little insight into the identity dynamics of men and masculinities, Connell (1994, 1995) and others have since looked to the work of Freud, Jung and feminist psychoanalysts to shed light on masculinity as an outcome of identity work. In so doing, Connell in particular has made yet a further substantial contribution to the burgeoning sociology of masculinity. However, despite the important developments occurring in this sociology since the 1970s, the influence of structural functionalism, particularly in respect of unitary notions of men and women, remains. The nature–nurture dualism continues to bedevil not only the 'everyday world' but also many of the sociological and psychoanalytical explorations of men and masculinities.

Back then to the initial question: is masculinity illusion or reality? To put it succinctly, masculinity is *both illusion and reality*. Thus it is coming to understand how this apparent paradox is sustained that is the key to appreciating the social, political and individual importance of masculinities. One can have some sympathy with those who wish to see an underpinning logic or causality to masculinities. For this perspective seems to speak to our common-sense and everyday experience of gender relations and gender difference. When we turn and face the violent and dysfunctional behaviour of males and the material inequalities of gender, it is easier to excuse them as biologically and functionally determined rather than as the material outcome of some complex sociological process or psychoanalytic illusion. Similarly, to explore the construction of sexuality and gender, as many functionalists and psychoanalysts do, in terms of the fraught but inevitable outcome of a tussle between essential truths, primary instincts, sexual urges and a necessary 'civilizing process', while a seductive notion, is only part of the story. Order, functionality, roles and certainty may appear, to many, to be what sustains the 'everyday world', but that world is not given; it is highly contingent and in a constant state of flux.

Interestingly, this social contingency is also apparent to those who are concerned with the demise of 'gender traditions' and what they see as an ensuing 'social disruption' (see, for example, Fukuyama, 1997). Increasingly these writers, and others of a similar conservative persuasion, turn to the world of science for 'answers'. However, science itself is not inevitably neutral, for its practices and assumptions are invested in discursive properties. Nevertheless, science beckons to us as a new 'religion', the new font of 'truth' and knowledge, the new legitimizing order (Lyotard, 1994). As such, it is not surprising that when geneticists and sociobiologists examine sex and gender they assume the possibility of finding 'objective' answers and solutions to the inconsistencies that surround us, and themselves, as gender beings. I suggest that there are theoretical tools that can be used to better understand how men and masculinities exist as simultaneously illusion and reality without recourse to mythology or scientism, and these ideas are developed further in this book. However, in undertaking any critical examination of men, it is important not to lose sight of the material consequences and political dimensions to masculinities and their associated myths and ideologies. With violent crime by men on the increase across the Western world (Hatty, 2000) and men's violences taking multiple forms (Dobash et al., 2000; Hearn, 1998b), it is evident that, while masculinities may be illusory, the material consequences of many men's practices are quite real enough.

FURTHER READING

Brod, H. and Kaufman, M. (eds) (1994) *Theorizing Masculinities*. Thousand Oaks, Calif.: Sage.

Buhle, M. J. (1998) *Feminism and its Discontents*. Cambridge, Mass: Harvard University Press.

Franks, S. (1999) *Having None of It: Women, Men and the Future of Work*. London: Granta Books.

Levant, R. F. and Pollack, W. S. (eds) (1995) *A New Psychology of Men*. New York: BasicBooks.

Segal, L. (1999) *Why Feminism? Gender, Psychology, Politics*. Cambridge: Polity.

2
The Personal and the Political
Men and Feminism

In the previous chapter I raised the point concerning the importance of recognizing the personal–political dimensions to the study of men and masculinities, drawing particular attention to the material inequalities that surround gender differences. Nevertheless, while making this emphasis, I also recognize that there are those who will be uncomfortable with this approach, possibly seeing it as lacking 'objectivity', as 'politicizing' sociology or as part of an 'endemic political correctness'. One aim of this chapter is to respond to such concerns, mainly by drawing attention to the fact that genders and masculinities are not neutral concepts, but, like notions of race and nationhood, they are imbued with political tensions, conflicts and alliances. However, unlike race and nationhood, gender has only relatively recently been widely understood and recognized as a contested political arena.

Countless wars have been initiated and fought over issues of national identity, and most societies, at some point in their history, have tried to 'justify' their political oppression of ethnic minority groups. Two of the most blatant examples of racism during the last century were Nazi Germany and Afrikaner-led South Africa. Both countries, quite rightly, experienced vehement condemnation for their policies; the ideologies and thinking that informed Nazism and apartheid are now recognized by most as being inhuman and barbaric.[1] Yet another form of apartheid, one that continues to politically marginalize and segregate women, continues in a number of countries, often without any orchestrated international censure or denunciation. Indeed, it can be argued that notions of political correctness, perversely, dissuade many in the West from denouncing, for example, the treatment of women in Islamic societies and the maltreatment of Islamic women in the West. One reason for this may be because few if any countries or societies can claim not to have been underpinned, at some point in their history, by gender inequality. Most still are. In terms of governments and nation states, there are no innocents here. The demands for gender justice that such marginalization provokes has, however, been voiced by women for centuries (see Rendall, 1985), taking a particular form in the twentieth century as modern feminism and the women's liberation movement (Greer, 1970). The point that I am making, then, is that the critical study of men and masculinities has a personal–political dimension to it, as would, in a not dissimilar way, the study of black and white power and identities in those societies where racism is an implicit or explicit feature.

This recognition that individual men and women are not, indeed cannot be, totally exempt from the political consequences and implications of their personal actions, has long been a central tenet of feminism, espoused by all streams of feminist thought from radical (see Dworkin, 1981) through to poststructuralist (see Elam, 1994). It is not only that the personal is political in terms of the power dynamics by which the public and private are defined and constructed (Cohen, 1997), nor is it only an emphasis on resolving 'personal problems though political action' (Pateman, 1983, quoted in MacInnes, 1998: 137). Following Griffin (1996), I would argue that the individual is politicized into a collective discourse, which subsequently informs and creates the categories by which women and men exist as fluid 'epistemic communities' (see also Assiter, 1996). To assume that the personal is a somehow privileged apolitical space, a 'defence against invasion by the wider system' (Craib, 1994: 134), appears somewhat naive given what we know of the gendered public and private realms (see also chapter 5).

However, this said, one cannot assume that all men are oppressors (of women) or that all women are victims (of men). While some feminists would concur with such a view (for example, 'Redstockings Manifesto', 1970), many would not (for example, hooks, 1995). Nevertheless, once the point is made that men and masculinities exist in a political context, then the issue arises as to how such a context can be critically interrogated and understood theoretically. What light can be shed on this hitherto relatively invisible yet fundamental part of the social web? This brings me to the second aim of the chapter, which is to explore the concept of men as a political category and the various and contrasting responses to feminism, by men, during the past four decades.

The chapter begins by looking at the 'masculinity in crisis' thesis. Is there such a social phenomenon, or is it something of a 'moral panic' articulated by those, men especially, who consider that feminism somehow threatens the 'social fabric', and, not least, them as men? Such issues cannot be understood without analysing the debates surrounding men and women as political categories, and these are examined under the heading 'Men as a political category'. It is argued that women and men are political categories, but categories that are grounded not in biology but in discursivity. Whether or not one concurs with the notion of men and women as political classes or groupings, what does seem evident is the influence of feminism as a political discourse, especially across the Western world. Somewhat inevitably, men have responded to this 'challenge' to their power and subjectivity in contrasting ways, and these responses by men to feminism will be examined in the section on 'Men's responses to feminism'. The final section explores the debates surrounding men changing, together with some of the epistemological issues arising from the reshaping of men's subjectivities.

A crisis of masculinity or a moral panic?

A discourse of crisis

Considering the inequalities of contemporary gender relations, the notion of a crisis of masculinity would appear to many to be quite bizarre. For how is it possible that men and masculinity are in 'crisis' given the continued, worldwide, material inequalities that favour males and men? Despite the obvious contradiction, the notion of a male crisis is very prevalent at this juncture in history; indeed it pervades many of the social, political and academic debates about men. To underline this point I will use three recent public expositions concerning men and masculinity that cut to the heart of the issue. Each is quite different in context but together they illustrate the depth and extent of the phenomenon. The first is a quote from Susan Faludi's book *Stiffed: The Betrayal of the Modern Man* (1999):

> Why don't contemporary men rise up in protest at their betrayal? If they have experienced so many of the same injuries as women, the same humiliations, why don't they challenge the culture as women did? Why can't men seem to act? . . . Men aren't simply refusing to 'give up the reins of power', as some feminists have argued. The reins have already slipped from most of their hands, anyway. (ibid.: 603)

Faludi's US-based thesis is that modern man has been 'betrayed' by a combination of factors, notably a sexist consumer culture that commodifies and objectifies the male; the loss of economic authority; the weakening and reshaping of men's relationship to the world of work; the public exposure of dominant notions of masculinity to ridicule and censure; and the failure of men, as a gender group, to 'rebel' against their emasculinization by 'the culture'. Central to Faludi's argument is that feminism has contributed to the undermining of patriarchy and the male paradigm of control. Although this process has forced countless numbers of men to reconsider previously held beliefs about male roles and dominant masculinities, it has also, inadvertently, left men with a crisis of confidence. For men are increasingly caught in the pincers of a culture that still expects them to 'be at the helm', yet also requires them to engage in reflexive analysis of their masculinity: 'Men have no clearly defined enemy who is oppressing them. How can men be oppressed when the culture has already identified them as the oppressors, and when they see themselves that way?' (ibid.: 604). Faludi sees the 'answer' to this dilemma in women and men uniting in rebellion against their common enemy, that is 'the culture', which, she argues, is at the centre of this 'betrayal of modern man'. However, just what this 'culture' is, and how it has come to exist external to the wider constitution of gender power relations, is not explored by Faludi. Indeed, her understanding of culture – and power – as monomorphic is, I suggest, inherently flawed. Nevertheless, Faludi's text is significant in that it can be read as an attempt by a feminist to align with others (non-feminists) in declaring 'no more sex war' (against men) (see, for example, Lyndon, 1992).

The second commentary on the 'male crisis' is based on a recent study (Scase, 1999) that forecasts the changing shape of households in Britain during the first decades of the millennium. Widely reported in the UK press, the study suggests that due to the fact of women's increased 'opportunities and choices in their lives', particularly over the roles they can play, more women are choosing (happily) to live alone 'unfettered by the demands of a husband and children' (*The Guardian*, 1999: 6). Juxtaposing this observation with the suggestion that 'macho stereotypes' are a contributing factor in the 60 per cent increase in suicides by young British men between 1991 and 1997, the case is put that while a 'brave new world dawns for (single) women', (single) men face an increasingly 'sad, lonely and unhealthy' existence, being unable to cope physically, emotionally or psychologically with their isolation. The sense of urgency that such notions engender for many commentators is captured in the following quote: 'The findings are a red flashing light telling us that there is something badly wrong in our culture. If we do not transform young men's lives, we face an uncivilised future' (Adrienne Katz, director of the UK charity, Young Voice, quoted in *The Observer*, 1999: 13).

Underpinning these warnings as to the sad state of twenty-first century man is additional research in the UK and Japan. For example, a recent UK study reveals increasing numbers of adult males choosing to continue living in the parental home (ONS, 2000) rather than marry or cohabit; men choosing to stay 'with mum' until their late thirties rather than be independent. This data is interpreted as men's inability to grapple with the challenges now posited on them by women's new found independence, as a retreat from responsibility. While in Japan – a country considered by many to be a bastion of misogynistic practices and beliefs, yet also experiencing similar shifts and changes in terms of traditional gender roles – concern for the 'Japanese male psyche' is now apparent. Increasingly, such commentators on Japanese contemporary society are highlighting concerns over, not only the psychological well-being of Japanese males, but also the inflexibility of maleist-orientated Japanese culture (Zinberg, 2000; Makino, 2001).

The apocalyptical implications arising from a masculinity in crisis are well caught in my third account, which draws on two reviews of the film *Fight Club*. Released in late 1999, this film, based on the novel by Chuck Palahniuk, starring Brad Pitt and directed by David Fincher, was presented and marketed as a 'glorious satire of our "crisis of masculinity" '. The following quotes, taken from the internet site *Movie Review Query Engine*, were written by American males, both amateur reviewers, who submitted their accounts and opinions of the film for publication across the web.

> 'Fight Club' is, by and large, an effective film that surrealistically describes the status of the American male at the end of the 20th century: disenchanted, unfulfilled, castrated and looking for a way out. The beginning of the film is pitch perfect, chronicling the desperation and despair of modern living in a society where comfort is the measure of success. It's the ultimate visual statement of the question: Are you working for your car or is your car working for you? A consumer society that emasculates men. No rite of passage into manhood, no lion or bear to kill. In an era where men do not have missions, in the urban wilderness, what is there to hunt? To dominate? To kill? (Clifton, 1999)

> If there is one thing that 'Fight Club' unabashedly displays, it's that the era of the sensitive male is over. Men do not gush with gooey sentimentality. Restraint is only a temporary state of mind. There is an animal inside all of us, and it's aching to break out. But the rules of society and the pleas of our local community beg us to be kinder and gentler. Thus, we brush aside any feelings of aggression and replace them with happy thoughts and trance music. But just once, I'd like to catch up to that guy who cut me off and run him off the road. (Yen, 1999)

On this particular web site there were over 170 reviews of *Fight Club*, many of which were entirely sympathetic with the above expressions of male angst and barely suppressed anger, if not hatred, at the 'culture' (*pace* Faludi) that has brought men to this 'desperate plight'. However, not all men had an identical reading of the film. One male reviewer labelled it 'silly, pretentious and idiotic' (Foley, 1999). A further described it as 'an avalanche of silliness', the only danger being that 'some people will actually take it seriously' (Edmonds, 1999). A third noted, rather chillingly, that 'the film is technically flawed, but coming in the wake of rage crimes like Littleton it could not be more timely' (Leeper, 1999).[2]

None of the above quotes or analyses 'proves' that there is a crisis of masculinity. What they do show is that a discourse of masculinity in crisis has emerged to some prominence. That is, across many societies, most notably but not only in the Western world, the idea that men are facing some nihilistic future, degraded, threatened and marginalized by a combination of women's 'successful' liberation and wider social and economic transformations has become a highly potent, almost common-sense, if at times contested, understanding of men at this point in history.

The crisis discourse in politics and public policy

Education Significantly, the male crisis discourse has seeped out of cultural discussion and is now increasingly being used to inform public policy. For example, the discourse is being utilized by politicians to account for male educational 'underachievement' (for discussion, see Epstein et al., 1999; Francis, 2000; Lingard and Douglas, 1999; Arnot, David and Weiner, 1999). With politicians in the USA, Australia, Germany, the UK and Japan all grappling with the question of 'what to do about the boys?', and research in the UK showing females now outperforming males across the educational spectrum for the first time (Elliott-Major, 2000; for discussion, see Francis, 1998, 2000), many, mostly male, politicians and policy makers talk of a new gender crisis, one revolving around males. The power of the male crisis discourse is revealed in the fact that it enables politicians of all persuasions to declare that equal opportunities have gone too far in promoting equality for girls, and that attention should now turn to addressing the low self-esteem and particular 'needs' of boys (Kenway, 1995). In short, rather than welcome the emergence of new and powerful femininities and see girls' educational achievements as the new norm in Western societies, politicians sense the cultural turn is one that now allows them to identify males as the new 'disadvantaged'. Not only does this rhetoric fail to account for class and ethnic variations in male educational achievement (see Mac an Ghaill, 1994; Sewell, 1997), it also speaks to the masculinist paradigm at the heart of education; that is, a cultural logic that posits masculinism, encapsulated in individualistic competition, outcome, achievement, work ethic and performativity, as both the purpose and defining character of education (see also Prichard, 2000). This debate is also explored by Connell (2000), who argues that the school setting provides its own particular gender order, albeit one frequently themed through the powerful 'heterosexual "romance" pattern of gender relations' (2000: 161). This prevailing masculine/feminine dichotomy is also revealed in Becky Francis's (1998, also 2000) research that explores some of the dominant (re)constructions of gender identity engaged in by primary school children. However, Francis's research also reveals and explores the capacity of these same children to adopt more flexible responses to images and messages of gender stereotyping in schools and elsewhere. In all these studies, as in similar research, the school setting reveals itself to be both a conduit for dominant ideologies/discourses of gender and a vehicle for the validation of a particular form of masculinity. At the same time, however, it is itself a setting under change. And part of this change, as currently experienced in the educational systems of many Western countries, is the reconfiguring of classroom and education achievements by some boys and girls. It is the fascinating but complex dynamic surrounding and signalling these educational changes that proponents of the male crisis discourse fail to grapple with. Instead, they prefer to lend spurious legitimation to the concerns of those, for example, in the men's movements, while conveniently failing to recognize or acknowledge that this so-called new gender inequality is completely reversed once women and men leave education for paid employment (see also Blackmore, 1997, 1999).[3]

Health The male crisis discourse is also enlisted to 'account' for men's health issues, particularly those concerned with heart disease, forms of cancer, stress, suicide, smoking, drinking and mortality rates. To be sure, research concerned with examining the relationship between men's health and forms of masculinity is not new (Connell, 2000), and, as Connell notes, patterns of male health have to be understood in terms of ethnicity, class, culture and economics. Nevertheless, the availability of the male crisis discourse has enabled those who would seek to polarize gender differences to do exactly that, but under the rubric of a 'men's health crisis'. One consequence of this is that while there are important associations to be made between dominant expressions of masculinity and men's mental and physical well-being (for discussion, see Sabo and Gordon, 1995) the power of the male crisis discourse distorts or hides these connections. It does this by polarizing the debate into one of competition for health resources between women and men, while also enflaming the 'moral panic' and ensuing backlash against feminism and women's issues generally.

Crime A third area where public policy and the male crisis thesis connect is crime and criminality. Historically, law and order debates have often used general concerns regarding the behaviour and morality of males to inform policies on crime and punishment (Collier, 1998). For example, mid-twentieth century studies undertaken by Thrasher (1936), Whyte (1943) and Cohen (1955) encapsulated, at the time, many peoples' anxieties and fears about dysfunctional, potentially violent and criminal males, usually working-class young men. Similarly, the emergence or visibility of so-called 'dangerous others' (Collier, 1998) in society is not new, particularly when these 'others' are identified to be black males (see Westwood, 1990; Shilling, 1993). Thus, when taken from a historical perspective, it is possible to see issues of race, ethnicity and class linking with concerns around men to produce a particular moral panic of a period. However, as has been discussed, there is a further legitimizing process at work in the contemporary male crisis discourse, one which in its articulation turns attention to the contribution of women (feminism) to men's situation. For while most crime continues to be the province of males, the crisis of masculinity discourse suggests that the inability of many men to cope with the new expectations of women (feminism), combined with the demise of traditional work patterns and male roles, makes them especially vulnerable to engaging in forms of resistance that lead on to criminal behaviour. This discourse has particular potency when used in connection with the criminality of boys and youths (for example, Phillips, 1993). As Collier (1998) argues, the contemporary 'trouble with boys' thesis can be enlisted by politicians and commentators to argue that equal opportunities, 'political correctness' and feminism have gone too far, to the point that they are perceived as directly implicated in the current male crisis. In short, women's new-found expectations and achievements are a social problem, not a social good – not least because they serve to put those males who are seen as most likely to offend (working-class white and black youths) in an untenable situation whereby their 'natural' masculine inclinations have no ready outlet. Thus the relationship between feminism, male criminality and redundant and dysfunctional forms of masculinity is reified.[4]

Procreation A final example of where public policy meets the male crisis concerns birth control and reproductive law. In the USA increasing publicity is being given to the number of conflicts between women and men over procreative matters. These conflicts centre around 'sperm wars' (Sheldon, 1999, 2000) and illustrate, for some commentators, a new chapter in the ubiquitous battle of the sexes. This conflict arises from the apparent deep fear of some men that their body fluids are being 'stolen' by women to produce babies they did not want but now have to support. In the new so-called 'postfeminist' era, these hapless men become the 'disposable sex' (Farrell, 1993), tricked into parenthood by women and condemned by law to be economically responsible for their child. This antifeminist perspective argues that women's new-found social and economic power has resulted in them acquiring unfair (legal) advantage over men, particularly in procreative matters. The result has been to render men 'neutered' (Phillips, 1999), disempowered and marginalized: 'first women stole men's jobs and earning power, now their body fluids' (quoted in Sheldon, 2000: 12). However, Sheldon (2000) argues that this understanding 'is flawed and misleading' in that it fails to recognize the conservative (maleist) culture informing the legal structuring of procreative disputes. In short, while the 'procreation realm' (Marsiglio, 1998) is increasingly complex and subject to legalistic frameworks, the inherent sexual division of labour is not changed, particularly in its manifestation as the nuclear family.

Whether the public–political concerns be education, crime, procreation or health, underpinning the male crisis discourse is the sense of threat and disruption to the social order that may well accrue if men are unable to redefine themselves in a postfeminist era. Caught between the expectations of (feminist-inspired) political correctness and their 'inherent' masculine desire to control and dominate (women), men are seen, to use Faludi's term, as 'stiffed'. In short, twenty-first century man faces a bleak, unforgiving future, unless, that is, 'we [*sic*] can transform men'.

The male crisis in perspective

Despite its reductionistic underpinnings, the notion of a homogenous body of men 'in crisis' is now commonplace in many contemporary studies of men, with numerous experts urging males to find their 'authentic selves', outside of the stereotypical machismo that damages and 'imprisons' them. In seeking to problematize 'modern masculinity', increasing numbers of counsellors and others suggest that the 'major male identity crisis' requires males to 're-assess their masculinity' by adopting roles that are 'relevant to modern times' (Hodson, 1984: 2; also Clare, 2000; Gillette and Moore, 1991; Horrocks, 1994; West, 1996; Biddulph, 1994).

Within the sociology of masculinity there are a number of responses to such a discourse or thesis. In particular, it is important to draw attention to the main discourses being used to reify this 'crisis'. First, the idea of a 'crisis of masculinity' speaks of masculinity in the singular; usually white, heterosexual and ethnocentric. Moreover, the masculinity posited is ahistorical and absolute, with men perceived as an homogenous group lacking class, ethnic, sexual or racial differentiations. Men are, paradoxically, understood to be somehow simultaneously powerful and threatening, yet also rendered powerless by external (often feminist) forces. Drawing on (pseudo)psychoanalytical models, males are seen as riven with barely controlled urges of sexuality and violence (*pace* Freud), their attempts at 'self-civilization' being in constant tension with their innate aggression. Mythologies of an 'ancient conquering' masculinity are unproblematically reified within an 'inner male psyche', now seen as damaged through consumerism and/or 'domestication' (*pace* Jung). Following from this, the 'need' for men to find their identity in fraternal projects and missions is emphasized (*pace* Bly), as is the radical juxtaposition of masculinity to femininity, particularly in terms of dominance over 'Others', women especially. The assumption that an ordered society is dependent on the maintenance of a given functional gender order (*pace* Parsons), is increasingly being presented alongside a homogenous view of men as a unitary, complementary, category of identity, imbued with 'natural' traits and dispositions. Politically, few studies undertaken by men into the 'male crisis' declare a profeminist position; an exception is Biddulph (1994). More frequently, they can be identified as part of the 'men's studies' genre (*pace* Bly) and thus personally/politically antipathetic towards feminism (for discussion, see Canaan and Griffin, 1990). Theoretically, the studies are often underdeveloped, relying on simplistic Freudian or Jungian understandings of self and identity; that is, one where the 'true self' is located in some inner psyche, under layers of socialization processes and inhibitions, many of which, being informed by dominant gender codes, are now seen as inappropriate in a 'modern society', if not basically flawed. Both sex role theory and structural functionalism are also prominent in many of the writings, though the theoretical connections tend to be implicit rather than explicit.

In short, many writings on the crisis of masculinity assume that men and their masculinity are homogenous and biologically indivisible, sustained by a natural order that has been severely threatened by women's 'misguided' attempts to transform the gender 'balance'. Importantly, and what is of concern, feminism is seen by many to be the guilty party in all this. Thus, the crisis of masculinity thesis can also be read as a form of backlash against women in general and feminism in particular (Lingard and Douglas, 1999). At this point we can see that the crisis of masculinity thesis can be used to divert attention from the power effects of men's largely still dominant position across the social sphere. Certainly, traditional notions of masculinity do come with a price for men, particularly in respect of their ability to develop empathy, understanding and emotional intimacies (see chapter 5). Men who invest heavily in controlling and instrumental forms of being put much at risk, notably relationships with children and partners. However, this problematic of men/masculinities must be placed in the wider context of continuing gender 'power plays' (Francis, 1998). The so-called feminization of labour, seen by some to have arisen from dramatic economic changes in the West and understood by Faludi and others to be a significant factor in the crisis of masculinity, can be more accurately described as a re-masculinization of organizational culture occurring from the 1960s to the present day (Kerfoot and Knights, 1993; Roper, 1994; Whitehead, 1999c), bringing with it work intensification and job insecurity for both men *and women*. As Francis (1998) argues, most workplaces cannot seriously be considered 'feminized', given that childcare support is still minimal and that rights over maternity and paternity leave continue to be wholly inadequate in most Western countries. In short, it is important to recognize that 'the meanings and fantasies accompanying the equation of men and power are largely undisturbed' (Segal, 1999: 161), despite several decades of feminism. Once again, accounts and understandings of gender (difference) can be seen to play across a complex landscape coloured by both the nature–nurture dualism and harsh political and material realities. Despite the complexities, it is important to keep an eye on the political inferences of a male crisis. As Robinson rightly warns, 'there is much symbolic power to be reaped [by white men] from occupying the social and discursive position of subject-in-crisis' (2000: 9).

However, despite these reservations, it would be unfair to totally discount the extensive research that has revealed something of the 'predicaments' of men at this juncture in history. Indeed, that is certainly not my intent. One should not be dismissive of the profound changes that have occurred in the economic and social structure of many modern societies, and the impact that, for example, women's increased presence in employment, education and politics has wrought. New and future generations of men, certainly those in post-modern, post-industrial societies, may well find that any adoption of traditional (dated) masculine postures is dismissed by women as sad and ridiculous. Across both the public and private sectors, more women are asserting their independence, and in so doing are challenging, directly or inadvertently, the dominant stereotypes and traditional notions that have long reinforced gender differences and inequalities (for example, Maile, 1999). These movements have consequences for men and masculinity, as writers across the sociology of masculinity accept, and, yes, many men have suffered, emotionally and materially, as a direct result of transformations outside their immediate influence (for discussion, see Connell, 1995; Robinson, 2000; Rutherford, 1992; Segal, 1997; Seidler, 1997). Caught in a vortex of gender, social and economic change, many men, particularly those lacking the necessary social or cultural capital to protect themselves from such changes, are increasingly denied respite in traditional relationships and the self-validation elicited by fraternalistic male breadwinner work patterns.

Yet in recognizing that for particular groups of men, especially the long-term unemployed and low-skilled, discourses of feminism may well be difficult to reconcile with their own lack of power and opportunity (Segal, 1999), it is important to put the 'crisis of masculinity' in a historical perspective as well as a contemporary one. For while it may appear so, the notion of masculinity in crisis is not new. In the USA, Herb Goldberg forewarned of a male crisis in his 1976 text *The Hazards of Being Male*. In 1977 both Paul Willis and Andrew Tolson alerted us to some of the identity consequences for those white, British males whose sense of masculinity was primarily invested in a fast diminishing, working-class, breadwinner, factory-floor work culture. If we go back a generation from the 1970s to the 1950s, the research by Hacker (1957) and Hartley (1959) into the state of American men's masculinity posits an almost identical thesis. So by any account, Western males can be seen to have been in a 'crisis' for over fifty years now. Yet the debate did not originate even in the 1950s. For the belief that 'soft' or emasculated males are a danger, a threat to the social and national good, certainly prefigures contemporary debates. Suzik's (1999) study of the creation of the American Civilian Conservation Corps reveals concerns in America in the early 1930s that young men had been emasculated by the effects of the Great Depression. Similarly, Edley and Wetherall (1995) remind us that the Boy Scouts of America were formed in 1910, precisely to create a new generation of 'masculine males' (p. 74). And in his study of the development of the sex role paradigm, Pleck (1981) notes that the theory resonated with concerns at the time of the First World War over the capacity of US males to be fit for national service. If we go back even further to the 1800s, a century during which countries such as the UK and the USA experienced profound if not traumatic social and economic movements, concerns about men (of all classes) and their decadence, morality, sexuality, carnality and lack of domestic and civilizing traits were never far from social and political discourse (Kimmel, 1996; Roper and Tosh, 1991). Indeed, the nineteenth-century writings of Marx and Engels identify a 'lumpen proletariat', which they describe as a 'threatening substratum' of society, a predominantly 'male rabble', feckless and lacking self-control (for discussion, see Mann, 1992). Finally, Faludi's thesis that American males are suffering an emotional crisis as a consequence of a rampant contemporary consumerist–feminist 'culture', is placed in context by Kimmel's (1995b, also 1987b) historical analyses of nineteenth-century writings on men, which reveal that 'fantasies of masculine retreat' from 'feminization and consumerism' have been a key theme of writings by and on American men for over 200 years.

Public concern over men and masculinity is clearly not confined to the late twentieth and early twenty-first centuries, a fact that should not surprise us once we recognize something of the historical and social conditions under which masculinities 'exist'. As descriptors, neither men nor masculinity are fixed: they always have been and always will be somewhat transitory generalizations of identity, inadequate in themselves for revealing the subjectivities of the individual male. However, so much is invested in these descriptors, both in terms of power and ideas of social well-being, that anxieties and moral panics concerning men are readily manifest across the social (and worldwide) web. This does not make the crisis real in any absolute sense – though for some individual men anxieties concerning their sense of (masculine) identity may well be quite vivid. What the crisis of masculinity thesis does do, is reveal to us the importance of understanding men and masculinities as discursive; that is, dominant, subordinated and political ways of talking and thinking about men in multiple cultural settings.

Men as a political category

It is not possible to critically interrogate the contemporary debates concerning a 'crisis' of men and masculinity without recognizing the categorical and political implications of such accounts. Men do not exist in some neutral, benign context, but, by definition, exist in relation to women. As such, their existence, somewhat inevitably, has political implications. In emphasizing this fact, profeminist writers such as Stoltenberg (1977, 1990) and Hearn (1987, 1998a) have described men (and women) as a gender class, sustained by the power, prestige and privileges that patriarchy bestows on the male. The notion that men exist as a distinct class does have some value, for it unambiguously posits women and men in a political arena, with potentially quite contrasting opportunities to access power and privilege and, thus, material well-being. As Monique Wittig argues, a central aim of feminism is to strive for the elimination of these political categories of 'man' and 'woman', in the process freeing all individuals from their historical, ideological fetters:

> it is our historical task, and only ours (feminists) to define what we call oppression in materialist terms, to make it evident that women are a class, which is to say that the category 'woman' as well as the category 'man' are political and economic categories not eternal ones. Our fight aims to suppress men as a class, not through genocidal, but political struggle. Once the class 'men' disappears, 'women' will disappear as well, for there are no slaves without masters. (Wittig, 1992, quoted in Hearn, 1998a: 806)

As is discussed in chapter 3, the 'juridico discursive' (Foucault, 1980; also Sawicki, 1991) model of power, generally assumed in the notion of 'class', locates power as a centralized source, and is thus inadequate in terms of understanding the (micro)processes of resistance, differentiations and networks of collusion across and within the gender categories of woman and man. Gender *political categories* is, I suggest, a more appropriate term, for it signals the possibility of power differentials without reducing women and men to predictable or culturally uniform classes of being. Yet in presenting the case for seeing men as a political category it is equally important to draw attention to how such a category is sustained, not only by men's supposedly instrumental desire for power over women, but through the more subtle and arguably more profound conditions of discursive association; that is, the dominant, privileged knowledges that serve to reify the 'historically transitory' (Hearn, 1998a) category of men.

The discursive connection

When individual men voice their anger at women and feminism for supposedly emasculating them through political correctness and/or domestication, they are not speaking as neutral observers. On the contrary, they are overtly, or at least implicitly, positioning themselves as gender representatives speaking for and of the category 'men'. An individual's ability to do this is greatly enhanced by recourse to some 'natural knowledge', which is usually offered as a precursor of common sense. As Petersen observes, despite being presented as given, such knowledges are not apolitical:

> Natural knowledge has served to 'naturalise' relations of power, seen clearly in the discourse on sexuality and discourse on sex differences. The idea that there exists a prediscursive natural or biological realm, separate from and unaffected by a cultural realm, or relations of power, is one that is deeply inscribed in Western thought. [Such] conceptions of sex/gender are premised on, and insistently refer to, a tradition of viewing culture as malleable relative to nature: that is, culture, rather than nature, is the thing that can, and indeed should, be changed. (1998: 121)

The notion of a 'crisis' of men/masculinity can be seen, then, as a desire to change culture in order to maintain a 'natural' gender order. Implicit in this notion is, first, some men's desire to continue or return to a given set of power relations between women and men which is, in the main, materially advantageous for them; second, evidence of some men's attempts to reinforce or construct a particular sense of masculine identity that provides them with a feeling of potency in an increasingly insecure world. However, the ensuing belief that something is 'fundamentally amiss' with contemporary gender relations is only tenable if one assumes that a previous natural state of affairs has now given way to an 'unnatural' state. Importantly, one does not have to 'believe' in natural gender differences in order to enlist this as a discourse to support and reify a particular political position. It is sufficient that such a discourse exists. At this point it can be seen that notions of men and masculinities have the capacity to produce 'truths' and 'knowledges' through their discursive properties, in the process reinforcing women and men as political categories. As Foucault puts it:

> Discourses are practices that systematically form the objects of which they speak. . . . Discourses are not about objects; they do not identify objects, they constitute them and in the practice of doing so conceal their own invention. (1972: 49)

In Foucauldian terms, the discourse of 'crisis of masculinity' has the capacity to constitute man as nature, while concealing the (politicized) invention invoked in such a notion behind a language of 'natural traits'. At the level of factual 'truth' the crisis of masculinity does not exist; it is speculation underpinned by mythology. Nevertheless, what is factual is that such a discourse exists in the public domain, possibly enhanced through the tabloidization of (ever-present) gender shifts. Consequently, the 'man' as speaker reveals himself to be a member of a political (gender) category that exists in some tension with other categories, in this case most notably that of 'woman'. This is not primarily a struggle over power and material advantage – though there is that dimension; it is a struggle over dominant discursive representations of masculinity and their relationship vis-à-vis femininity. Clegg describes such a dynamic as follows:

Language defines the possibilities of meaningful existence at the same time as it limits them. Through language we constitute our sense of ourselves as distinct subjectivities through a myriad of 'discursive practices', practices of talk, text, writing, cognition, argumentation, representation generally. The *meanings of* and *membership within* the categories of discursive practice will be a constant site of struggle over power, as identities become posited, resisted and fought-over in attachment to the subjectivity that constructs any particular individuality. (1998: 29; original emphasis)

The centrality of language to notions of men and masculinity is the subject of increasing interest across the sociology of masculinity. As research by Scott F. Kiesling indicates, men draw on the discursive resources and terms associated with dominant masculinity to substantiate fraternal networks and reify power frameworks (2001; also Johnson and Meinhof, 1997; see also chapter 7). To be sure, the ways of being male/man which such languages suggest are highly idealized if not mythical in origin; nevertheless, the material consequences of such actions are very real. A further test by which to emphasize the centrality of language to gender is to pose the following (hypothetical) question: 'If we ceased to talk about women and men would women and men cease?' The answer, I suggest, is yes. For the language we use to define and identify 'women' and 'men' is identical to that which we draw on for self-signification (Butler, 1990, 1993), and, as Clegg indicates, there is no self external to its discursive existence. In recognizing this we confirm not only the unlikelihood of us ceasing to use sex and gender differences as pivotal identity constructs, but also the relationship of identity to power. Thus in positing women and men as unitary categories – a socially expedient fiction – we also expose, and, ironically, reify, the political dimensions of these categories. As the discursive fictions of 'woman' and 'man' become signified through social intercourse, so are accompanying myths and 'truths' enlisted to give some grounding to that which is ultimately ephemeral. However, as Foucault (1970) stresses, discourse is not merely about speaking; it also signals who can speak and act, under what conditions and, importantly, which voices and knowledges are privileged by and within this discourse: '*Man* appears in his ambiguous position as an object of knowledge and as a subject that knows' (Foucault, 1970, quoted in Ball, 1990: 14; my emphasis).

In making the case for seeing women and men as political categories, I can fully appreciate why many individuals would baulk at being located in a particular gender community and thus declared 'politicized'. I am well aware that not all gay men, for example, see themselves as part of the gay movement, many being keen to disassociate from any such personal–political invention (for example, Rankin, 2000). However, whatever an individual's preferences, behaviours, dispositions and so on, the fact remains that political categories do exist. Gay, woman, black are politicized identities operating at a macro level across society, and their importance as points of relation to the 'Other' in terms of identity construction cannot be overemphasized, any more than can the political implications of being a gay man. If one doubts this, one only has to look at the continued heated debates within the most democratic societies concerning, for example, the rights of gay and lesbian people, institutionalized racism, and women and abortion. Individual women and men may not wish to directly contribute to these debates, but the outcomes of these political issues will impact, at some level, on them and their families. In short, to deny association at an individual level, which is one's privilege, is not to be excused association at a societal level.

Being within a political grouping is no predictor of behaviour, so I am not suggesting that political categories are deterministic; nor am I suggesting that being woman, gay and/or black inevitably secures that person in a given community of practice. What I am suggesting is that we should recognize women and men as discursive subjects but existing within political categories across the social web. To deny this reality is to fail to recognize that gay, black, white, lesbian, heterosexual and so on exist in any political dimension beyond the individual.

Men's responses to feminism

Marking differences

The manner in which the personal and political are acted out by men in their gender and sexual relations with women and other men, is, of course, variable and largely unpredictable. Such contingency of expression, having less to do with biology than with the social and cultural setting, also reminds us that constantly shifting idealized representations of masculinity can be subject to public and private tensions at any particular historical moment. As has been discussed, many of the more 'traditional' notions of masculinity, and the associated practices of men, have come into conflict with feminism and the changing expectations of increasing numbers of women. This, of itself, is not necessarily problematic for either women or men. Indeed, as Wittig (1992) argues, such confrontation, when it leads to change and equality, remains a key aim of feminism and feminist scholarship. As such, many (pro)feminists welcome the idea that modern man is under some pressure to change his attitudes and practices towards women. At the very least, notions of 'men in crisis' indicate that feminism, as a coalition of diverse but complementary political discourses, is not easily ignored. Indeed, I would argue that all men, in some form or another, have had to, or will have to, consider their relationship to the questions, criticisms and demands of feminists. But not only of those women who consider themselves feminists. For the discourse of women's rights has extended beyond feminist scholarship and is now present, to some degree, in virtually every aspect of the social network.

Not surprisingly, men's desire and ability to accommodate feminist discourse within their subjectivity has, to date, proved quite varied. As is discussed below, for most men the process of cultural and personal 'adjustment', which feminism demands, is neither readily nor easily undertaken. One consequence of the unease that women's rights triggers in some men is to retreat to extreme antifeminism. The crisis of masculinity thesis may be largely fictional, but the existence of men as a political category is not, a fact that is made further apparent by the antagonism towards feminism/feminists that many of those in, for example, the 'men's movement' display. Increasingly, such men are prepared to publicly associate themselves with a fierce antifeminist position, often 'justifying' such stances in terms of the need to hold onto some obscure 'masculine heritage' (for example, McAulay, 2000).[5]

It is safe to assume that there have always been differences amongst men in their attitudes and responses to the notion of gender equality. However, since the mid-1970s these differences have become more marked as increasing numbers of men, across Western societies especially, aligned themselves with the various social movements emerging in response to feminism. One of the earliest examinations of this phenomenon was undertaken by Clatterbaugh (1990), who focused on the following six major perspectives seen to have arisen in North America since the 1970s.

1 The conservative perspective This is an antifeminist perspective that draws on both biological and moral standpoints to argue that traditional gender roles should not be changed. In opposing feminist agendas, conservatives believe that men and masculinity are indivisible, a natural and functional synergy created through evolutionary processes and society's innate need for structure and order (for example see Gilder, 1973).

2 Men's rights perspective Proponents of this perspective argue that while women have benefited from feminism, this has only served to create new injustices and a new sexism against men. Men's rights advocates seek to bring about legislative changes of benefit to men, particularly in the areas of divorce, child custody, sexual harassment and domestic violence prosecution (for example, see Goldberg, 1976).

3 The spiritual perspective Otherwise known as the *mythopoetic* movement, adherents to this perspective draw on various Jungian and Freudian theories to argue that masculinity is formed deep in men's psyche. While some of those in the mythopoetic movement are not avidly antifeminist (for example, Rowan, 1987), many are. Exemplified by the works of Robert Bly, advocates of the spiritual perspective believe that feminism and the women's movement are emasculating men from their 'inner selves', in so doing denying men access to the archetypal myths and rituals that would otherwise enable them to experience growth and self-discovery (for example, see Bly, 1990).

4 The socialist feminist perspective Drawing on Marxist understandings of social relations and production, men socialist feminists seek to highlight the alienation men experience when subjected to the systems of production in a capitalist society. Broadly aligning with a Marxist feminist perspective (Hartmann, 1981), men advocates of socialist feminism argue that masculinity has become symbolized and inculcated by material greed competitiveness and a narrow, intense and damaging focus on waged labour. In seeking an 'antisexist society', adherents to this perspective are closely aligned with a pro-feminist agenda (for example, see Tolson, 1977).

5 *The group-specific perspective* This is less a coherent, homogenous movement of men, and more a loose coalition of (usually profeminist) perspectives informed by the specific experiences of, for example, black men (Staples, 1986), gay men (Edwards, 1994), Jewish men (Brod, 1994) and Latino/Chicano men (Mirande, 1997). Within this genre, writers such as Alfredo Mirande (1997) are now openly calling for a Chicano/Latino men's studies. In many ways, not least through their critique of ethnocentric and standardized discussions on men and masculinity, group-specific scholarship can be linked to similar feminist writings on the (marginalized) narratives and experiences of gay women and black women (for example, see Ferree, Lorber and Hess, 1999).

6 *The profeminist perspective* Adherents of this perspective are, along with socialist feminists, generally considered the most closely aligned to feminism and feminist agendas. However, in being sensitive to the (historical) power of malestream accounts to both define women's realities and, thus, potentially appropriate feminism (for discussion, see Hall, 1990), profeminists, being men, do not consider themselves feminists as such. Rather, profeminists are men who seek to develop 'a critique of men's practice' informed by feminism (Hearn, 1987), while recognizing that their position as men is founded on continuing inequalities between women and men (Heath, 1987). In this respect, profeminist perspectives can be placed in contrast to certain writings in the 'men's studies' field. Many feminists have expressed concern that some 'men studies' perspectives, while presented as contributing to an analysis of men and masculinities, are often less concerned with feminist agendas and less explicit in their personal–political orientation vis-à-vis feminism (for discussion, see Canaan and Griffin, 1990; Skelton, 1998; also Whitehead, 2000).

Political polarizations

Since Clatterbaugh published his study, the polarization of the various socio-political groupings of men in relation to feminism has become acute. Profeminist men in academia have made significant contributions to the critical debates on men and masculinities, indeed their work for the most part informs this book. Similarly, more men, and not only white American males, appear prepared to critically reflect on themselves as masculine subjects in the postmodern, post-industrial age, in so doing, engaging in ways of being that are closely aligned with feminist agendas, if not seeking a (political) solidarity with women (see, for example, Falabella, 1997; Gutterman, 2001; Jackson, 1990; Makori, 1999; Pease, 2000; Rutherford, 1999; Seidler, 1997; Stoltenberg, 2000; Swedin, 1996). Across all four continents there is evidence of a slowly developing awareness amongst men of the issues facing them as individuals and as a political gender category (for discussion, see Connell, 1998; also Sweetman, 1997). It would be inaccurate to describe such profeminist engagements as a 'social movement'; they are more reflective of a loose coalition of interests. Nevertheless, there is some degree of transnational profeminist cooperation and organization, most notably represented by groups such as 'Men for Change', 'National Organization of Men Against Sexism', 'Real Men', 'National Organization for Changing Men', 'International Association for Studies of Men'; journals such as *Achilles Heel*; and internet sites such as 'MensNet', 'PROFEM mail list' and 'XY Magazine'.[6]

In contrast to the loose organic cooperation amongst profeminist men, what Clatterbaugh identified to be the spiritual, conservative and men's rights perspectives are now increasingly coalescing into a fully fledged and politically active antifeminist men's movement. In a recent study of contemporary men's groupings, Messner (1997) labels this movement 'essentialist retreats', identifying the mythopoetic men's movement (MMM) and the recently launched Christian Promise Keepers (CPK) under this heading (see also Schwalbe, 1996). Messner is careful to identify not only the commonalities but also the differences between these two groups, noting that the MMM is in some dialogue with profeminist men (see Kimmel, 1995a). Nevertheless, in several key respects the MMM and CPK are identical, that is in their antipathy towards feminism, their fear of men's emasculinization (by 'modern culture' and feminism) and their belief in a deep essential masculinity. Of the two groups, the Christian Promise Keepers, launched in the USA only in 1990, is the most vehemently opposed to feminism, and the most politically active with several hundred thousand members. The CPK combines a right-wing Christian fundamentalism with an anti-gay, anti-lesbian stance, all presented and packaged under the image and ideal of a traditional male breadwinner family. Politically and ideologically, both the MMM and the CPK have close associations with elements in the American Republican Party and the British Conservative Party, and each movement finds adherents amongst white, working-class, lower-middle-class males (Leibowitz, 1996) and those in the white supremacist movement (Ferber, 2000). The CPK's belief in the sanctity of a patriarchal marriage, functional sex/gender roles and natural gender differences resonates with those on the political right who wish to see a return to what they describe as 'traditional moral values' (see, for example, Gilder, 1973; Murray, 1990).

Despite (or because of) overwhelming evidence that marriage, traditional gender roles, and male breadwinner families are in a steep decline (Creighton, 1999), the MMM and CPK tend to attract those who yearn for some mythical, distant, Victorian age where men can (re)assert their 'Zeus power' (Messner, 1997). In this respect, the concept of 'essentialist retreats' is an apt descriptor of these antifeminist movements. However, in their political stance and presentation, the CPK are a threat not only to feminists, but also to those women and men who do not consider themselves feminists. First, as an antifeminist movement the CPK seeks to promote patriarchal values and relationships; it signals opposition to women exerting choice over reproduction, particularly abortion; it contributes to the right-wing understanding of the underclass as a product of 'dysfunctional families' (see, for example, Murray, 1990); it argues that public and private roles are necessarily gendered; and it questions the place of the single parent (mother) in a 'functioning', 'stable' society. Finally, and in common with men's rights groups, the CPK argues that feminism has 'gone too far', resulting in men's oppression and 'feminization' by the ideology of political correctness (see, for example, Evans, 1994).

While the beliefs of those in the men's movement may appear, to many, to be seriously out of kilter with the *Zeitgeist* of the postmodern age, it is important to recognize that such perspectives will never be fully extinguished from social discourse, any more than will racist views. There always has been and always will be resistance to gender justice. While feminism has succeeded in making sexism and misogyny generally socially and politically unacceptable, some men do seek to resist this. In so doing, they are drawing on common-sense notions of gender difference in support of their political/social ambitions, though clearly their fundamental concern is over an apparent loss of power and material advantage.

However, in itself, the men's movement does not, I believe, pose a significant threat to women's equality; not least because their pronouncements have an increasingly freakish quality. Importantly, the processes of change in gender relations are now too broad and deeply rooted across the Western world to be halted by any single movement, while feminist politics and issues of women's equality are increasingly acquiring purchase worldwide (see chapter 1). Nevertheless, there can never be cause for complacency, and any notion of a 'postfeminist' age is decidedly premature (Whitehead and Barrett, 2001). This is particularly so in an era when 'scientific facts' are so readily tabloidized and promoted to 'explain' gender differences, and when right-wing political parties continue to surface, for example, in major European states (see Mudde, 2000).

If the political and personal polarization between profeminist men and those engaged in an 'essentialist retreat' represents one significant response of men in relation to feminism, a second interesting direction is that taken by those men whom Clatterbaugh described as representing the 'group specific' perspective. By definition this group is necessarily diverse, not representing one particular position. However, I will focus on two key perspectives, that of black and Latino men, and that of gay men.

Black and Latino men, black and Latino masculinities

Any understanding of black men and masculinities cannot be undertaken without first recognizing the ideological and discursive parameters within which black/blackness is represented. The binary oppositions that crudely contribute to the reification of gender difference are no less apparent within the black/white dichotomy. As Derrida (1972) has argued, binary oppositions are generally implicated in discrete relations of power and privilege. Thus to write *white*/black, *British*/alien, *American*/Mexican, *European*/African is, as Hall (1997: 235) notes, to 'capture this power relation in discourse'. Similarly, in the same way that one can locate women as a gender class while still recognizing the diversity within that group, so it is possible with the notion of 'black'. Black(ness) does not represent a homogenous, closed ethnicity but is, as Marriott puts it, 'a bewildering diversity of subject positions, social experiences and cultural identities' (1996: 186). As 'woman' exists as the 'Other' to 'man', formed through the gendered power effects within which is constituted a positive/negative ambivalence towards self-identity, so is the white 'Other' in part constituted in relation to the racialized 'Other' of the black, Chicano and Latino person (Bhabha, 1986; Fanon, 1986; Hall, 1996, 1997; Mirande, 1997; Moodley, 1999; Stecopoulos and Uebel, 1997). Thus the term 'black' exists simultaneously as a conduit for identity construction and as a personal–political position. Both the identity and the politicization of people of colour is, then, grounded only in respect of their location by and within this political–cultural configuration.

In providing sophisticated and revealing insights into the complex political and sociocultural ideologies of race and ethnic identities, writers in black and Latino/Chicano masculinity studies have utilized an array of resources from psychoanalysis through to cultural studies. It is not possible in this brief section to do justice to the sheer depth and diversity of this impressive scholarship; however, black and Latino feminist and profeminist writers such as bell hooks (1991), Angela Davis (1983), Michelle Wallace (1979), Maxine Baca-Zinn (1982), Joseph Carrier (1976), Robert Staples (1982), Richard Majors (1986) and Alfredo Mirande (1997) have been particularly influential. As within the broad 'church' of feminism, there are significant personal and theoretical differences amongst the community of critical writers on black and Latino masculinities, for example, in their utilization of (poststructuralist) Derridean techniques or (structuralist) Barthesian semiotics (for examples, see Stecopoulos and Uebel, 1997; also Hall, 1997). However, as with feminist writers, there remains one important point of commonality amongst those who seek to make critical contributions to racialized gender politics, and that is the recognition that people of colour are inevitably engaged in or touched by a gendered anti-racist struggle (Cherrie and Anzaldua, 1981; Davis, 1983; hooks, 1995; Mirande, 1997; Staples, 1986). Thus, while differences are evident across and within black/Latino communities and critical gender scholarship – for example, between women and men writers (Wallace, 1979; also Franklin, 1995); between gay and heterosexual Latino/Chicano males (Almaguer, 1995; Mirande, 1997); between black British and Asian British males (Mac an Ghaill 1994); and between black feminist and black maleist definitions of black (national) masculinity (Carby, 1998) – unities are not only possible but emerging. Indeed, for writers such as bell hooks the ties that bind black women and men are unique, if not beyond the 'conceptualization of bourgeois white women':

> Throughout our history in the United States, black women have shared equal responsibility in all struggles to resist racist oppression. Despite sexism, black women have continually contributed equally to anti-racist struggle, and frequently, before contemporary black liberation effort. There is a special tie binding people together who struggle collectively for liberation. Black women and men have been united by such ties. They have known the experience of political solidarity. It is the experience of shared resistance struggle that led black women to reject the anti-male stance of some feminist activists. This does not mean that black women were not willing to acknowledge the reality of black male sexism. It does mean that many of us do not believe we will combat sexism or woman-hating by attacking black men or responding to them in kind. (1995: 521)

There is little doubt that the belief in and call for unity that bell hooks articulates is put under strain by the blatant misogyny of some black males, thus reminding us that notions of political unification and action, be it around race, sexuality or gender, are fragile and can never be assumed. This point is underlined by the sexist attitudes of many in the black power movement of the 1960s (Walker, 1976); by the avid misogyny and homophobia of many prominent black cultural figures, notably hip-hop acts such as 2 Live Crew and Ice Cube (for discussion, see George, 1998; McDowell, 1997; Rodman, 2000); and by the contrasting views and responses that the Washington DC 'Million Man March', undertaken in 1995 by predominantly African American males, elicited from black men and women (for discussion, see Messner, 1997). While increasing numbers of black and Latino men recognize that social justice cuts across not only race but also gender and sexuality (Mirande, 1997), many men of colour continue to seek dignity and respect through the stylized display of an often aggressive, misogynistic 'cool pose' (Majors, 1986). In so doing, black men alienate many black women, particularly black feminists; while their performances, although possibly enabling for them, merely serve to reinforce racialized heterosexual images (Wallace, 1979; also chapter 6).

Yet despite many unresolved tensions between women and men of colour, unities and coalitions are evident. Indeed, as Marriott (1996) and Mirande (1997) note, in terms of academic writing, black and Latino cultural studies now constitute a new theoretical (pro)feminist paradigm, within which critical understandings of race and masculinities form a central feature. In contributing to this paradigm, women and men from across all cultures and ethnic groups are making significant contributions to our understanding of black, Asian, Chicano and Latino masculinities and their interrelationship with, for example, education and resistance (Mac an Ghaill, 1994); notions of (white) national manhood (Nelson, 1998); cultural representations and national identity (Carby, 1998); social class (Hondagneu-Sotelo and Messner, 1994); literary fiction (Nowatzki, 1999); sexuality (Mercer and Julien, 1988; Staples, 1995); management (Moodley, 1999); psychotherapy (Moodley, 2000); language and symbolism (Hall, 1997); display, power and resistance (Majors and Mancini, 1992); stereotypes of machismo (Mirande, 1997); imperialism (Mercer and Julien, 1994); blackness and embodiment (Dyer, 1986); black queer theory (Mercer, 1992); and Latino sexuality (*travesti*) theory (*Sexualities*, 1998).

Gay male liberation and queer theory

As with black and Latino men, gay males can be seen to exist in an ambiguous yet highly visible relationship to the 'white heterosexual male'. It is a relationship that, as with 'woman', is largely framed within a political category that serves to constitute and locate its members as 'Other' (Beauvoir, 1973). Similarly, it follows that as with the political categories of 'woman' and 'black', gay men (and lesbians and *travestis*) can simultaneously be seen to represent an homogenous (marginalized) group while being self-evidently constituted and riven by radical diversity and difference, a fundamental condition of all non-grounded subjects (see Rajchman, 1995; also *Sexualities*, 1998). Of course, the very existence of these categories, and their potentiality as discursive 'subject positions' (Hollway, 1989), requires the existence of 'the Other' to separate, distinguish and validate that which would otherwise remain myth and illusion. The political (and personal) emerges, then, in both the utilization of the given culturally and spatially specific identity significations taken up by gay males, and in the material actualities that are a condition and outcome of this process. The forms of representation that serve to ground and substantiate gay male cultures and sexualities will, inevitably, be heavily mediated by dominant but shifting social codes and values. However, no societies or cultures are constituted in a political benignity. Indeed, such a concept is probably oxymoronic. Thus, whether homosexuality is celebrated or repressed – or, for example, whether gay and lesbian couples are recognized in law – is clearly never simply a matter for gays and lesbians but will remain to a large degree subject to the discursive power and potency of 'compulsory heterosexuality' and the homophobia that is its condition and consequence (Connell, 1995).

This paradoxical and often tense positioning of gay male sexuality in the wider political domain is not a new phenomenon, for 'sodomitic subcultures' (Merrick, 1999) have generally existed in ambivalent relationship to dominant social codes and gender orders (see also Hawkes, 1996). Nevertheless, as Weeks notes, sexuality has now become a 'constitutive element in postmodern politics' (1995: 83; see also Simon, 1996), being adopted as a platform for both the conservative and the liberal across the political arenas of left and right. This heightened politicization and publicization of gay male sexuality does not, however, automatically prefigure a greater openness or accommodation around sexual difference. As Foucault puts it: 'What is peculiar to modern societies, in fact, is not that they consigned sex to a shadow existence, but that they dedicated themselves to speaking of it *ad infinitum*, while exploiting it as *the* secret' (1978: 35; original emphasis).

Foucault's comment reveals something of the paradoxical conditions under which contemporary expressions of sexuality now exist. First, powerful mythologies continue to envelop all sexualities, thus ensuring that a 'secretive' element aids their (commercial) exploitation; second, there is evidence of the moralistic unease that narratives and discourses of sexuality elicit for many people (Weeks, 1991); and, finally, the political–personal contestations surrounding sexual differences and symbolic representations of sexuality remain vivid, being no less apparent today than, for example, in Victorian England (see Edwards, 1994; Hall, 1997; Nead, 1990; Weeks and Porter, 1998).

Gay male sexuality (and identity) continues, then, to be subject to a mix of populist tabloidization and ignorance and some private and public reflexive articulation. However, the increased speaking of gay male sexuality can also be understood as a political response, particularly by gay males, to the social and political configuration surrounding 'Other' sexualities, manifested in Western societies, especially the USA, during the latter half of the last century. For although it is evident that gay males have always existed across most societies in some politicized form, the mix of conditions under which the gay male liberation movement took off in the 1970s is highly pertinent for understanding the complexities of personal–political association. The black, youth, lesbian and women's liberation movements of the 1960s, together with the Stonewall Rebellion (see Marmor, Sanders and Nardi, 1994), laid the foundations and created the impulse for a coalition of the gay movement with other 'Others', such as lesbians, struggling against a dominant white, male heterosexual constituency (Adam, 1977). This coalition, in turn, connected with gay and non-gay profeminist men similarly influenced by feminist and anti-racist politics. As Messner (1997) discusses, the consequence of this configuration of events was to prove profoundly significant not only for gay male liberation, but also for the newly formed scholarship on men. First, 'gay communities' assumed a more public visibility across most Western societies, creating geo/socio/economic conditions within which gay males felt some freedom to adopt quite diverse and often overt expressions of homosexual representation and identity. Second, gay rights assumed a more prominent place across the political landscape, being a banner under which gay males, and their supporters, could align themselves as a social movement. Third, as with the writings on black and Latino masculinities, gay male scholarship created new subjects of knowledge, challenged traditional understandings, shifted identity boundaries and constructs, especially around language, and provided insights into gay men's personal–political alliances and friendships (see Edwards, 1994; Nardi, 1992a, 1999; Petersen, 1998; Seidler, 1992a; Seidman, 1996).

However, in the process of presenting themselves as a 'movement', the gay liberationists also exposed the contradictions that exist as a condition and a consequence of 'identity politics'. For example, while disrupting stereotypes of the homosexual as 'effeminate' and womanlike, many homosexual subcultures merely serve to reinforce stereotypes and definitions of hegemonic masculinity (Altman, 1982; Connell, 1995; Messner, 1997), in the process contributing to the (essentialist) reification of that which originally served as a point of oppression of gays and was, thus, to be resisted (see also Segal, 1997). Consequently, in coming to political and public prominence, emerging out of what Foucault describes as the 'sexual shadows' and into something of a limelight, the gay male movement has become, for many gay men, a 'unity of many contradictions' (Edwards, 1994: 29). Communal expressions of gay male 'solidarity', while a valuable and visible platform for politicizing gay male rights, do signal, then, the tensions and paradoxes that can exist for individual gay men – not only for gay men as a group, but also in respect of their relationship with heterosexual males, men of colour, lesbians and women across the political spectrum. For example, political associations and possibilities between (pro)feminists and gay liberation are not straightforward, nor are they inevitable, one area of conflict being the essentialism underpinning much of the gay liberation discourse (for discussion, see Edwards, 1994; Stanley, 1982; Weeks, 1991, 1995). Such ambivalences are further complicated by the multiplicity of discursive subject positions and the capacity of the individual to exist within, and across, for example, black/gay, Jewish/gay, Asian/gay, Latino/gay categories of being.

As this chapter seeks to emphasize, membership of a political category is no predictor of attitude, behaviour or, indeed, personal–political position. Being a gay male does not, in itself, presume nor construct individuality. Associations and coalitions can be momentary, fluid and multiple – they are not essentially grounded. Yet, like woman, lesbian and black, gay male is a politicized category by virtue of its relationship to dominant white, male heterosexuality. This tension between the personal and the political is one that gay male scholarship continues to grapple with. In so doing, many writers in this field are turning their attention to queer theory.

Queer theory Queer theory is an attempt to disentangle gayness from any essential or biological underpinnings, associated dualisms and 'naturalness' surrounding sex, gender and sexuality, in the process challenging homophobic discourses and normative heterosexuality (Petersen, 1998). Drawing on poststructuralist and postmodern understandings of identity and being, queer theorists seek to question any notion of a coherent 'identity politics' inherent in the gay and lesbian movements. Instead, the term 'queer' is adopted as a fluid locus and label of resistance to dominant heterosexual meanings and definitions (Berry and Jagose, 1996; Butler, 1993; Laurentis, 1991).

> The term 'queer' emerges as an interpellation that raises the question of the status of force and opposition, of stability and variability, *within* performativity. The term 'queer' has operated as one linguistic practice whose purpose has been the shaming of the subject it names, or, rather, the producing of a subject *through* that shaming interpellation. 'Queer' derives its force precisely through the repeated invocation by which it has become linked to accusation, pathologization, insult. This is an invocation by which a social bond among homophobic communities is formed through time. (Butler, 1993: 226; original emphasis)

A key factor in queer theory is the recognition that languages, meanings and movements are not neutrally constructed, nor indeed ahistorical (Sedgwick, 1994), but are, in fact, invested with power properties that have the potential to constitute the discursive subject as 'Other' and therefore as 'less than'. Thus in stressing differences and the existence of multiple, contradictory subjectivities, especially through taking up and engaging in postmodern sexual stylizations, proponents of queer theory argue that 'identity categories are necessary and dangerous illusions [and] that the effort to define "who we are" inevitably involves regulations and exclusions' (Petersen, 1998: 102; for discussion, see Butler, 1993). Central to this understanding is the reappropriation by gay men and lesbians of the term 'queer' from its hitherto homophobic meanings, and an open, celebratory engagement, if not pre-occupation, with what are perceived to be counter-hegemonic sexual signifying practices such as transsexuality, bisexuality and cross-dressing.

Queer theory can be seen to be an avid political statement and celebration of difference from the compulsory heterosexual 'norm' that otherwise validates and constrains the possibilities for multiple, contra-sexual and identity expressions. However, despite the political possibilities that queer theory engenders, many feminists have noted with concern the underpinning rigidity and stereotype that often accompanies queer theory as everyday practice, sexual or otherwise. Lynne Segal, for example, makes the following observation in her examination of queer theory:

For all its commentary on gender and sexuality (available to those already enlightened), self-styled postmodern performances of flexible self-invention become more problematic, the closer the inspection of them. *The consumption of transsexual desire is the most decisive form of gender consolidation, notwithstanding its literal enaction of gender construction.* (1999: 63; original emphasis)

Drawing on the observations of, amongst others, Roger Lancaster (1998), Jay Prosser (1998) and Alan Sinfield (1998), Segal questions the supposedly liberating effects that accompany queer theory's exposure of the contingency and volatility underpinning gender identity. As Segal wryly notes:

> After feminism, after gender theory, after queer theory, after all the flaunting of the inherent instabilities or fluidities of gender and sexuality, the problem remains: we still live in a world haunted by cultural and personal fixations on sexual opposition. (1999: 65)

In sum, gay liberation movement and queer politics have their genesis in the feminist and profeminist agendas that are now, for many, common currency across the political and social landscape. Gay male Liberationists did not merely respond to feminism, they formed alliances with both lesbian and straight women who were also struggling against an oppressive dominant heterosexual masculinity and those men who articulate such. However, alliances are inherently unstable and, as with black and Latino men, as many differences exist within these political categories as exist outside them; though recent research by Peter Nardi (1999) does highlight the centrality of 'friendship/kinship' as a central aspect in the lives of many gay men (see chapter 5). Such tensions as already exist within the multiple subjectivities of momentary coalitions are further problematized by the desire of some individuals to draw on narratives of 'naturalness' in order to 'secure' that ever elusive sense of grounded sexual and gender identity. Consequently, queer theory has emerged as an attempt to release individuals from the constraints of both biological determinism and the dualistic thinking that provides the very basis of (contra)identities such as black/white, woman/man, gay/straight. However, to what extent or degree male, phallocentric, homophobic politics are undone or merely revalidated by queer theory remains a question for discussion and further research.

Concluding on changing men (and women)

Whilst it is axiomatic that feminism is about change, the importance of subsequent gender transformations in respect of men is often downplayed or overlooked by those social commentators concerned with shifts in gender relations. Yet, clearly, any understanding of gender equity must involve men changing, though whether this would extend, to use Stoltenberg's phrase, to men 'refusing to be men' (1990) is extremely doubtful (for discussion, see Pease, 2000; Segal, 1997). Nevertheless, feminism has never been limited to changing the balance of power between the genders. Of equal, if not more importance, is individual men recognizing their own gender as an inhibiting factor to gender equity and gender justice, a reflexive state that is entirely possible. Yet male fraternities, and the associated desire by most men to be aligned with the political category of male, often stops individual men challenging sexism even if, as individuals, they are politically disposed towards feminism. These contradictory factors informing male subjectivities illustrate why the sociology of masculinity, and the subsequent critical spotlight it can shed on the hitherto shadowy performances of masculinities and men's lived experiences and practices, is so central to feminist praxis.

As the above accounts of the various and contrasting responses of men to feminism reveal, the political cannot be divorced from the personal, for the actions of men do have personal–political consequences. However, of all the various movements of men arising in response to feminism, only the socialist and profeminist men openly declare their alignment with the broad aims of feminists. And even this alignment is not unproblematic. Most feminists are more than happy to see profeminist men critically engage in the study of gender, but many add a note of warning. For example, Hall argues in favour of men studying men and masculinities, but only so that 'we will understand much more about how men's power is reproduced' (1990, 237). Hanmer warns against perceiving 'the study of men to be about liberating men' (1990: 29), while Canaan and Griffin (1990) state that men contributing to the sociology of masculinity should 'come out' politically if they are not to marginalize women's knowledges and feminist work by creating a politically suspect 'men's studies' –

a point supported by prominent profeminist writers such as Connell (1998), Heath (1987), Morgan (1992) and Hearn (1994).

The powerful ways in which discourses around women and men can be used politically is evident from the crisis of masculinity thesis. From Australia to Japan, from the UK to California, an examination of the male crisis discourse reveals much about contemporary global gender relations and shifts in women's subjectivities, though whether or not these dynamics open up the possibility for the 'deconstruction of men' (Hearn, 1999) is less clear. What is clear is that many men are using this discourse as a political platform from which to atttempt to reverse any material benefits to women arising from equal opportunity legislation and feminist politics more generally. It is particularly worrying that this discourse is subsequently finding its way into social policy.

From an analysis of the contrasting ways in which men have responded to feminism and to their subsequent critical engagement with their own sense of being men/masculine, it is evident, then, that the personal is fully complicit in the political economy of gender. However, not all men writers who have contributed to the sociology of masculinity agree with this point (see Craib, 1994; MacInnes, 1998). For example, in an interesting realignment of this notion, MacInnes (1998) argues that *'the personal is not political: the personal is what makes the political possible'* (1998: 135; original emphasis). Basically, MacInnes suggests that diverse forms of identity politics, such as those around sexuality, race and gender, mistakenly assume a socially constructed self, and thus place undue emphasis on the agentic capacity of the individual to democratize her/his personal life. MacInnes's point is important, for like many realist social theorists, he desires a return to 'collective struggle against material exploitation and inequality' (1998, 136); that is, he is concerned that opportunities for political action have been lessened by the centralizing of the self, and the subsequent privatization of political struggle prefigured by identity politics (for example, Beck and Beck-Gernsheim, 1995; Giddens, 1991).

While I have some sympathy with MacInnes's desire for 'communal action' to change inequalities, I believe his understanding of the complexities of human subjectivity is somewhat incomplete. It is quite evident from the contrasting responses of women and men to feminism, of black and white women and men to anti-racist politics, and of gay and non-gay women and men to sexual politics, that the point at which political discourse emerges into private action is quite different for each individual. There can never be an assumption of collective, political interest. Such a notion would require a homogenous coherent subjectivity, possibly grounded biologically, together with the subsequent ability of the individual to first, exist external to discourse/ideology and, second, to be able to speak, *and be heard*, in the singular and absolute to a diverse and shifting audience. Language itself is so highly politicized (for example, binaries, dualisms) and so subject to multiple (Derridean) interpretations that any communal–political alliances are inevitably riven with contingency, misinterpretations and the fluidity of transitory cooperations. But saying this is not to argue that all social and political experiences and opportunities are subject to an elementary conflict between individuals competing for limited resources (for example, see Duke, 1976), or that political coalitions are inevitably subverted by individual instrumentality. The Nietzschean reductionism that such views presume seems to me altogether too simplistic towards human action and potential. Nevertheless, there are elementary conditions in the social field that will, I believe, always disrupt or compromise the possibility of communal action, beyond that which is evident in momentary social movements (for discussion, see Porta and Diani, 1999). This is not to say that one should not try to engage and develop a communal politics, but sociologists (especially feminists) should be both wary and aware of the discontinuities between political public presentations and private actions.

Feminism, and the subsequent responses of men in respect of changing gender relations, provides an opportunity, then, to consider the importance of subjectivity and self-reflexivity to personal, political positions. Certainly it can be argued – as do, for example, Assiter (1996) and Stanley and Wise (1993) – that women exist, by virtue of their political categorization as an 'epistemic community'. Whether this constitutes an overarching and determined womanist epistemology, in so much as women's insights can be deemed to provide a unique knowledge of women's oppression and men's oppressiveness, is less certain, as is the related notion of a single feminist standpoint (for elaboration, see Francis, forthcoming; McLennon, 1995; Harding, 1991; Hartsock, 1983; Hekman, 1990; Holmwood, 1995; Smith, 1988). Nevertheless, the *possibility* that the (feminine) subject can draw on a particular, politicized, set of knowledges, thus giving voice to a gendered reality that exists 'out there' for the political category woman, seems quite evident (see Kristeva, 1986). Moreover, such a notion is entirely compatible with the poststructuralist concept of the discursive postmodern subject (Hekman, 1999). So for women, any 'new femininities' and the feminisms they draw on, can be argued to be personal–political positions, reinforced by the individual's exposure to various, gendered, power relations (for example, Laurie et al., 1999). Yet what still remains unresolved, though of vital importance to this analysis, is the gendered subjectivities of men – can they change?

Well clearly, given the evidence thus far, individual men can change, in the process adopting anti-sexist positions, sharing public and private roles with women, and learning to appreciate, if not enjoy, being unconstrained by traditional notions of masculinity (see Christian, 1994). However, one has to concur with the scepticism of David Morgan (1990) when he asks 'why would men want to change – what (materially and in terms of power) can they gain from this?' (see also Hearn, 1994; Heath, 1987). It is no accident that much of the critical debate carried out by men into men and masculinities, and discussed above, has come from those marginalized, in a similar way to women, by dominant discourses of heterosexuality and male power, that is, gay men and men of colour. Such groupings draw on a set of understandings forged through direct immersion in, and often confrontation with, gender and racial politics. It has to be said that far fewer white heterosexual men, particularly those from lower socio-economic groupings, are engaging with critical gender discourse. Those white heterosexual men who have aligned themselves with feminist agendas appear, in the main, to be academics or men with a particular cultural capital. In other words, those men positively engaging with feminism (profeminists), and who represent the broad 'male majority' in terms of colour and sexuality in Western societies, are mainly those who feel less directly threatened (materially or ontologically) by feminism.

Certainly my own research into men and masculinities supports the view that any notions of a universal shift in men's gender awareness is still premature (Whitehead, 2001b). For many men their gender, as a key if not determining factor in their life experiences and history, remains unseen if not incomprehensible to them. As Michael Kimmel succinctly puts it, the reason for this continuing gender blindness stems from most men's inability to see themselves as men:

When I look in the mirror . . . I see a human being – a white middle
class male – gender is invisible to me because that is where I am privileged. I am the norm. I believe most men do not know they have a
gender. (Kimmel, cited in Middleton, 1992: 11)

For too many men there is little occurrence of the self-reflexivity that
writers such as Giddens (1991) and Beck and Beck-Gernsheim (1995)
suggest is elementary to social transformation and gender equity in
the late modern age (see also chapter 5). This is not surprising,
perhaps, for as Kimmel and Middleton observe the notion of the male
self-reflexive subject is problematic precisely because 'men don't see
what they are seeing when they see themselves' (Middleton, 1992:
11). In this respect, in asking whether men, as a political category,
can change positively, one may well conclude on a pessimistic note.
Yet I would qualify this. For it is clear that recognizing the force and
rigidity of gender differentials world-wide, often enacted in a brutal
manner and sometimes in the name of religious ideology, is to be able
to reflect that maybe Western societies, by way of comparison, have
moved, are slowly moving, towards some degree of gender equity. I
hasten to add that this is only a tentative observation, not a predic-
tion of imminent Utopias.

FURTHER READING

Kimmel, M. S. (ed.) (1995) *The Politics of Manhood*. Philadelphia, Pa.:
  Temple University Press.
Messner, M. A. (1997) *Politics of Masculinities: Men in Movements*. Thou-
  sand Oaks, Calif.: Sage.
Nardi, P. M. (ed.) (2000) *Gay Masculinities*. Thousand Oaks, Calif.: Sage.
Robinson, S. (2000) *Marked Men: White Masculinity in Crisis*. New York:
  Columbia University Press.
Stecopoulos, H. and Uebel, M. (eds) (1997) *Race and the Subject of
  Masculinities*. Durham, NC: Duke University Press.

3
Power and Resistance

Many sociologists would contend that much of their research is inevitably concerned with the character and distribution of power. Certainly the issue of power is never far from debates around gender. Indeed, men's power is probably the central theme of feminism in so much as it necessarily conditions and prefigures all other debates. While the desire to see men change, discussed in the previous chapter, is a key concern of feminists, such movements in the gendered subjectivities of men can be seen to trigger, if not require, transformations in the relations of power, not only between the political categories of women and men, but, more importantly, between individual women and men. For example, it was never enough that some (heterosexual) men sought self-exploration and shifts in terms of their masculine subjectivity through the men's groups that were prominent in the late twentieth century. While welcome and important individually, such engagements inevitably come back to issues of childcare, men's violences, domestic work, sexual divisions of labour in organizations and home, heterosexual men's personal support for the rights of gays and men's active support for gender equality across both the public and private spheres generally. Yet many men find such personal–political engagements anything but straightforward, not least because they require a renegotiation of a power relationship as much as a personal one. In this respect, traditional gender relationships can be seen to be much less problematic for men, for equality is largely only in appearance and is masked by the apparency of women's power in the domestic sphere. While many heterosexual men may say they would wish for an equal relationship with a woman, far fewer appear willing to live the actual consequences of this on a day-to-day basis, for it requires them to adopt a non-centralist position in the relationship; that is, a position where they exist not as central, but as jointly peripheral. The essentialistic retreats by men, discussed in the previous chapter, can be said to represent traditional men's failure to accept and accommodate such a necessarily peripheral position, one that comes in tandem with women's increasing assertion and exercise of power. In short, it can be argued that for women to acquire power, men have to give it up.

In exploring the interrelations of gendered power in the specific context of men and masculinities, this chapter will draw primarily on two theoretical perspectives. The first is a 'juridico-discursive' model: one that is fundamentally concerned with power as structure, albeit problematically exercised and experienced in part as a result of being configured by contesting pressures. This model draws heavily on notions of gender order, hegemony, ideology and patriarchy. The chapter then turns to poststructuralist understandings of power. These theories place a greater emphasis on the discursive subject as product of, and mitigating factor in, the exercise of power. Within poststructuralism, the concern is to understand the productive as well as oppressive dimensions of the power/resistance equation, the relationship between the subject and power, and the regulatory consequences of privileged knowledges.

Structural models of gender power

Juridico-discursive theories

The term 'juridico-discursive' arises from the work of Michel Foucault (1980, 1983; see also Sawicki, 1991), who used this descriptor to locate and critique traditional social theories that understand power as hierarchically sourced (from top down), materially based (economically driven), possessed (by group or individual) and primarily prohibitive (coercive). While there are numerous examples of the use of such theorizing in sociology, the most visible are in the three basic theoretical positions of constructionism, critical structuralism and functionalism. Max Weber's (1930) work is an exemplar of constructionism in that he defined power as primarily the exercise of will in the face of resistance, be it through individual or group action. In identifying power as largely derived and legitimized through different types of authority, Weber provides insights into the role of bureaucracy, the state and government in constructing, maintaining and negotiating (between) contesting vested interests. The Weberian model of power as socially enabled and constructed through legitimatization processes, while largely embedded in dualistic models (for example, state versus individual), is somewhat more nuanced than the critical structuralism exemplified in Marxist and neo-Marxist theories. For Marx, power struggles are elementary to human history, being the means by which material inequalities are maintained, not through the actions of individuals, but by social classes. The particular form of social stratification seen to have emerged in modern capitalist societies is viewed by Marxists as fundamentally divisive and elitist, with the beneficiaries being those placed at the top of the economic infrastructure (for example, see Miliband, 1989). Social stratification is also central to the third position, that of Talcott Parsons's notion of functionalism. However, there is one key difference in so much as functionalists view stratification as fundamental to maintaining social order and stability in society. In this respect, the emphasis is less on power as conflictual and more on the importance of shared values, and the use of power by authorities and dominant groups in ultimately balancing conflicting interests to the benefit of wider society.

For critical gender theorists, the above concepts, whether largely granted or not, have one key omission and one commonality. The commonality is that these theories are mostly the products of men – malestream theory. The omission (not unrelated to the commonality) is that the theories fail to recognize bureaucracies, the state, government, dominant groups, authorities, divisions of labour and capitalist organizations as being largely controlled, managed and structured by men. Thus the realization that men, as a political category, are the main beneficiaries of the material inequalities exposed in these models of power is missing. This gender blindness in much social theory has of course now been substantially exposed to critique and analysis by feminists. Nevertheless, the hierarchical model that underpins juridico-discursive understandings of power has served to inform key concepts in feminist and profeminist debate, most notably in respect of the concepts of patriarchy, hegemonic masculinity and the gender order.

Patriarchy

Kate Millett (1970) is generally recognized as the first feminist to introduce the term 'patriarchy' into contemporary feminist scholarship. A radical feminist, Millett sought to emphasize the overt and often hidden 'sexual politics' that men practice in order to maintain their established hegemony over women. For Millett, key tools in this exercise of male oppression are the ideologies at work in masculinist definitions of gender and sexuality, a hegemonic process facilitated by the fact that social, economic and political institutions rest in male hands:

> our society, like all historical civilizations, is a patriarchy. The fact is evident at once if one recalls that the military, industry, technology, universities, science, political office, and finance – in short, every avenue of power within society, including the coercive force of the police, is entirely in male hands. (Millett, 1970: 25)

Millett's analysis of patriarchy was one that sought to understand how women become conditioned into colluding in their own oppression. Millett's answer to this question was to suggest that women were pressured to accept inequality with men through the power of sex role stereotyping underpinned by the social stigmatization of those women who 'sought to escape the confines of socially correct "feminine" behaviour' (Eisenstein, 1985: 6).

While Millett stresses the ideological forces pressuring women to consent to the prevailing power-structured relationship of gender, other feminists are more explicit in their emphasis on the role also played by physical force and its threat:

> Patriarchy is the power of the fathers: a familial-social, ideological, political system in which men – by force, direct pressure, or through ritual, tradition, law, and language, customs, etiquette, education, and the division of labour – determine what part women shall or shall not play, and in which the female is everywhere subsumed under the male. (Rich, 1976: 57)

The notion of patriarchy that writers such as Millett and Rich develop is one most closely in tune with a juridico-discursive model of power, though while there are differences between, for example, Marxist, radical, socialist and psychoanalytical feminist concepts of patriarchy (for elaboration, see Tong, 1993; Hearn, 1987), the stress on (men's) power as hierarchically located, oppressive and ideologically substantiated remains true for each. Thus for many feminists, a key strength of the concept of patriarchy lies in its ability to describe the ideological and material conditions of gender inequalities and oppressions across multiple sites, while locating the primary antecedents that inform such (Coward, 1983). For example, many feminists have developed dialectical models of patriarchy and capitalism that seek to theorize the interrelated materialist, class and gendered processes of (re)production manifest in the interconnections of both capitalism and patriarchy (for example, see Delphy, 1977; Walby, 1986). Following which, writers such as Cockburn (1991) have argued for the continued use of the term patriarchy in feminist scholarship, not least because it signals that 'female subordination is *systemic*' (1991: 6; original emphasis), durable and global.

Despite the emotive power of the term and its continued use in academia, patriarchy has been subject to increasing critique by feminists. Hargreaves, for example, catches the concern many feminists have towards patriarchy as a theoretical model when she states: 'the concept of patriarchy implies a fixed state of male oppression over women, rather than a fluid relationship between men and women which is complex and moves with great speed at times' (1982: 115). Similarly, Elshtain (1981) argues that patriarchy speaks of a dated, maleist, Victorian view of women as 'morally pure victims'. More recently, Pollert (1996) has suggested that, 'as a short-hand descriptive tool to indicate male-dominance it [patriarchy] may have a role. But, more often, its use indicates confusion' (1996: 553). Hargreaves, Elshtain and Pollert (also Kandiyoti, 1988; hooks, 1981) are concerned that patriarchy is not only reductionist, but, moreover, is unable to explain and analyse male dominance and its differentiations across multiple sites. Pollet, in particular, critiques the Althusserian circularity implicit in the term patriarchy; that is, that it fails to prise open and illuminate the points of resistance, change and difference (amongst women). Thus while patriarchy may usefully be deployed to describe the surface lived experiences (public and private), for many women the term speaks only to 'abstract structural dynamics' and 'abstract theorising' (1996: 655), divorced from the subtleties of gendered interaction.

Pollert's 'health warning' on the use of the term patriarchy is instructive. For it alerts us to the dangers of assuming a concrete structure within which the individual either struggles to little or no avail or, in Althusserian terms, is subsumed under an ideological apparatus that has successfully inculcated any critical faculty and awareness. If one concurs unreservedly with Cockburn's (1991) view that patriarchy continues to be a universal and systemic state, such a perspective might be tenable; yet the evidence for this, as Pollert argues, is less apparent. On the contrary, as has been discussed, there is ample evidence to show that women do successfully resist and overcome male dominance across both the public and private spheres and are increasingly doing so across numerous, diverse societies. Likewise, issues of class, race, ethnicity and sexuality need to be introduced into the analysis if one is to capture something of the (localized) experience and dynamic of male dominance, beyond simple overarching description. Consciousness-raising of women and men over issues of gender is neither straightforward nor without its points of tension and resistance (Eisenstein, 1985), but I would suggest that feminism has emerged as the most subversive, critical and, consequently, powerful social discourse during the past 100 years. And while this process is resisted by many men, the absolutist implications of patriarchy cannot capture the (gathering) success of the feminist dynamic, nor the potential for further gender transformations in favour of women (and, by implication, men).

Hegemonic masculinity

If the use of patriarchy as a readily available tool to describe male dominance has been a character of much feminist scholarship, this is even more so in respect of profeminist writings. To be sure, and as was discussed in chapter 1, with few exceptions the first wave of critical writings by men on the sociology of masculinity were noticeably 'power-blind', failing to offer any substantive critique of male dominance as men's exercise of (gendered) power. However, this situation changed dramatically in 1985 with the publication in *Theory and Society* of an article by Tim Carrigan, Bob Connell and John Lee. Drawing on a juridico-discursive model of power, Carrigan, Connell and Lee argued for an understanding of masculinity that recognized dominant interpretations and definitions of being masculine to be embedded in and sustained by (male-dominated) social institutions such as the state, education, corporations and the family. They stressed that masculinity was not merely a psychological innateness of the social self (the Freudian or Jungian model) or a product of functional and largely static sex roles. Rather, Carrigan et al. sought to stress the interplay of praxis and structure, where masculinity becomes recognized as a vital, historical, component in the armoury of male dominance; informing the 'gender system' while serving to validate and reinforce patriarchal power (see also Kaufman, 1987). In connecting the institutional aspects of male power with the collective practices of men, Carrigan et al. sought to describe, identify and expose the character of a dominant form of masculinity that they termed 'hegemonic masculinity':

> The ability to impose a particular definition on other kinds of masculinity is part of what we mean by 'hegemony'. Hegemonic masculinity is far more complex than the accounts of essences in the masculinity books would suggest. It is not a 'syndrome' of the kind produced when sexologists like Money reify human behaviour into a 'condition' or when clinicians reify homosexuality into a pathology. It is, rather, a question of how particular groups of men inhabit positions of power and wealth and how they legitimate and reproduce the social relations that generate their dominance. (1987: 179)

> 'Hegemony', then, always refers to a historical situation, a set of circumstances in which power is won and held. The construction of hegemony is not a matter of pushing and pulling between ready-formed groupings, but is partly a matter of the *formation* of those groupings. To understand the different kinds of masculinity demands, above all, an examination of the practices in which hegemony is constituted and contested – in short, the political techniques of the patriarchal social order. (1987: 181; original emphasis)

> The most important feature of this [hegemonic] masculinity, alongside its connection with dominance, is that it is heterosexual. (1987: 180)

The impact of the above analysis on the sociology of masculinity, and critical gender research generally, cannot be overstated. At a time when much of feminist scholarship was still drawing unproblematically on the concept of patriarchy, Carrigan, Connell and Lee shifted the debate forward significantly, not only for the sociology of masculinity but also for feminist theory generally. The concept of hegemonic masculinity achieves what patriarchy fails to achieve: it offers a nuanced account of the processes and relationalities of femininity–masculinity and male power while staying loyal to the notions of gender and sexual ideology, and male dominance. Hegemonic masculinity not only succeeds in signalling the multiple, contested character of male practices; it does so in the context of larger formations of gender structure. Thus feminist and profeminist scholarship has at its disposal a complex yet accessible theory from which to critique and interrogate men's practices in multiple settings, while also a) recognizing that such processes do not go uncontested and b) maintaining a strict adherence to the concept of male power as structural.

Since the introduction of this concept in the early 1980s, Bob Connell in particular has proceeded to offer quite substantive examinations of hegemonic masculinity. This includes: utilizing hegemonic masculinity as a theoretical tool to understand the means by which men's dominance over women is institutionalized and achieved 'within a balance of forces, that is, a state of play' (1987: 184); illuminating the 'patriarchal dividend' (1995: 79) and advantage which hegemonic masculinity offers the majority of men; and emphasizing that hegemonic masculinity, while increasingly representative of a 'global, corporate form of masculinity' (1998), does not go unchallenged or unresisted by women and by those men exhibiting subordinated or marginalized expressions of masculinity.

Despite having very close associations, hegemonic masculinity differs from patriarchy in that there is less of an essentialist assumption about the outcome or conditions under which this gender power play is experienced and enacted. For while the fundamental premise remains that male power is a 'hegemonic project' (Connell, 1995), embedded in ideological and material structures, there is space for ambiguity – and change. Thus Connell can claim that women may resist hegemonic masculinity, while also stating that dominant forms of femininity actively collude or are 'complicit' in enabling the supremacy of hegemonic masculinity (1995: 77). Similarly, while it is stressed that 'not many men meet the normative standards [of hegemonic masculinity]' (1995: 79), and even that 'many men live in some tension with, or distance from, hegemonic masculinity' (1998: 5), hegemonic masculinity remains the 'guarantor' of men's dominant position and the 'currently accepted strategy' for 'defending patriarchy' (1995: 77). Finally, and importantly, it is not necessary to offer a general descriptor of hegemonic masculinity, but to posit that 'a hegemonic form of masculinity [is] the most honoured or desired in a particular context' (1995: 77).

Not surprisingly, the concept of hegemonic masculinity has become almost *de rigueur* for those critical gender theorists who turn their attention to men and masculinities. The power of the term lies in the fact that the theorist can align themselves with the notion of patriarchy and male dominance, while mitigating any reductionistic oversimplifications through use of a concept that speaks of fluidity, multiplicity, difference and resistance, not only within the category women but also amongst men. Moreover, in utilizing this concept the theorist is then excused having to engage in any deep analysis of the actual practices of men, it being taken as given that dominant patterns of masculinity exist and thus contribute in some 'knowing way' to a larger project of domination by men over women (see Connell, 1987).

The theoretical model of hegemony underpinning the concept of hegemonic masculinity owes much to critical structuralism, in particular to Antonio Gramsci's (1971) neo-Marxist analysis of class relations (also Williams, 1973). Thus the concept assumes power as, fundamentally, a contested entity between social groups, in this case women and men. The agentic capacity of the individual is recognized, but this potential for free will and transformation exists in a state of constant tension and struggle with ideological and structural determinants. The ideological forces at the disposal of and enlisted by powerful groups and individuals emerge from the 'fact' of the existence and structural character of this (pre)social condition. So key structural entities such as the state, education, the media, religion, political institutions and business, being historically numerically dominated by men, all serve the project of male dominance through their capacity to promote and validate the ideologies underpinning hegemonic masculinity. In the same way that (neo)Marxists understand contested class relations to be immanent to the social, so the concept of hegemonic masculinity takes as given the 'project' of cultural and numerical dominance of heterosexual men across not only key decision-making arenas but also across society generally.

As an overarching descriptor of the conditions of possibility between the political categories of women and men, hegemonic masculinity clearly has some usefulness. Importantly, it can signal the existence of dominant and subordinate patterns of male behaviour across various sites, particularly institutions, while indicating how such patterns may contribute to the material actualities of gender inequality. However, the concept of hegemony that informs 'hegemonic masculinity' has some weaknesses. First, despite the emphasis that neo-Marxists such as Gramsci and Williams place on the transformational potential within the notion of hegemony, their underpinning thesis is one of polarization between competing groups. For while a neo-Marxist definition of hegemony appears to rely less on the classical Marxist base–superstructure distinction, in the final analysis all that is offered is a fine tuning of conflict theory (for example, Duke, 1976), with the actions of groups and individuals reduced to a desire or search for material advantage, ideology being the key tool at their disposal in this quest. Second, actually pinning down a strict definition of hegemony is not easy; it is, as several writers have noted, a very 'slippery concept' (Rojek, 1995). Consequently, while purporting to bridge the structure and agency dichotomy, but lacking an adequate analysis of the subject, the notion of hegemony falls prey to being open to quite different interpretations and utilizations by critical theorists. For example, Carrigan, Connell and Lee describe hegemony as 'a political technique of a patriarchal social order' (1987: 181), an unreservedly structuralist position. In contrast, Hall (1997) implies that hegemony can be interpreted as close to a Foucauldian model of power; that is, power as circulatory rather than hierarchical. For Hall, hegemony is less about domination and more about negotiation, with cultural representations being a 'key site' in these processes.

Although offering a more nuanced interpretation of male dominance than patriarchy, hegemonic masculinity ultimately suffers from the same deficits, for it posits an intentionality behind heterosexual men's practices (a 'will to power' if you like) while suggesting that women and gay men are somehow excluded from this otherwise innate desire to dominate and oppress. Even those men who would wish not to associate with hegemonic masculinity are somehow inevitably drawn into living their lives in a constant state of tension with this dominant form of masculine being. As can be seen, the circularity of patriarchy is not overcome, for the question remains as to how and why (some) heterosexual men 'legitimise, reproduce and generate their dominance' (Edley and Wetherall, 1995: 129), and do this in spite of being in a social minority vis-à-vis women and 'other' men. As will be argued below, to assume that such conditions are the product of ideological and structural dynamics is to marginalize or make invisible the subject. All that is seen is the structure, with some insights into (contested) patterns of behaviour. The individual is lost within, or, in Althusserian terms, subjected to, an ideological apparatus and an innate drive for power. In attempting to reconcile the inconsistencies between this deterministic model of (male) power on one hand, and the (changing) multiplicity of masculinity on the other, hegemonic masculinity has to resort to an understanding of the social as, ultimately, a contested arena. To be sure, both women and men are understood to be subjected to this process, and thus adversely affected, albeit in different ways (Connell, 1995). Consequently, it is overly simplistic to say that 'men are the winners'. Nevertheless, the theoretical language and assumptions that many scholars bring to the term hegemonic masculinity leave little room for ambiguity, the term being increasingly used as a blanket descriptor of male power (see also Whitehead, 1999a, for discussion).

Hegemonic masculinity is, then, as reductionistic a term as patriarchy. It is not deterministic because hegemonic masculinity takes great care precisely *not to predict* men's behaviours. Indeed, proponents of the term hegemonic masculinity suggest that only a minority of men express and perform to its pattern. Just what hegemonic masculinity actually is, then, is never illuminated, yet somehow this 'culturally exalted pattern of masculinity' serves to 'stabilize a structure of dominance and oppression in the gender order' (Connell, 1990: 83). As Donaldson accurately notes, there is little of substance in the 'models of hegemonic masculinity' (in the media and so on) that form the exemplars for heterosexual men to follow. Indeed, as Donaldson goes on to argue, these hegemonic models are often exposed as having 'feet of clay' (1993: 647). Following Donaldson, one is obliged to ask just who these exemplars are. Is it John Wayne or Leonardo DiCaprio; Mike Tyson or Pele? Or maybe, at different times, all of them?

The fundamental inconsistency in the term hegemonic masculinity is that, while it attempts to recognize difference and resistance, its primary underpinning is the notion of a fixed (male) structure. It is not surprising, then, that confronted with the circularity of this agency–structure dualism, many critical gender theorists ultimately ignore this tension and resort to locating hegemonic masculinity within a wider patriarchal state. However, as has been shown, this fails to understand the character of hegemony and fails to offer a means by which to theorize women's and gay men's exercise of power and their ability to resist oppression. The key commonality through all the various understandings of hegemony is the notion of resistance and (potential) transformation – the inherent contingency of negotiated positions (for example, see Sage, 1998). As has been discussed, hegemony can be interpreted as emphasizing the *lack of total dominance* (of any one group or class). Neo-Marxists such as Williams, for example, have stressed that hegemony is never complete, never totalized, and is always subject to the power of individual and collective struggle. However, the concept of hegemonic masculinity disabuses this possibility, not least because its very fluidity signals its 'ability' to be any male practice, anywhere, anytime. Following this interpretation, hegemonic masculinity will always be with us; it can never be overcome – even with the complete overthrow of patriarchy; it will just move, change and shift, but like mercury its fundamental character will remain untouched. The reason for this is quite simple: what appears a subordinated masculinity in one site always has the potential to be a hegemonic masculinity in another.

Once critically examined, the notions of 'patriarchal hegemony' or 'hegemonic structure' reveal themselves to be oxymorons. And while it may appear a seductive theoretical device, conflating patriarchy with hegemonic masculinity merely results in a 'lost subject' (woman and man), subsumed under a blanket, often bland, descriptor of male dominance, with little accord given to the exercise of resistance. What hegemonic masculinity reveals is that within the rich and varied gamut of men's practices, patterns will emerge, and some will inevitably dominate in specific locales and, in so doing, contribute to the larger conditions of inequality and points of oppression. To adopt Pollert's critique of patriarchy, hegemonic masculinity is a useful shorthand descriptor of dominant masculinities, but its overuse results in obfuscation, in the conflation of fluid masculinities with overarching structure and, ultimately, in 'abstract structural dynamics'.

Gender order

Possibly recognizing the theoretical limitations of patriarchy, and many feminists' critique of the term, Connell has contributed to the development of a slightly more malleable concept, that of the 'gender order' (Matthews, 1984). Following Matthews, Connell describes the 'gender order' as 'a historically constructed pattern of power relations between men and women and definitions of femininity and masculinity . . . the structural inventory of an entire society' (1987: 99; also Carrigan, Connell and Lee, 1985).

For Connell, the gender order is immanent to the capitalist system, sexual politics, gender ideology, the sexual division of labour and all processes of human production. Operating within a 'gendered logic' (Connell, 1987: 105), the acts of force, violence and oppression (against women and 'Others') by heterosexual men point to a '*structure* of power, a set of social relations with some scope and permanence' (ibid: 107; original emphasis). Thus the gender order signals the systematic pursuit of power by heterosexual men, but the possibilities of (gender) power struggles being won by women and gays. Thus Connell can argue that 'hegemony, subordination, and complicity, as just defined, are relations internal to the gender order' (1995: 80).

This emphasis on the self-sustaining relationship between the gender order and hegemony partly overcomes the incompatibilities that arise when hegemony and patriarchy are conflated. In this case, the gender order can be seen as an attempt to put some theoretical distance between the absolutist and hierarchical concept of patriarchy, while recognizing that gender relations are inevitably complex, fluid and dynamic. The key benefit for the theorist is that they do not lose their commitment to a juridico-discursive model of power. However, the problem remains as to what degree subjects (individuals) are constructed and/or enabled by this process. In attempting to straddle, yet again, this tantalizing gap between structure and agency, quite imaginative models of gendered power have been developed by some profeminist theorists. For example, Messner and Sabo attempt to develop a 'non-hierarchical theory' of gender that does not result in what they term 'watered-down relativism or theoretical anarchy' (1990: 10). Their attempt to unite the structure–agency divide relies on a model of different theories of oppression in the form of a wheel:

> At the hub, constantly keeping the wheel in motion, is the historical dynamic of structural constraint (which includes structural, ideological, and characterological oppression) and human agency (which includes critical thought and resistant, informative action). The spokes of the wheel represent various forms of oppression: class, race, gender, age, and sexual preference (others can certainly be added). The rim of the wheel represents social theories of liberation, whose role it is to link the spokes in such a way that the hub can move the wheel. The fact that the spokes of the wheel are linked to one another at the hub and at the rim of the wheel shows that all forms of oppression, although relatively autonomous, are still dynamically interdependent. (Messner and Sabo, 1990: 11)

Despite the imaginative model being offered here, all that is posited is the possibility of agency, but ultimately agency that is relational to 'a wider array of systems of domination' (1990: 11), the gender order being 'a dynamic process that is constantly in a state of change' (ibid: 12). This is a contradictory and obscure argument. For although dynamism (agentic capacity) is recognized, domination (structure) remains. Consequently, in this account, all that can change are the different forms of oppression (of women by men). Women and 'Others' remain oppressed, (heterosexual) men remain the oppressors, enabled by a gender order that validates men's acts of oppression and does this in large part through the success of hegemonic masculinity to act as the 'exemplar' in the ideological and material subordination of women. Consequently, for Messner and Sabo (also Connell, 1987, 1995) to suggest that gender power relations 'unfold within changing structural contexts' is to reduce masculinities and femininities to predictable, and thus reductionistic, relations of power. The individual is, once again, absent from both history and theory, having been made invisible within a system of domination that changes, and yet somehow never changes.

Masculinism

The final theoretical concept that I will examine within the structural (juridico-discursive) model of power, is masculinism. Introduced by Arthur Brittan in 1989, the concept of masculinism has had far less impact on the sociology of masculinity than either hegemonic masculinity or the notion of a gender order. Yet masculinism is an inter-

esting and pertinent example of an attempt to recognize male dominance as a material actuality; hierarchical forms of masculinity as
privileged and powerful within given settings and contexts; and the
fact that gender structures are neither permanent nor immune to
subversion. To be sure, masculinism still speaks of a set of power
relations as juridico-discursive, but Brittan's analysis was an early
attempt by a profeminist theorist to contribute to the feminist-
inspired 'demystification of patriarchy'. Brittan sets about this task
by locating masculinism and masculinity as quite different:

> Those people who speak of masculinity as an essence, as an inborn
> characteristic are confusing masculinity with masculinism, the mascu-
> line ideology. Masculinism is 'the ideology that justifies and natural-
> izes male domination, as such it is the ideology of patriarchy.
> Masculinism takes it for granted that there is a fundamental difference
> between men and women, it assumes that heterosexuality is normal,
> it accepts without question the sexual division of labour, and it sanc-
> tions the political and dominant role of men in the public and private
> spheres. (1989: 4)

Masculinism is, then, the point at which dominant forms of masculinity and heterosexuality meet ideological dynamics, and in the
process become reified and legitimized as privileged, unquestioned
accounts of gender difference and reality. As an ideology, masculinism can be seen to be threaded across both the public and private
spheres, connecting with, for example, dominant forms of organizational culture, militarism, gender representation and a sexual division
of labour. Brittan also stresses the multiplicity of masculinity, thus
recognizing there are countless ways of men expressing their manliness, across different times, places and contexts. However, he also
argues that men's practices contribute to formations of male dominance in many fields, though he is anxious to avoid any essentialist
position that might arise as a result of unproblematically conflating
masculinities with men's power, particularly heterosexual men's
power. While recognizing that class, economic and political structures
are moulded in such a way as to materially advantage heterosexual
men, Brittan suggests that this hierarchical heterosexual structuring
of gender relationships is not inevitable or permanent. Brittan states:
'My position is that it is always in the process of being reinterpreted
and subverted . . . in the last instance heterosexualism is tentative and
problematic' (1989: 18).

Of course, such qualification only really works once it has been declared to what degree one is prepared to stress the element of tentativeness within the formation of heterosexual and masculine power structures. Back again to the structure–agency dualism: and here Brittan is somewhat at odds with the analyses presented by Connell, Messner, Sabo and others. For their position is, in the final instance, unambiguously structural. By contrast, in seeking to problematize patriarchy and its inherent ideologies, Brittan is opening the door for a more nuanced and subversive account of power, one that recognizes the subject as an important actor and conduit for the (de)construction of any given set of power relations. As is discussed below, my response to this question of 'tentativeness' is to draw more heavily than Brittan, and certainly Connell, on a discursive understanding of (gender) power. Nevertheless, it seems to me that the concept of masculinism makes a valuable contribution to the sociology of masculinity. For critical structuralists the concept is readily aligned with notions of gender order, patriarchy and hegemonic masculinity. For what masculinism does is highlight the ideological dimensions and possibilities within masculinity as dominant practice(s) in given settings. Similarly, for poststructuralist theorists, the concept of masculinism can also be retained as a theoretical tool. But only with one important proviso: the ideological framework and assumptions must give way to a *discursive* understanding of power. Thus masculinism becomes a dominant discourse rather than a dominant ideology. To some, this may appear an arbitrary distinction. It is not. As has been discussed, critical structuralist concepts offer no theoretical basis on which to examine the otherwise 'lost subject': the individual posited as caught in a set of power relations that attest to a larger will or determination to oppress and dominate by actors who are themselves somehow removed, external to or hierarchically positioned vis-à-vis this ideological condition. The use of such structuralist terms as hegemonic masculinity assumes that by his instrumentality and skill, or by his powerlessness in the face of ideological forces, the (male heterosexual) actor is able to maintain a structural condition in his favour. In the final analysis, ideology posits a strategic intentionality and internal logic to power, held a priori by actors and enabled by a 'pre-existent truth situated elsewhere' (McNay, 1992: 25). However, as will now be discussed, despite its polemical appeal, such a notion of prior will is itself untenable within a sociology of masculinity that seeks to emphasize the possibility of change, resistance and transformation.

Power as discursive

Bringing back the resisting subject

The 'absent subject' in notions of hegemonic masculinity, patriarchy and gender order exposes the fundamental weakness in the concept of a juridico-discursive model of power. For despite their allusion to resistance and agency, critical structuralist perspectives ultimately subsume the individual (subject) under a cognitive, strategic and assured deployment of power by rational actors, individuals who are themselves somehow excluded from the ideological forces that 'they deploy'. Consequently, complex gendered power relations are reduced to an 'oppressor–victim' dualism, in which multiple subjectivity and self-identity processes are made invisible by the power of political categories of gender and sexuality and their ideological and material forces. As was discussed in chapter 2, understanding heterosexual and homosexual, or woman and man, as discursive political categories is not to deposit in these terms essentialistic and predictable behaviours. On the contrary, such terms can, I suggest, make an important contribution to the development of theories that retain recognition of multiplicity and difference, both key components in contemporary understandings of masculinity. But to talk of multiple masculinities on the one hand and unchanging structures on the other is not only idiosyncratic; it is dangerously reductive. It is dangerous to assume, first, that heterosexual men function as a strategic group with the primary motivation being the taking/holding of power; second, that 'Other' groups, such as feminists, gays, blacks (and profeminists) are somehow 'innocent of divisive, exclusionary, and oppressive tendencies' (Grimshaw, 1993: 56). As many feminists have noted, both assumptions speak to the underpinning 'Utopian vision' in much feminist work, a vision that must, by definition, assume a rationalist, modernist and ultimately humanist subject, a 'gendered deep self [that] continues through adult life and cuts across divisions of race, class, ethnicity, and so forth' (Fraser and Nicholson, 1990: 20; also Sawicki, 1991).[1]

A Foucauldian analysis

If concepts such as patriarchy and ideology are subject to much critique by feminists and others, and open to contrasting interpretations, the same can be said, several times over, for Foucauldian analyses of power. Foucault's writings have deeply troubled many feminists, for not only was there an absence of any critical gender analysis in his work, his argument that power is inherently productive and therefore positive, yet unstable and therefore not reducible to a given source, appears to undermine the very roots of feminism. Toril Moi is one of a number of feminists who warn against being 'seduced' by Foucault's 'ploys', the danger, as Moi sees it, being the 'depoliticisation of feminism' (1985: 95). However, as Foucault himself pointed out, his ideas are best deployed as a 'tool box', wherein the theorist picks, mixes and 'bends', if necessary, his array of intriguing, compelling, often elusive, concepts. It is with this qualification in mind that, through this book, I engage with Foucault's work and similar poststructuralist writings, the aim being to demonstrate that such theories can be usefully deployed in the sociology of masculinity. In this respect, I am contributing to what is now emerging as a third wave within the critical study of men/masculinities. This 'third wave' has its roots in identical developments in feminism and sociology more generally and is evident in the work of, for example, Segal (1999), Saco (1992), Pease (2000), Kerfoot and Knights (1993, 1996), Petersen (1998), Collier (1998), Nixon (1997), Moodley (1999), Gutterman (2001) and Jefferson (1994), each of whom has usefully integrated postmodern and/or poststructuralist perspectives in their critical study of men and masculinities across diverse empirical sites.

A further proviso in drawing on Foucault is to note that his emphasis on the relationship between power and the self changed significantly over the course of his working life. Originating out of a structuralist tradition, Foucault's early work on power (for example, *Madness and Civilization* (1965), *The Birth of the Clinic* (1963), and *Discipline and Punish* (1975)), was quite reductionistic, its main differentiation from Marxist theories on power being that Foucault did not give primacy to the state but to the body as the site at which the individual becomes 'dominated', 'subjected' and 'controlled' through disciplinary (discursive) regimes enabled by the omnipresent 'panoptic gaze' (see chapter 6). In these works Foucault sees the (sexualized) human body as the recipient and centre of an endless Nietzschean struggle between opposing 'power blocs', a historical condition wherein force prevails over meaning as the ultimate human condition. Discursive regimes of power are, for Foucault, inevitably bound up with systems of knowledge, to the point that he argues 'there is no power relation without the correlative constitution of a field of knowledge, nor any knowledge that does not presuppose and constitute at the same time power relations' (1975: 27). Although Foucault is, in these works, developing a devastating critique of both Enlightenment rationality and its associated myth of an innately moral humanist subject, his understanding of the production of 'docile bodies' (and knowledge) as directly implicated in the processes of (capitalist) production owes much to Marxism and is, in the final analysis, 'an essentially monolithic account of power as domination' (McNay, 1994: 64, also 1992). In his middle period, exemplified by *Power/Knowledge* (1980) and volume one of *The History of Sexuality* (1978), Foucault begins to deconstruct the notion that power is purely repressive and hierarchical, and only operative through 'the limited field of juridical sovereignty and State institutions' (1980: 102). In dismissing the idea of power as centralized, 'appropriated as a commodity' or functional to the benefit of a given structural order (1980: 98), Foucault stresses the symbiotic relationship between power and resistance. In so doing, Foucault develops further his concept of the discursive subject as a social and historical construct, fragmented, decentred, but, crucially, enabled by the very circularity of power at large in the social web. The body remains the primary point of subjectification by regimes of power, but it is now understood by Foucault to be marked and created as a subject (and thus categorized as an individual) by these very same dynamics. Thus the symbiotic relationship between power and the subject is revealed both in the individual's subjection to those 'laws of truth' that constitute various discursive regimes and in the simultaneous marking and identifying of the subject as an individual – an enabling, positive moment of (self) creation.

In his final period, exemplified by 'Technologies of Self' (1988b, also 1988a), Foucault moves much closer to the question of agency within the discursive parameters previously elicited. He comes to see the self as created as a 'work of art', not in a prior sense of there being a prediscursive subject, but through the self-disciplining techniques of the 'practices of self' that are at the disposal of the subject (as individual) seeking self-signification (see also Butler, 1990). The question for Foucault is now less on how individuals are subject to the powers of others, and more on how subjects (individuals) come to create their own selves and 'realize their own desires' against a scenario partly constructed by their own artistry. In making this point in 'Technologies of Self', Foucault reflects back on his earlier work and his future direction:

> Perhaps I've insisted too much on the technology of domination and power. I am more and more interested in the interaction between oneself and others and in the technologies of individual domination, the history of how an individual acts upon himself, in the technology of self. (1988b: 19)

What follows is a brief selective appropriation of Foucault's work on power. This is not in any way intended as anything more than a precursor to what I consider to be the possibilities of further research that seeks to connect Foucault's work and poststructuralism more widely with what is, in effect, a third-wave sociology of masculinity. In examining key Foucauldian concepts I am drawing primarily from Foucault's middle period. His later excursions into desire and self-creation are further discussed in chapter 7.

The discursive subject of power

The first point to stress is that the concept of discourse being used here is quite different from that of discourse as linguistic analysis. Too often the two are unproblematically conflated by theorists, and in the process the vitally important relationship of language/practice with the Foucauldian notion of an ungrounded self is lost. In poststructuralist terms, discourse refers not only to both language *and* practice, but also signals the means by which the subject is enabled and marked as an *individual*, the individual being a product of discourse. An example of discourse conflation is apparent in the work of Pease (2000), an otherwise interesting and useful examination of the relationship between notions of the postmodern and profeminist masculinity politics. He argues, for example, that 'women's oppression is not purely ideological or discursive' but also material (ibid:

34); that 'hegemonic masculinity may be considered as a dominant discourse' (ibid: 35); and that while differences amongst men clearly exist in the postmodern age, nevertheless 'we must avoid the danger of losing sight of patriarchy' (ibid: 31). As I have argued above, it is not possible to hold on to both a structuralist and poststructuralist position, and any attempt to do so is untenable, not least through the quite different understandings of power and the self that each position speaks to. Similarly, any notion that the material is somehow excluded from discourse is a misreading of poststructuralist theory, as is the attempt to retain the concept of patriarchy in the postmodern age. Such confusions can lead to a further problematic conflation, that of postmodernism and poststructuralism. Though closely related, the terms are fundamentally different. Postmodernism is, in the final analysis, a theory of the post-modern (note the hyphen). Thus it has a contemporary and historical relevance, mainly for Western societies, in that it clearly connects to the Enlightenment and to wider discussions concerning what Lyotard (1994) describes as the end of metanarratives and dominant knowledge forms in late capitalist societies. In contrast, poststructuralism is a set of theoretical tools, ranging from Lacanian pyschoanalysis through to Derridean deconstructionism, that together, and in part, provide means by which to interpret, understand and locate the subject in the social network, in the process providing insights into (non-grounded) identity, the self, power/resistance and subjectivity. In this respect, poststructuralism could well be around for eons, unlike postmodernism, which is historically located in the moment.[2] With this distinction in mind it can be seen that the discursive subject is not a contemporary phenomenon. Taken from a poststructuralist perspective, there have only ever been, and only ever will be, discursive subjects.

So what is discourse and how does it relate to power? In Foucault's terms discourses are more than the means by which individuals are reified and confirmed as individuals, for discourses carry knowledge and truth effects through their capacity to signal what it is possible to speak of and do at a particular moment and in particular cultural settings. The centrality of discourses to understanding and interpretation means that they are the very fabric of the social web. Discourses are the means by which we come to 'know ourselves'; perform our identity work; exercise power (in contrast to 'holding power'); exercise resistance; pronounce or deny the validity of knowledges and 'truths'; communicate with others and 'our selves' through the reflexive process; and subjectively engage with the world around us. Discourses are not restricted to any one society or culture but permeate all social environs. It is through discourse that beliefs, rituals and truths surrounding, for example, gender, sexuality and race, become manifest and dominant. But always there are counter-discourses at large. Consequently, though both dominant and sub-ordinated discourses exist, the sheer multiplicity and dynamism of discourses precludes the possibility of a final, totalizing, all-oppressive, social order:

> We must not imagine a world of discourse divided between accepted discourse and excluded discourse, or between dominant discourse and the dominated one; but as a multiplicity of discursive elements that can come into play in various strategies... Discourse transmits and produces power: it reinforces it, but also undermines and exposes it, renders it fragile and makes it possible to thwart it. (Foucault, 1984: 10, quoted in Ramazanoglu, 1993: 19)

The truth effects of dominant discourses can be understood to have normalizing and regulatory capacities in so much as they produce knowledges that are implicated in the construction of historically specific regimes of power. In contrast to notions of ideology, these regimes of power are not the product of individuals external to discourse, but they may indeed come to serve the interests of political categories such as men, though the predictability of this is not given. Thus power can be seen as immanent to the social condition and to the very being of subjects who inhabit this web. However, in contrast to a juridico-discursive model of power, poststructuralist perspectives understand power as exercised in contrast to being possessed (by a founding subject); productive rather than primarily repressive; and circulating the social network as opposed to being hierarchically situated.

> Power must be analysed as something which circulates, or rather as something which only functions in the form of a chain. It is never localised here or there, never in anybody's hand, never appropriated as a commodity or piece of wealth. Power is employed and exercised through a net-like organisation. And not only do individuals circulate between its threads; they are always in the position of *simultaneously undergoing and exercising* this power. (Foucault, 1980: 98; my emphasis)

In his early and middle periods, Foucault's propensity for seeing a 'will to power' as the underpinning drive behind subjects' engagement in the social web led him to a deterministic position not too dissimilar from Marxism and similar critical structuralist perspectives. Thus, at an extreme level, such an analysis would see struggles for power between opposing groups as ultimately configuring not only all social life, but the production and emergence of (dominant) discourse itself. Such a perspective draws close to the concepts of hegemonic masculinity and patriarchy, but only if the theorist seeks to privilege conflict over consensus and negotiation. Moreover, to follow this notion to its logical conclusion, one has to posit the self as a founding subject, for how otherwise would the subject be in a position to rationalize this pursuit of power and engage its practices in a cognitive, prediscursive fashion?

In his later work Foucault came to recognize the reductionistic implications of this earlier analysis, and also the inherent contradiction that it posits. Consequently, Foucault sought to emphasize the importance of desire to be (an individual) as the 'inner drive' of the discursive subject (see chapter 7). So it is with this qualification in mind that I suggest Foucault's analysis of power should be explored in terms of men and masculinity. For rather than see gender relations as a Nietzschean power struggle between opposing forces of dark and light (man and woman), it is more appropriate to see gender as a process of identity work, *but a process with political implications and manifestations*. These political dimensions are apparent in the material actualities of gender (see chapter 1), in the categories of woman and man that exist as discursive regimes of truth across the social network (see chapter 2) and in the experienced embodiment of gender (chapter 6). However, the power of these regimes of truth does not lie in their ability to ultimately discipline all bodies. Such a priori purposefulness is not within their capacity. Rather, the power of discursive regimes of (gender) truth lies in the very language that dichotomizes, and thus brings into existence, the gendered and sexualized status of the body – woman and man, straight and gay (Petersen, 1998; Lloyd, 1984; Butler, 1990; Weeks, 1991). The key, then, to understanding the subject's relationship to power is to see the subject (individual) as immanently connected to discourse, as embodied and inculcated through discourse, but also with the capacity to (discursively) reflect on this condition – the limits to this reflection being the discourses available and at its disposal in any setting.

The concept of resistance can be seen, then, to be a central and consistent element in Foucauldian analysis, and, indeed, to be fundamental to his concept of power. As Foucault puts it, 'there are no relations of power without resistances; the latter are all the more real and effective because they are formed right at the point where relations of power are exercised' (1980: 142). Thus the very dynamic of discourses precludes both totality and predictability. Within Foucauldian analysis the question as to whether we are bound by structure (the state and so on) or able to exercise total free will (agency) becomes a meaningless question.

To illustrate this point I will use the example of young Asian women. Increasing numbers of young Asian and Muslim British women are removing themselves from what many experience as oppressive patriarchal family and cultural backgrounds, a cultural shift with profound implications for their sense of identity and femininity (see Dwyer, 1999). Whilst this process may not go unresisted by their families and wider community (see Shain, 2000), the opportunities for Asian British women to resist what is at times direct and violent oppression (Burke, 2000) arise because the discursive possibilities to do so become available to them through education, cultural pluralism and similar knowledge experiences. But they cannot completely make this transition outside of their culture. They cannot become as far removed from an Asian culture as, for example, a white woman of the same class, education and age. What young Asian and Muslim British women appear to be doing in this situation is creating a new self, but not in any fully agentic, rational, holistic or cognitive fashion. The new self that is created emerges through an engagement in new discourses and through becoming open to the possibilities that arise for them as a consequence of imagining new, multiple, ways of being a woman. As Dwyer's research shows, young Asian and Muslim British women are constructing alternative discourses of femininity that are informed by class, cultural and educational factors, but the process is neither fully agentic nor fully proscribed. Any discursive identity shift is undertaken in part in negotiation with, and in resistance to, dominant discourses. Yet in 'imagining new futures' for themselves (Dwyer, 1999) these young women continue to occupy the political categories marked by the terms 'Asian British woman', and there is little or nothing they can do about this. How each woman lives out her life within the discursive possibilities and political categories that locate her reveals her degree of agency or choice. In short, there is no absolute structure; there is no absolute agency. Even using the terms is problematic because they are so value-laden in respect of most sociological perspectives.

Understanding power/resistance as exercised, rather than as ontologically distinct and grounded in the individual, points to the ambiguities and contingencies of each aspect of the 'power process' – gender, race, class and so on – operating across the social web; not existing in some uniform, distinct fashion but as contested 'social vectors of inequality' (Cooper, 1994: 450). Similarly, recognizing the elementary character of resistance offers a means for understanding how certain knowledges and 'truths' simultaneously flourish and threaten. For example, feminism has become a global discourse, beyond the closeted cells of Western academia, yet it remains, for many, an 'F' word, not to be spoken in certain company. Yet despite their threat to masculine power regimes, once out in the public domain discourses of feminism have been unstoppable, the attempts by many, usually men, to stifle their replication having little or no effect. But we should not be too surprised at this: feminisms exist precisely because masculine power regimes exist; feminisms are a point of dynamic resistance, providing their own distinct knowledges, truths, practices, not merely as a point of opposition but by offering ontological possibilities through pronouncing and identifying distinct (womanist) epistemologies (for example, see Stanley and Wise, 1993). Thus resistance indicates a point at which the discursive subject might achieve a sense of ontological purchase. For through the moment and engagement of resistance individuals can experience the unifying effects arising from the consensus and acknowledgement that their particular knowledges and practices are valid. Feminism, gay liberation and the women's movement would be examples of where the exercise of resistance offers a sense of personal, political and (inter)subjective unifying potential for the fragmented subject. But the possibilities of identity work offered by such processes are not confined to any particular group. Indeed, Robinson (2000) suggests that a similar process of identity politics is now occurring for white males through their taking up the crisis of masculinity discourse.

One way to appreciate the dynamism of discourses is to recognize their virus-like properties. Discourses have seductive and contagious characteristics, for without them the subject has no means or markers of identity. The belief system that exists through discourse becomes a compelling anchor from which the contingent subject holds on to a particular reality. This virus factor in discourses is heightened by the unbounded contemporary character of language and practice circulation as it has become enabled through technology, the media, global travel and so on. Discourses themselves travel, cannot be totally eliminated by force and cannot be silenced. Indeed, to force the subject to deny or renounce a knowledge or 'truth' through violence or the threat of violence is to resort to the 'final solution', a tacit acknowledgement that the discourse (and the subject it enables) is more powerful than the oppressor. In short, the extinction of an individual does not inevitably result in the extinction of a discourse. In this respect, discourses are infinitely more powerful and effective than physical oppression. History has seen countless examples of individuals being prepared to withstand torture, persecution, even accept certain death, rather than renounce a belief system.

Indeed, it can be argued that discourses have the potential to exist as violence, as well as arising from or being a consequence of violence. For example, the extensive and detailed research by Daniel Goldhagen (1996) into how the non-Jewish German people colluded in the persecution of German Jews, to the extent of becoming 'Hitler's willing executioners', is a disturbing study of the power of discourse; in this case the centuries-old anti-Semitic discourse that flourished in Germany well prior to the 1930s. This discourse laid the cultural possibilities for individuals to 'justify', if not contribute to, the horrors of the holocaust. As Goldhagen argues, anti-Semitism is not genetically rooted in the psyche of the German people; it is a discursive condition that stays alive, in part, through the historical cultural belief systems that have come to define what it means to be a 'true Aryan'. In this respect, the holocaust was a condition of possibility within the discursive landscape of Germanic culture long before it became a horrific reality. Similarly, it can be argued that the oppressive and violent regime of Saddam Hussein, described so effectively in Cockburn and Cockburn's (2000) study, is sustained as much by his ability to discursively position himself as the 'legitimate' resister and enemy of, first, the Iranian and Israeli peoples and, subsequently, the West as by his terrorization of the Iraqi population.

Foucauldian analysis signals that (gender) power and oppression can exist across a multitude of social environs, not all of them describable as masculinist or the province of the male. Discourses of femininity also have power effects and exist within a discursive gender regime, enabled in part through the power relationships of gender categories. Similarly, oppression and dominance do not inevitably correlate with physical power and strength. There are numerous examples of both the potentiality and power of femininities, and of the oppressive characteristics of apparent physical weakness. Examples might be the power a frail, aged, bedridden woman can exert over her male or female carer; the personal/political power evoked by the likes of Nancy Reagan, Winnie Mandela and Hillary Clinton; and, not least, the power of the 'hand that rocks the cradle'.

Fashion is possibly a more potent threat to dominant discourses than force. For discourses go in and out of fashion across the social web, an often incomprehensible and unpredictable condition beyond the ultimate control of any given individual or group. This is an inevitable characteristic and consequence of globalized economies and the increasing movement of people and knowledges. The dominance or subjugation of certain knowledges, practices or ideas may be momentary or may be persistent. Thus we can say with some certainty that dominant notions of masculinity or manliness will persist across the social web. What cannot be predicted is just which practices, assumptions or understandings such dominant discourses of masculinity will come to speak to.

The variety and diversity of discourses of gender is immediately apparent in the increasing plurality of masculinities themselves. Ways of talking, thinking, representing and practising masculinities are highly variable, crossing cultural and social boundaries with a speed that was unthinkable even two decades ago. Certainly, I would argue that discourses of masculinity, no matter how variable, do have a commonality, this being their given association with the male, but, beyond that, much is open to representation and interpretation by the identity-seeking subject. However, to understand masculinities as discursive is not to ignore the power effects of masculinities: their potentially oppressive properties, the material actualities of gender inequality and the political dimensions of identity work. The individual cannot hold power, but (he) can exercise it through the utilization of dominant discourses of masculinity. In so doing, the individual contributes, possibly unknowingly, to political categories of gender and to the power regimes that configure them. And herein lies the subtle but important difference from juridico-discursive models of (male) power. For Foucauldian analysis allows the subject in, both in terms of being subject to discursive power regimes and as, simultaneously, a contributor to and active player in the social enaction of gender, and, thus, in instances of dominance. Applying this concept to men, what emerges from this analysis is a *masculine subject*, a discursively bounded and enabled individual locked within a political category not directly of its making (see chapter 7). This political category 'man' offers a direct and powerful means for identity validation, and in so doing reconstitutes its own discursive power regime. The masculine subject is not a 'free subject' in any pure, humanistic or spiritual sense, but is subjected to the disciplinary conditions elementary to discourse. Such disciplinary techniques are, as will be discussed, saturated through the body, our sense of embodiment and accompanying notions of sex and sexuality. We cannot wholly escape them, but we necessarily draw on them to become that socially and self-validated individual. For men, the question is not whether they take up masculine discourses as practices of self-signification, but rather which masculine discourses to engage in. And here, whatever choice is available is heavily localized and thus constrained by numerous variables such as age, cultural capital, body, health, ethnicity, geography, nationality and, not least, the unique history of that subject as individual.

Summary

This chapter has explored the concepts of power and resistance in respect of men and masculinity through analysis of two key, but quite opposing, sociological perspectives. The first perspective, a juridico-discursive model, posits power as hierarchical, fundamentally oppressive, cognitively and ontologically valid and enabled, and materially based. Located in constructionist and critical structuralist perspectives, the juridico-discursive model has been influential in both feminist and pro-feminist first-wave and, especially, second-wave scholarship, coming to inform related concepts such as patriarchy, gender order and hegemonic masculinity. However, despite the potency of such concepts and the emotiveness they engender, they have fundamental inconsistencies and weaknesses for understanding the dynamic and fluid relationships between the political categories of gender and between individual women and men. Most notable in this regard is their inability to provide a theory of the (gendered) subject (individual) as an active yet constrained factor in the reproduction of dominance, and in the resistance to dominance.

The second model of power examined, a discursive model, is largely informed by Foucauldian poststructuralist theory. This model sees power as circulatory, exercised rather than held, and immanent to both the social condition and the production of individual subjectivity. In providing a non-determinist theory of the subject, the discursive model has been, and is being, increasingly utilized by third-wave feminist scholarship. In this respect, an aim of this chapter, and indeed the book, is to contribute to this theoretical direction, in so doing providing further understanding of the processes of power and resistance within and across the political categories of woman and man.

In connecting a discursive model of power with masculinity this chapter has introduced the concept of the *masculine subject*. In so doing, the case has been made for seeing males and men as discursively informed masculine beings, a state of gender signification enabled, not least, by virtue of gender being the primary identification that holds them (and females) on entry into the social web. As is elaborated in chapters 6 and 7, masculinities provide a set of symbolic and material practices, the engagement of which by the discursive subject enables gender identification to be socially validated and materially embodied. Thus the subject is both *subjected to masculinity* and *endorsed as an individual by masculinity*. In recognizing that masculinity exists as wider cultural formations, in post-structuralist terms being a regulatory practice and dominant knowledge form, I suggest that the term *masculinism* best illustrates the potentiality of such a gendered manifestation. However, this is to understand masculinism as a discursive rather than an ideological condition. While existing in multiple forms and expressions, masculinity as discourse can be seen to both inform and validate a larger political condition through its relationship to femininities and the 'Other'. Recognizing that all gendered discourses and exercises of power largely reflect the circumstances of their immediate expression, chapters 4 and 5 will examine such conditions and enactions of masculinism and masculinities across the public and private spheres.

FURTHER READING

Connell, R. W. (1987) *Gender and Power.* Cambridge: Polity.

Faudion, J. D. (ed.) (1994) *Michel Foucault: Power. The Essential Works 3.* London: Allen Lane/The Penguin Press.

McNay, L. (1992) *Foucault and Feminism.* Cambridge: Polity.

Ramazanoglu, C. (ed.) (1993) *Up Against Foucault: Explorations of Some Tensions Between Foucault and Feminism.* London: Routledge.

Sawicki, J. (1991) *Disciplining Foucault: Feminism, Power, and the Body.* New York: Routledge.

4
Public Men

Critiquing and deconstructing gendered public (production) and private (reproduction) domains has long been a core aim of feminist scholarship. One of the first feminists to make explicit the power relations buttressing the public and private was Mary O'Brien (1983). Located in a Marxist–feminist perspective, O'Brien's thesis was that malestream thinking, wherein man has been assumed to 'make history', privileges the public (masculine) world of production over the private (feminine) world of reproduction, thereby creating and reinforcing the ideological and material conditions for the continuation of patriarchal relations. For O'Brien, the political, but ultimately artificial, separation of the public and private serves to continue 'the generic oppression of centuries' (1983: 92) by positing the fate of the private (reproduction, family, relationships – women) in the hands of men.

O'Brien's analysis made an important contribution to second-wave feminist scholarship in so much as it laid an empirical and theoretical framework from which to understand the political importance and sensitivity permeating the personal and private realms. This analysis resonated with feminist insights, developing through the 1980s and 1990s, into the 'sexual division of labour' (Beechey, 1987; Dex, 1985; Walby, 1988), 'women's multiple roles' (Franks, 1999; Hochschild, 1989), the 'non-status' of women's work (Oakley, 1974), the ideology of the male breadwinner family (Davidoff and Hall, 1987), sex inequalities at work (Game and Pringle, 1984; Reskin and

Padavic, 1994) and the patriarchal conditions of capitalist production (Walby, 1986). Profeminist writers such as Bob Connell, Michael Messner, Andrew Tolson, David Morgan and Jeff Hearn shed further light on the specific interconnections of men, masculinities and the public worlds of work, unemployment, politics, sport and leisure. As these and other feminists/profeminists attest, the public sphere is, by any definition, a powerful one; being the malestream-informed historical vehicle, space and catalyst for determining and conditioning patriarchal relations and the gender order (Hearn, 1992).

In respect of males' sense of identity, the public domain can be understood to be the historically gendered arena where males engage with and replicate those behaviours and practices which, in their particular context, define manhood and manliness. The public sphere is a place that males are supposed to inhabit naturally, a place they must colonize, occupy, conquer, overcome, control. It is the site where men come to be (men). So what is meant by the 'public domain'? Jeff Hearn describes it as:

> all that happens in public, and not domestically, not in private; that which happens in organisations, militaries, public workplaces, factories, offices, churches, and corporate institutions, and in the street and other widely visible open spaces. (1992: 2)

As Hearn goes on to recognize, this definition, while usefully fixing a clear separation from the private sphere, is also problematic, for it draws on the very dichotomies that underpin gender distinctions and, thus, individual relations between women and men. Recognizing this, with intent to deconstruct the public–private dualism, is now a central aim of postmodern and poststructuralist 'anti-dualist' perspectives (see Butler, 1990). As Butler and other third-wave (pro)feminists argue (see Petersen, 1998), the language we use to make sense of difference, indeed to critique power relations, is itself directly implicated in these very same complex dynamics. Discourses of gender coexist within a dichotomy that takes as given 'natural' differences between the sexes. Thus to speak of the public and private is also to connect with those dualisms that serve to reinforce dominant notions of femininity and masculinity. For example, to talk of public and private selves is to speak of what are considered socially and culturally appropriate performances – emotions, behaviours, actions – by women and men in public. Similarly, the word 'domes-

ticity' is not gender neutral, any more than are the labels 'professional' and 'leader'. Each is laden with assumptions and appropria-
tions that, in discursive terms, reinforce a culture of masculinism –
the cultural dominance of the male (in the public sphere). If such a
condition is doubted, one need only cast a cursory eye on probably
the two most influential public spaces – politics and business. There
are, as yet, no governments or dominant political parties where
women form the majority of elected representatives (for example, see
Whitehead, 1999b); a point emphasized at the largest ever gathering
of world leaders for the UN Millennium Summit in New York in September 2000, where out of over 180 heads of state only seven were
women. An equally severe marginalization of women occurs across
Western business and corporate life where fewer than 10 per cent of
senior executive positions are held by women (IoM, 1998).

It is clear that women may well be occupying much of the space
that defines the public sphere, but they are not occupying, in any great
number, those public spaces where power is exercised, not least
because in very many countries they are prohibited by men from
doing so.

To be sure, men do not dominate all aspects of the public domain.
Indeed, there is evidence that certain parts of the public sphere are
becoming problematic spaces for men to occupy. For example, the
increasing exposure of some men's abusive practices on children has
created a climate of uncertainty for males working with young
people. Teaching infants in UK schools is no longer seen, by some,
as a suitable occupation for men. And research suggests that fewer
men are applying to become teachers, in part because of apprehen-
sion at being labelled as 'a bit funny' (Ferudi, 2000; Thornton, 1999).
Even those public arenas such as politics, sites traditionally dominated by males, find themselves increasingly subject to critical
scrutiny over their equal opportunities record (see Singh, 1998) and
how this might connect to men's practices within these sites. Groups
and individuals are more likely to voice their concern at the continued absence of women and black people in politics than ever before,
and male-dominated political parties ignore these protests at their
peril (see Fawcett Society Report, 1997; Whitehead, 1999b; Watt,
2000).

A further warning in the use of the terms 'public and private' when
speaking of gender concerns the overlay of meanings existing within
each term. For example, while using the descriptor 'public' we cannot

assume practices in this domain to be public. Put simply, what is in the public sphere is not necessarily in the public eye. Indeed, somewhat paradoxically, the public worlds of men are often very private, with men's practices often obscured behind ritualized behaviour, bounded by fraternities and frequently embedded in misogynistic attitudes and sexual stereotype (Cheng, 1996; Barrett, 1996). To be sure, there is now increasing attention being brought to bear on the public and private lives of men, and few male-dominated places remain untouched by the critical gaze of feminism. But the opening up of these spaces has not been easy, there being, not surprisingly perhaps, resistance to this by many men. One reason why the public world of men is a sensitive arena is the power that configures it. As many who work in organizations and politics recognize, the power that comes with hierarchical position can appear very real, and once assumed it is hard to relinquish – though, as was discussed in the previous chapter, one has to be wary of assuming power either as a fixed, absolute material condition or as uncontested.

A final and important consideration when talking of (gendered) public and private distinctions concerns permeability and slippage. The public and private spheres are not solid entities, any more than they are impermeable and secure. To be sure, it is a characteristic of many organizations that they assume, if not require, a separation between work and home, and it certainly suits many workers to have it construed as such. For as Hochschild's (1997) research shows, despite the increasing number of companies with so-called 'family-friendly policies', men (and women) are not, in any great numbers, taking advantage of any relaxation in work–home divisions to spend more time with their families. Indeed, recent research in the UK indicates that many more women than men would prefer to spend more time at work than at home (DfEE, 2000) – an indication, perhaps, that the private sphere is, for working mothers especially, a place of emotional stress and multiple roles, rather than a haven of tranquility within which to pursue creative activity.

Any notions of public–private compartmentalization are further problematized at the level of our emotions. Feelings of anger, frustration, love, anxiety and passion are not easily switched off as we physically move from home to work and vice versa (see Fineman, 1993). Similarly, intimate relations are not produced solely in the private world, while (masculinist) practices at work can readily become (masculinist) practices at home. So despite attempts to present or construct them as distinct and compartmentalized, the public and private domains interact, interrelate and intrude on each other. This is increasingly so in the high-tech age when countless homes have e-mail and Internet facilities and the work/home boundaries become subsequently eroded and more fluid. At the very least there is slippage between the discourses that inform the public and private domains. And while the public and private necessarily coexist as dichotomies, each creating by its own presence the existence of the other, this is not to assume that, as discursive subjects (individuals), we exist in such a compartmentalized dualist state.

Recognizing the all-encompassing character of the 'public domain', there are clear limits on the focus that can be brought to bear within this volume. Attention is given, then, to those arenas that constitute much of the public domain and where males are particularly visible in their display of masculinity; that is, the world of work, management and professions. The final section will explore feminist critiques of two central, but often overlooked, aspects of the public–private dualism – leisure and time. First, though, I will consider in more depth the characteristics that serve to define the gendered 'public' world of men, in particular men's ontological and mythological association to the 'heroic male project' and the building of 'empires'.

He's leaving home: the heroic male project

Myths and icons

Despite having such a clear, totalizing definition, the 'public domain' is not as straightforward as it appears, and not merely for reasons already stated. For there is a further characteristic to the public domain that needs to be addressed, that is the mythological and heroic narratives that are its basis. For the world of men (the public domain) can be seen as, and is often presented as, mysterious. Middleton describes it as:

> this elsewhere that is vast and pervasive, [a] world from which boys
> are excluded by their own sex, the same sex that is supposed to have

created it. Men's work is a mystery, and mysteries create awe and longing (as many religious leaders have known). (1992: 41)

This mythical aspect of men's public–private lives is captured in the notion of 'man as (lone) hero': the adventurer/explorer/conqueror trapped in a cycle of return and departure as he exposes himself to new challenges; with a drive to achieve that is not, apparently, of his choosing but comes from 'deep' within his psyche. Although the imagery here is often presented as a 'heroic male project', this process is not simply one of self-aggrandizement or self-sacrifice. At an ontological level, the cycle of leaving serves to create the conditions and possibilities for alleviating the male's ever-present existential uncertainty and self-doubt. This theme is a potent one in the mythologies surrounding men, spawning countless books and films. In terms of twentieth-century masculinist imagery, one can see the heroic male project writ large in the imagery of the singularly obsessed, but reticent, Olympian (e.g., Michael Johnson, Steve Redgrave), the charismatic Arthurian politician (e.g., Jack and Robert Kennedy) and the macho leader of the male gang or 'rat pack' (e.g., Frank Sinatra). Examples in literature are too numerous to detail but Joseph Conrad's *Heart of Darkness* and its film relation *Apocalypse Now*, Tom Wolfe's *Bonfire of the Vanities* and its film relation *Wall Street*, Jack Kerouac's *On the Road* and the many 'road' films that have derived their formula from such imagery – all succinctly capture an aspect of this mythological masculine subjectivity. For example, Kerouac's book begins with this passage:

> I first met Dean not long after my wife and I split up. I had just gotten over a serious illness that I won't bother to talk about, except that it had something to do with the miserably weary split-up and my feeling that everything was dead. With the coming of Dean Moriarty began the part of my life you could call my life on the road. Before that I'd always dreamt of going West to see the country, always vaguely planning and never taking off. Dean is the perfect guy for the road because he actually was born on the road. (Kerouac, 1957: 3)

Taking one particular critical gender reading of this text reveals a man searching for relief from the emotional exigencies brought on by fear of death, relationships and the unseen, unspoken of 'other'. Release and comfort come in the form of another man, not (apparently) a gay man, but a fraternal friend, a buddy who symbolizes a rugged (heterosexual) independent, heroic and mysterious masculinity. So within the first few lines the reader is introduced to the reticent male hero, a loner and individualist, 'leaving home' for the road, to find himself once more. Later on in the book, the hero, Dean Moriarty, succinctly describes his philosophy of always being ready to 'leave': 'I'll tell you Sal, straight, no matter where I live, my trunk's always sticking out from under the bed, I'm ready to leave or get thrown out' (ibid: 251). This narrative produced by Kerouac was not, however, merely fiction. For Kerouac lived out his impossible, endless quest for 'love over the next hill' (Rutherford, 1999: 16) in a real, but tragic, way. Never able to fulfil this longing, Kerouac resorted to drink and died a drunk in his mother's house.

Despite its inherent flaws, the image and mythology of man leaving home to engage in a heroic project maintains a resounding presence in most societies. We see the mythology at work in the notion of 'man as hunter'; the adult male subjecting himself to the rigours and dangers of the wild, far removed from the comfort of (female) home, enduring these trials for the very sake of 'my family's well-being'. Yet despite their absence from the main scene, which such notions suggest, women play a key role in the imagery of 'man in his world'. They exist, usually, as the purpose, the vulnerable, the flight from, the prize, the sought after, the protected. 'Woman' is omnipresent, yet necessarily curtailed by the masculine mysteries invoked by the images of man doing 'his own thing'. Woman is the Other that necessarily exists in order to allow man to assume his central role. Indeed, at a practical level, women are usually the ones who make the necessary sacrifices of time and energy in order to supply the means and space for men to exercise their heroic project. Thus no matter how far the man travels, emotionally or physically, there remains this umbilical cord to the female, an attachment that carries the potential to nurture yet destroy (the male). This image of woman as nurturer–destroyer is powerfully symbolized in the famous 1940s Western, *The Searchers*, starring John Wayne and directed by John Ford. In this film the male hero does not appear to choose his heroic project, but rather has it forced upon him by the compelling need to do his duty as a man – the 'protector of woman', a situation that simultaneously defines yet destroys him (see also Coyne, 1997; Donald, 1992). The ambivalence, if not threat, contained in women's relationship to the heroic male project is symbolized equally vividly in the comic strip superheroes *Batman, Flash Gordon, Superman* and *Popeye*, each of whom exists, in part, as, paradoxically, an asexual hyper-masculine man caught in an unresolved relationship with 'woman' (for elaboration, see Middleton, 1992; Pecora, 1992; Thomas, 1999). In the 'real world', the dilemmas of the heroic male project, together with their irresistible character, are caught in the timeless images of men trudging resolutely off to war, waved off by their womenfolk.

Despite usually being presented as such, it is apparent that the public domains of men do not merely provide a means and space by which to 'provide for the family'. For the arenas that constitute the public sphere contain both rites of passage for males and validations of masculinity, heterosexuality and brotherhood. As such, the homo-erotic overtones that permeate the close and intimate male relationships of the public domain become juxtaposed with the overt and strident homophobia that often accompanies images of the rugged, male hero (see Berger, Wallace and Watson, 1995; Hall, 1997; Rutherford, 1997; Silverman, 1992). The tensions between these contrasting sexual(ized) discourses can inspire their own fantasies, interacting with national and racial differences to create, for example, the 'Blond Bedouin' mythology surrounding Lawrence of Arabia (Dawson, 1991); the 'pure Aryan' symbolism of Nazi Germany (Dutton, 1995); the sexually ambiguous, politicized black masculinity embodied by sportsmen such as Carl Lewis and actors such as Paul Robeson (Carby, 1998); and the boyish, tragic innocence of ill-fated young men, exemplified by soldier/poet Englishman Rupert Brooke, who, along with millions of others, sacrificed himself for an 'imperial mission' (Rutherford, 1997; see also Dawson, 1994). Despite their differences, such images and icons of masculinity play a vital role in mythologizing the heroic male project, for each in its way contributes to both the mysteriousness of what men do and what men are. Moreover, as potent images of the 'heroic male', such icons as Lawrence, the Aryan, Brooke, Robeson, are inevitably enlisted to serve, if not to be directly implicated in, a further project – building and defining empires.

A heroic male project – building empires

There is no more potent symbol of the heroism, potency, mythology and mystery of the male public domain than the idea of empire. A point reinforced by the fact that the empire-builders of history appear to have universally been men. When women do make an appearance on this stage they seem caught by countermanding discourses of (unfulfilled) maternalism (e.g., Elizabeth I), carnality (e.g., Catherine the Great), sexuality (e.g., Cleopatra) or innocence/naivety (e.g., Joan of Arc). Unlike for men, there appears to be no space for empire-building women to occupy that is not already tainted or undermined by the presence of their sexuality and/or gender. The Dr Livingstones, Sir Francis Drakes, and Cecil Rhodeses can leave home to carve out empires in the 'heart of darkness', and questions are seldom raised about who they left behind, or the sexual expectations that travelled with them (see Kent, 1999; also Paxman, 1999). Similarly, Caesar, Alexander, Hannibal, Hitler and Napoleon were first and foremost 'men of action', compelled, it would seem, to lead and conquer not to nurture. Attila, Shaka and Genghis Khan were barely domesticated, being brutal, ruthless men 'wedded' only to their armies.

While such 'icons' exist across all continents, the place that has for over 200 years probably best symbolized the pioneering 'instincts' of men is North America. Although contemporary Americans may be reluctant to talk of an American empire as such, the legends and images of Davy Crockett, George Washington, the Alamo, Wyatt Earp, General Custer, Abraham Lincoln, Gettysburg, Jack Kennedy and the Clark and Lewis expedition are of white, heterosexual, Anglo-Saxon masculinities writ large; broad strokes of male heroism and tragedy painted across a physical and metaphorical landscape where the female (and black and gay man) is reduced to anxious spectator as a continent is 'civilized' by a 'rugged masculinity' (for discussion, see Bleys, 1996; Hearn and Melechi, 1992; Nelson, 1998; Quam-Wickham, 1999). Such imagery has reached out now from its historical setting and taken root in that most American of contemporary masculine adventures – the conquering of space itself (for example, see Messerschmidt, 1996). Whether the physical setting be Wall Street, the Rio Grande or, indeed, the Space Shuttle, we can see the legend that is America continue to be infused with masculine mythology.

It is the fact of masculinity's illusory and fluid character that leaves it amenable to being manipulated in the promotion of empire. Indeed, masculinity (as discourse) has the capacity to be employed in any cultural validation that involves males. It is no surprise, then, that few if any empires have not been founded on the real and/or mythologi-

cal acts of men; moments of bravery, endurance and self-sacrifice that
have lent themselves to interpretation by politicians, populists and
propagandists and have been subsequently drawn on by the masses
for meaning and comfort. The point is not so much whether
Lawrence, Lincoln, Crockett, Caesar, Washington and so on were
great men, but rather that their deeds lived on in the national consciousness long after their physical demise, and in the process nurtured notions of national, gender and racial difference. Thus a
people's sense of themselves as a nation is sustained, in part, through
eulogizing the masculine performances of certain men. We can see
it at work today in contrasting states such as the Irish Republic
(Michael Collins), Jamaica (Bob Marley), Scotland (Robert the
Bruce), Russia (Stalin) and Turkey (Atatürk). Nations large and small
draw on the masculine mythologies and legends surrounding 'great'
men to give meaning and purpose to what are no more than political boundaries increasingly in crisis (Castells, 1998). The fiction of
the nation state is sustained, in part, by the fiction of hyper-
masculinity, a mythological condition that almost inevitably results
in the political and cultural marginalization of woman as a political
category (for example, see Hensman, 1992).

Beyond the particular forms of masculine subjectivity invoked
by militarism, dreams of conquest and accompanying physical
endurance (Barrett, 1996; Morgan, 1994; Kent, 1999), the nineteenth
and twentieth centuries witnessed the emergence of a new kind of
male empire-builder, a man who seeks to make his mark on and
change the world through his drive, energy, self-discipline, initiative,
but, most importantly, through his financial acumen. This man is a
leader, risk-taker, gambler, inventor–creator and, inevitably, a worka-
holic. He is the self-made man carved out in the image of Ford, Hurst,
Hughes, Goldwyn, Carnegie, Rockefeller, Beaverbrook. His contem-
poraries are global entrepreneurs such as Bill Gates, Donald Trump,
George Soras, Richard Branson and Rupert Murdoch. Smaller
empires of the self-made man may not extend beyond ownership of
a single MacDonald's franchise, yet his self-image would similarly be
as controller of both self and, importantly, others (men and women).
Those men with huge financial empires are seen as the archetypal
'winners' in the global capitalist contest, being assured, rich, lucky –
and ruthless. The images of maleness that surround the global entrepreneur are symbolically and materially expressed in masculinist
arenas such as Wall Street, Fleet Street, Manhattan and Hollywood.

However, unlike the singularly besuited (white) Rockefeller or Ford, contemporary global icons of (heterosexual) male potency are just as likely to include Ice T, Michael Jordan, David Beckham, Brad Pitt or Eminem.

Despite their plasticity, these and similar symbols of 'successful' twenty-first century (Western) adult manhood now stride out across a global male subconscious, with each country and continent having its own particular exemplar of this self-made man, rich beyond avarice, and, in some instances, apparently more powerful than the Caesars who ruled Rome. Again, the domestic, private realm of the female exists within these images, but rarely intrudes to disrupt or question, being enlisted only to reinforce a public image of (hetero)sexual potency and/or fatherhood. Women's relationship to this world remains conditional upon acceptance by those (men) who would recruit into it those in their own image (Collinson, Knights and Collinson, 1990). Connell (1998) describes the form of masculinity performed by the men (and some women) who exemplify the empire-building global entrepreneur as a 'transnational business masculinity', a discourse of maleness that has quickly taken root across an increasingly mobile, high-tech, global society.

The dominant images of masculinity captured in the opulent, potent, fast-moving yet elusive public world of 'successful' men construct a fantastical and compelling mythology for many males. Whether it be the clandestine military exploits of a country's Special Forces, the sexual pastimes of a porn king, or the conspicuous consumption of a rock star, the exaggerated behaviours and unreal lifestyle of such men only serves to reinforce the allure of their masculine display. The power of this imagery is particularly apparent within those glossy magazines targeted at young men – the 'lads'. Yet despite the powerful and seductive character of the images and the notions of leadership and empire-building that they trigger, for most men the public domain is a more mundane place. It is the world of paid employment, the world of often petty organizational politics, the world of pensions, (ir)regular salaries and corporate culture. For most men, any 'heroic project' begins when they leave for work.

Work, management and the professional

Men at work

As I have suggested, the drive or purpose behind many men's pursuit of a heroic project should not be seen simply as a cognitive drive for power – though, to be sure, the exercise of power may well reinforce many men's sense of their own masculine potency and should not be disregarded as an important motivator. Similarly, as feminist scholarship has clearly shown, the malestream dialectic that configures a distinct hierarchical separation between the public and private, materially benefits the political category of men while continuing to reinforce dominant discourses of gender. However, whether this results in a state of patriarchy depends to a great extent on one's definition of patriarchy (for discussion, see Walby, 1986). Indeed, as was discussed in chapter 3, from a feminist poststructuralist perspective the very notion of patriarchy is problematic. Nevertheless, whatever one's view of patriarchy, it is clear that if we are to acquire a deeper appreciation of men's relationship to the public sphere (whatever might define it), it becomes necessary to move beyond seeing work as extrinsically or intrinsically rewarding and to recognize its ontological connections; that is, paid employment provides an important arena through which the discursive subject can achieve a sense of identity – the accomplishment of being (an individual). In this respect, paid work is more than merely a provider of some material or social comfort or an opportunity to exercise power; it is a primary vehicle for the otherwise contingent and unstable subject to achieve a sense of self, to become grounded and located in the social world (for discussion, see Casey, 1995; du Gay, 1996; Knights and Willmott, 1999). The discursive subject comes to be an individual, in part, through (paid) work.

There are multiple ways such sense of individuality becomes realized. For example, paid work can provide temporal and spacial structures that themselves offer a sense of location and permanence; the activities of work take place within and across numerous organizational locations, each of which offers sets of knowledges, values and codes to be adhered to and/or acknowledged; work provides an immediate social label for the discursive subject, a label that is readily recognizable to others; these social labels offer simultaneous rejection and acceptance – that which I am defines that which I am not; and the often frantic activities of work can be deeply comforting as our sense of self is reconfirmed daily in our congested diaries, this filling of time and space serving to mitigate the existential anxieties that surround us all (see Giddens, 1991; Whitehead, 2001a). Of no less importance is the fact that work and organizations are gendered. More specifically, paid work has historically been managed, organized and predominantly engaged in by men, one consequence of which is that it has come to exercise a major influence on definitions and performances of masculinity.

The wider relationship between ontology and masculine identity is discussed in chapter 7; suffice to say at this point that men's search for ontological security through work is not straightforward. As has been emphasized, the public world of men is sustained through a rich, complex combination of myth, mystery and materiality. To compound this, there are clear divisions of class, sexuality, skill, profession, ethnicity, age, education, authority and status that define and permeate the multiple cultures within gendered workplaces (Cheng, 1996; Mills and Tancred, 1992; also Hood, 1993; Tolson, 1977). Men's sense of masculine self may be constantly reaffirmed at work; yet it is also subject to scrutiny and question. For example, unemployment may threaten some men's sense of self (Morgan, 1992; Walter, 1979), as may equal opportunities initiatives and the increased number of women in previously male-dominated organizational sites (Maile, 1999). New technology, while often seen as maleist in design and utilization, also creates organizational transformations that can undermine traditional displays of masculinity (Cockburn, 1983). Even those men-managers at the top of the career ladder and in male-dominated professions are not protected from the emotional disruptions that accompany rapid and uncontrollable organizational change (Roper, 1994).

Clearly, different men will respond to such work transformations in different ways, any attempt at generalization denying the capacity of the individual to make some changes to his or her subjectivity. But organizational change is now endemic, particularly so in the postmodern age, a time when the discourse of organizational and individual performativity (Lyotard, 1994) dominates work sites (Dent and Whitehead, 2001; Usher and Edwards, 1994).[1] In short, it is not simply that men go out to perform their heroic project at work unhindered – if they ever have. More than ever, individual men and women are under pressure to perform to and be measured against sterile sets of targets, indicators and external variables that are largely outside their immediate control (Casey, 1995). Performativity is both a consequence and a part cause of the long hours' work culture now so evident in the industrialized world. For example, recent UK government research reveals that one in five employees now works over sixty hours a week, including 14 per cent of fathers, with men generally twice as likely as women to work such long hours (DfEE, 2000). And this in spite of a European Union working-time directive that stops most firms making staff work more than forty-eight hours a week.

Yet while work pressures and insecurities have become endemic through globalization and the emergence of the knowledge economy (Rifkin, 1996; Sennett, 1998), with women moving inexorably into worksites previously occupied by men, paid work within the 'new' capitalist system of production retains values closely associated with dominant discourses of masculinity. In that respect, men remain a privileged political category in the world of work. For masculine values pervade organizational cultures, locating women and notions of femininity as the 'Other' and, thus, marginal – a point on which feminists and profeminists of all theoretical persuasions are agreed (Cockburn, 1991; Gherardi, 1995; Kerfoot and Knights, 1993; Morgan, 1992; Prichard, 2000). Morgan, for example, highlights many of the belief systems and values that still sustain the modern capitalist world of work and mirror the Weberian notion of the 'ideal-type' working man – instrumental, rational and independent:

> [This man] is aggressive, independent, unemotional, or hides his emotions; is objective, easily influenced, dominant, likes maths and science; is not excitable in a minor crisis; is active, competitive, logical, worldly, skilled in business, direct, knows the ways of the world; is someone whose feelings are not easily hurt; is adventurous, makes decisions easily, never cries, acts as a leader; is self-confident; is not uncomfortable about being aggressive; is ambitious; able to separate feelings from ideas; is not dependent, not conceited about his appearance; thinks men are superior to women, and talks freely about sex with men. (Fransell and Frost, cited in Morgan, 1992: 57)

Increasingly for many, this comprehensive listing of 'masculine attributes', far from being ideal, are likely to be recognized as poten-

tially damaging for those who would aspire to them. The patholog-
ical and emotionally damaging consequences of striving to live out
this unattainable masculine behaviour are evident from research into
those who seek, at any cost, to invest a sense of self through pursuit
of a 'successful career' (LaBier, 1986; Pahl, 1995). For no matter how
much they might try, most men are unable to seamlessly perform such
ways of masculine being, attempts at doing so only resulting in
damage to themselves and others (see also Kerfoot and Whitehead,
1998a, 2000). Yet there is overwhelming evidence that such attributes
remain highly regarded in business organizations (Cheng, 1996;
Kerfoot and Knights, 1993; Roper, 1994), global corporations
(Connell, 1998), the armed forces (Barrett, 1996, 2001), most public
sector sites (Christie, 2001; Prichard, 2000; Whitehead and Moodley,
1999), unions (Cockburn, 1983; Creese, 1999) and professional sport
(Messner and Sabo, 1990; McKay, Messner and Sabo, 2000). Thus
it is one of the paradoxes of the age that organizations supposedly
strive to engender so-called feminine traits of trust, team-working and
cooperation, in work sites where masculine values of instrumentality, competition and individuality are demanded through a work
culture of performativity (for discussion, see Fletcher, 1999). The
reason for this submersion of the feminine in organizational culture
is the (often unrecognized) dominance of masculinism. As Joyce
Fletcher puts it:

> there is a masculine logic of effectiveness operating in organizations
> that is accepted as natural and right . . . this logic of effectiveness sup-
> presses or 'disappears' behaviour that is inconsistent with its basic
> premises, even when that behaviour is in line with organizational goals
> . . . [with the result that] people who exhibit such behaviour *get dis-
> appeared* from the organizational screen. (1999: 3; original emphasis)

So work can provide both assurances and contradictions for men and
their sense of masculinity. Fraternities within an organization can
require, if not demand, a particular validating masculine display from
its (men) members; anything less rapidly making would-be participants' membership untenable (see Barrett, 1996). This is as true of
membership of the Yardies or the Mafia as it is of the NYPD, the US
Marines or almost any firm of solicitors, accountants or business con-
sultants. Yet while the performance of dominant notions of masculinity may well enable men (and women) to remain in work

settings, if not progress up the slippery career ladder, work and identity insecurities remain, never to be fully resolved. Not all men are at ease with a masculinist corporate culture, and many seek to address the inherent tensions of attempting to manage contrasting ways of being by focusing on their paid work to the exclusion of all else, particularly relationships and family. And there is a comfort in this act, for so long as the man sustains his undivided attention on work, he is avoiding looking into his life and values – and the costs his actions incur for him and others. Moreover, his sense of power and potency becomes reified in the workplace, whatever impotencies might exist for him outside it. He comes to live his life and exercise his being in what is ultimately an artificial, cultural–social configuration – the compartmentalization of the public and private. The singularity of this practice not only contributes to the mythology of men's heroic projects; it serves to reinforce a particular (traditional) understanding of masculinity. A further effect is that men come to be associated with commitment, dedication, careerism, presenteeism and singularity of purpose in many high-status, high-pressure organizations (see Singh and Vinnicombe, 2000). Not surprisingly, one consequence of this association of career pursuit with the male is that in virtually every corporation men are the most numerous, if not most visible, gender – especially at the top.

Men as managers

While there is a history spanning several decades to feminist analyses of work, it is only relatively recently that critical attention has been brought to bear on men's relationship to the world of management. Yet focusing on men in management is an interesting area of study for gender researchers, not least because, as Collinson and Hearn point out, 'most managers in most organizations in most countries are men' (1996: 1). As Collinson and Hearn go on to note, there has been a 'strange silence' surrounding the interrelations of men, masculinity and management, the outcome of a 'taken-for-granted association, even conflation, of men with organizational power' (ibid: 1). This state of gender relations is one that appears particularly resistant to change. In most Western countries, sites where feminism has had the most impact to date, women still account for no more than 10 per cent of managers and 3 per cent of company directors

(IoM, 1995, 1998). Similarly, despite several decades of feminist thinking, 'charismatic leadership' in organizations remains synonymous with men and masculinity, with the consequence that concepts of organizational authority usually draw on the visionary leader as the patriarchal/paternalistic 'head' of the 'family' (for discussion, see Collinson and Hearn, 2001).

Largely because of its inherent contingency, management is increasingly located within fashionable knowledges and practices that are designed to give the appearance of certainty and grounding. Often promoted by gurus of corporate culture, such understandings serve to lend an air of objectivity and professional credibility to that which is both elusive and subjective – the (total) management of individuals. Yet an analysis of contemporary management knowledges reveals the underpinning gendered assumptions informing managerial practices, thus reminding us that management knowledge and practice is not objective. Whether it be in the execution of performance appraisals (Thomas, 1996), Human Resource Management (Wajcman, 1998), Total Quality Management (Kerfoot and Knights, 1996), team-working (Benschop and Dooreward, 1998) or in the very construction of corporate strategies (Kerfoot and Knights, 1993), discourses of masculinity are threaded through the everyday world of organizational life. The 'successful' corporate manager may, in turn, be authoritarian, paternalistic, entrepreneurial, careerist, instrumental, ruthless, rational, unemotional and distant. While such stances do not preclude women, they do speak to dominant understandings of men and masculinity and, as such, provide a discursive framework against which males may perform as managers and as men, less hindered than women by counter-discourses of gender and sexuality.

However, despite overwhelming evidence of the strong connections between management and masculinities, conventional management theory offers few insights on this subject. Most management theorists have conspicuously failed to recognize the interrelations of sexuality, gender and power at work in organizational sites and invariably present organizational leadership as the given realm of the male (for discussion, see Collinson and Hearn, 2001; also Hearn and Parkin, 1988). The importance of such gender absence is highlighted in the fact that as management has become more 'professionalized' (for discussion, see Dent and Whitehead, 2001; also Roper, 1994), so has the requirement for aspiring managers to undertake formal education in 'managing people'. Again, by exploring the character of such education, the gendered assumptions and divisions at the heart of management are revealed.

The route that many aspiring senior managers take in order to move up to the higher echelons of corporate life is the Master of Business Administration (MBA). This highly valued (and expensive) programme is delivered in most universities and presented as both the panacea to the Durkheimian anomie permeating organizations and individuals (Anthony, 1994) and a quick route to corporate riches. However, one only has to look at the gendered composition of most university business schools, their curricula and their areas of research to see that women remain highly marginalized and masculinist values predominate (Kilduff and Mehra, 1996). And though in the US women form 35 per cent of full-time MBA students in top business schools, and in the UK 25 per cent, fewer than 10 per cent of women make it to senior management positions (THES, 2000). Again, this emphasis on the male connects directly with the dominant corporate culture of masculinism, a point not lost on many aspiring women managers.

We should not be too surprised, then, that as the gurus of leadership studies are almost overwhelmingly 'successful' men, their much sought after prognostications for organization and individual 'success' tend to neglect the presence of women in organizations and, thus, reinforce the particular gendered character of corporate culture (Collinson and Hearn, 2001). Of course, this situation in academia merely reflects what goes on across most organizational sites, be they in the public or the private sector. Feminism is very much an 'F' word not only in large corporations but in virtually every male-dominated part of the public sector from politics to education (Whitehead and Moodley, 1999). So the fact that an MBA programme offering students a close and rigorous exploration of feminist insights into men, masculinities and management is a rare beast should not unduly surprise us. As Sinclair (2000) wryly observes, raising issues of masculinities in management education usually renders the men participants 'speechless'.[2]

It is clear, then, that despite several decades of contemporary feminism, the world of management remains male-dominated to an extraordinary extent. There has been much written about this state of affairs by feminists, particularly in respect of the 'glass ceiling' and how women might 'shatter' it (for example, Davidson and Cooper,

1992; Flanders, 1994). Such texts, often written within a broad liberal feminist perspective, suggest to women that all they need to break through into management is a 'can do' mentality, one that reflects the 'real world' of work. Other feminists take a more jaundiced view of this 'real world', suggesting that the very culture it espouses denies the possibility of the caring, ethical environment central to a feminist activism (Hughes, 2000).

Whatever one's view on contemporary organizational life, it is evidently an arena where gender change is slow in coming. Feminist research has indicated several factors at work here. One of the earliest and most influential texts on men and management was written by Rosabeth Moss Kanter (1977). Kanter argues that the culture of most organizations values the Taylorist 'scientific management' approach, whereby the 'good' manager is seen to act in a rational, analytical, unemotional, distant, 'objective', instrumental and tough-minded manner. Such behaviour is 'infused with an irreducible masculine ethic', which assumes that only men have the requisite qualities of the 'new rational manager' (Collinson and Hearn, 1996: 12). Kanter goes on to make two further important observations; first, that senior managers have a tendency to appoint in their own image; second, that in order to break down this masculinist culture, the number of women managers in an organization needs to rise to a 'critical mass' of, say, 30 per cent of the management. The first point that Kanter makes is reinforced by research into public and private organizations undertaken by Collinson, Knights and Collinson (1990), Thom (1999) and Meehan (1999), while Davidson (1997) makes a similar point in respect of the black and ethnic minority woman manager (also Moodley, 1999).

With regard to Kanter's observation concerning a critical mass of women managers as 'change agents', there are still few if any organizations where such a numerical situation exists. Also, the 'critical mass' thesis fails to understand that what sustains men in management is not just numerical advantage, but, as Hughes (2000) and Fletcher (1999) argue, the competitive, aggressive culture that speaks of masculine, not feminine, values. This condition is clearly exacerbated by the pressures on managers to be instrumental and aggressive, behaviours particularly apparent in insecure, performativity-driven work sites. This discursive culture of masculinism is as much (if not more) of a barrier to women's career progression as the number of men at the top, for it is highly pervasive and difficult to overcome through 'simple' numerical change. Also, to assume that women can bring some value differences to management is an attractive proposition, but it is also dangerous. For it reinforces an essentialist view of gender while locking male and female into the gender dichotomy that underpins inequality. Though some feminists do consider that the 'alternative qualities' that women may bring to management could undermine maleist values and practices (Rosener, 1990), there is little evidence of this happening yet. Indeed, the durability and corrosiveness of contemporary management life is well captured in Judi Marshall's (1995) research, where she notes that even when women do acquire management positions, they are often left feeling disenchanted by the work culture they find themselves immersed in and move on, often to self-employment (for discussion, see Maddock, 1999; Ozga and Deem, 2000).

The deep personal unease that many women managers experience in male-dominated organizations often results from what Silvia Gherardi (1995) describes as women's 'schizogenic' relationship to organizational life; that is, the 'dual presence' that can occur for women managers and executives, wherein they are required to assume contradictory roles of (feminine) gender and (masculine) organizational being. This tension creates an internal conflict that is, for many women, never fully resolved. Such conflicts are less likely to occur for most men, for in being managers their sense of masculinity is not so compromised. On the contrary, management offers most masculine subjects a seductive and powerful identity validation, in that it speaks directly to what it means to be a 'successful man': purposeful, rational, competitive, ruthless, strong-minded and controlling (Kerfoot and Whitehead, 1998a; also Cheng, 1996; Collinson and Hearn, 2001; Kerfoot and Knights, 1993; Roper, 1994; Wajcman, 1998).

As was highlighted above, it is useful to understand work and organizational life as discursive webs wherein identity can be explored, performed and, to some degree, negotiated. However, the culture of masculinism facing women (and men) in management remains so pervasive that their identity performance is constantly mediated and interrupted by the masculine values that prevail. Thus women are denied access to the higher echelons of organizations in the way that most (white) men are, with the result that the masculine/managerial subject remains the privileged subject in management (see Kerfoot and Whitehead, 1998a, 2000; also Kerfoot, 1999).

Much of this analysis and understanding of contemporary managerialism raises the question: why would women, or men for that matter, want to immerse themselves in it? This question cannot be answered for every individual, but it is important to recognize that women are clearly capable of being as tough-minded, competitive, instrumental and aggressive managers as men, and are also vulnerable to the particular ontological seduction that management elicits (see Whitehead, 2001a). This seduction is extremely powerful for both women and men and should not be underestimated, reinforced as it now is by the values of organizational performativity. Indeed, one can speculate that more, not fewer, women will, in the future, wish to be managers in every sense of the term, and for a complex combination of ontological, identity, status and material reasons. In this event, any subsequent shift away from men's numerical dominance in management may well challenge many men's assumptions about their organizational and gendered status, leading to them experiencing confusion and unease as previous 'secure' gendered boundaries become eroded (Maile, 1999). Certainly Hochschild's (1997) research indicates that corporate culture is increasingly a more attractive proposition than domestic labour for many women. Understanding these interrelations of power, gender, management and identity requires a recognition that organizations are not absolute, unchanging or external to the actors in them (Calas and Smircich, 1993; Kerfoot and Knights, 1996). Rather than seeing the organization as prior to the individual, it is more useful to understand that the organization exists as a contingent discursive 'community of practice' (Bruni and Gherardi, 2001), wherein identities are performed, powers exercised and cultures developed. It is a process that both women and men are subject to but, by virtue of the dominant gender discourses at large across the social web, one that they usually experience quite differently.

In sum, despite several decades of equal opportunities legislation and rhetoric, within most organizations women managers remain reminded of their gender in a way that posits them as outside the mainstream, maleist culture, whatever their success as practising managers might be. By contrast, management is still strongly inscribed with a masculine logic and male value ethic, whereby the 'harder' practices of managing people remain irrefutably infused with dominant notions of masculinity. While there is, as yet, no place for woman in management that is not already circumscribed by men, masculinity and masculinism, the man in management remains both dominant and 'strangely' invisible. Having recognized this, it appears more appropriate to see the problem of gender inequity in management as less of a glass ceiling in need of shattering and more of a transparent cellophane packaging that wraps itself around the woman manager as she progresses upwards, making her visible, having the appearance of equality of access, but ultimately denying her the freedom to move and act without being subject to the masculine gaze.

Masculinity and professionalism

As with management and managerialism, so professionals and professionalism are also key concepts informing the myths and mysteries of the gendered public world of work. Indeed, it can be argued that dominant notions of professionalism are particularly powerful in that they contain beliefs, values and practices that not only serve to legitimize certain forms of work, institutional settings and bureaucratic environs, but also provide clear social and class-based demarcations for exclusion and inclusion. Yet despite their importance for understanding public sector power, critical examinations of professionals and professionalism have an intermittent history: they are usually conjunctive to ongoing debates concerned with new managerialism (Clarke and Newman, 1997; Dent, 1993), work practices such as human resource management (Legge, 1995) and the intersections of work and capitalist systems (Thompson, 1983). Such debates tend to draw heavily on notions of ideological practice (Collins, 1979; Murphy, 1988) and labour process perspectives (for discussion, see O'Doherty and Willmott, 2001). Partly as a consequence of this theoretical background, much of the research into professionalism has had little to say about gender and even less about masculinity. Where critical analysis of women's relationship to professional practice has taken place, it has, as Davies (1996) notes, largely drawn on the notions of closure and exclusion central to realist labour process theory (for example, see Crompton, 1987; Witz, 1992). Consequently, while such studies have made important contributions to illuminating the gendered character of professional practices, there has been little subsequent examination of professionalism in relation to gendered subjectivity and identity, a gap in academic knowledge that is particularly acute in respect of critically interrogating the relationship between men, masculinities and dominant discourses of professionalism. Nevertheless, despite having this rather mixed history, critical examinations of masculinity and professionalism are now emerging to some prominence, indicating yet another interesting direction in the sociology of masculinity.

One of the first studies to explore masculinities and professionalism was that undertaken by Bob Connell. He uses the example of engineering to make the important link between 'occupational cultures', professionalism and masculinities:

> Professionalism is a case in point. The combination of theoretical knowledge with technical expertise is central to a professional's claim to competence and to a monopoly of practice. This has been constructed historically as a form of masculinity: emotionally flat, centred on a specialized skill, insistent on professional esteem and technically-based dominance over other workers . . . The masculine character of professionalism has been supported in the simplest possible mechanism, the exclusion of women. (Connell, 1987: 181, quoted in Wright, 1996: 88)

Although, as Wright goes on to argue, the argument put forward by Connell for seeing professionalism as historically constructed around a single dominant form of masculinity assumes that different professionals have the same masculinity, Connell's analysis does alert us to the connections between the professional and the man. Also, by placing professionalism in a larger context of gendered occupational behaviours, we can see how differences between notions of femininity and masculinity come to inform every aspect of organizational life. These insights have been usefully employed in exploring gender and bureaucracy (Morgan, 1996b), masculinities and bureaucratic institutions (Woodward, 1996), masculinities and unions (Creese, 1999) and masculinities and technocracy (Burris, 1996; Cockburn, 1983; Roper, 1994; Wright, 1996). A common aim in all these studies is to highlight how certain 'valid' skills and privileged knowledges come to speak to a dominant form of masculinity, a condition that results in maintaining women's exclusion from the realm of 'the professional' and from similar powerful positions in the public sphere.

While an exclusion–inclusion dualism can be a useful tool for illuminating women's problematic relationship to professional life, it is, as Davies (1996) argues, inadequate for understanding the conditions under which women professionals exist in male-dominated, bureaucratic organizational sites. Davies considers that turning our attention to the relationship between masculinities and professionalism, and understanding their symbiotic connection as mutually sustaining forms of dominant discourses, offers insights into:

> not so much the *exclusion* of women, but on a particular form of their *inclusion*, and on the way in which this inclusion is masked by a discourse of gender that lies at the heart of professional practice. (Davies, 1996: 663; original emphasis)

Davies goes on to suggest that the woman/feminine is treated as 'Other' in professional life, a process of gendering that not only marginalizes woman as subject, but also subordinates 'the feminine' as a way of being and knowing. This understanding of gender and professions points towards recognition of how masculinity and professionalism interact and sustain many men's sense of themselves as professional at an ontological level.

In my own work (Whitehead, 2002) I have explored the connections between masculinities and professionalism in terms of understanding professional practice as a form of ontological validation of the 'masculine/managerial subject', a way of being (a man) that strengthens rather than weakens men's ability to exercise power as professionals and as men. Similarly, Kerfoot (2002) has examined the discursive conditions under which men managers pursue a sense of professional identity through their activities in organizational and managerial settings. Kerfoot's study draws attention to how the discourses of professionalism are overlaid by masculinity, and how predominant conceptions of what 'counts' as professional practice in given contexts reproduce and sustain a particularized mode of engaging with the organizational world. In short, the notion of 'being a professional' can be regarded as mutually interconstitutive of certain performances of masculinity and ways of being a man/manager. Such analyses are supported by the research undertaken by Barrett (1996, 2001) into the experiences of women officers in the US Navy and the strategies adopted by these women in order to resist being further marginalized in, what Barrett terms, a 'hyper-masculine' work culture. And through detailed ethnographic study of a young woman professional working in an Italian branch of an international company, Bruni and Gherardi (2001) highlight the power of dominant discourses of masculinity to act as legitimizers of both professional and gender practices and, thus, identities, a process of 'heterogeneous engineering' through which women come to embody and enact a gendered professional self.

From all the studies now emerging on the relationships between masculinities and professionalism, it is clear that while women are not necessarily always formally excluded from professional sites, they are, in very many instances, subjected to pressures to conform to, and accept as 'proper', masculine values and ways of being. These pressures do not inevitably come from physical or sexual abuse, though that threat is implicit in some organizational sites (see Barrett, 2001), but from the more insidious and difficult to negotiate prevailing cultural environment of the profession. To be sure, women are not passive in this process, but they do enter the professional site as 'Other', and they are likely to be constantly reminded of this position within most professional work settings. As Bruni and Gherardi (2001) note, an important consequence of the privileging of discourses of masculinity in professions is that, 'like capital or land', masculinity 'by birthright' gives men an advantage and resource in organizations that can be drawn on and utilized to their advantage and, thus, to the disadvantage of women.

In sum, the world of work, while no longer numerically dominated by men, at least in Western countries, remains a gendered world where masculine values and ways of being predominate. This is particularly so in respect of management and professional practice. In these sites, men remain the dominant gender group, with prevailing work cultures increasingly drawing on the discourse of performativity (defined as competitive and instrumental practice measured against the achievement of externally set targets within given timeframes). While there will undoubtedly be differences in the ways in which women and men relate to such cultures, the very essence of managerial and professional life increasingly speaks of a way of being that demands intensive engagement by its members to the exclusion and/or detriment of other aspects of living. It is this compartmentalization of the public and private which, as much as any other aspect of life in the twenty-first century, continues to provide men with their primary masculine validation. As will now be discussed, such compartmentalizations inevitably draw in, permeate and define non-work (leisure) and time itself.

Time to play

In this concluding section I will consider the importance of time as an emergent theme within the sociology of masculinity. In so doing I will pay particular attention to the notion of free time, or leisure time (Rojek, 1995). Singularly and together, critical insights into leisure and time have much to reveal about gender relations, men's practices, the exercise of power and, not least, the masculinist character of public and private spheres. Feminist research into leisure and time has clearly demonstrated not only how spatial constructs exist as gendered 'discrete' entities in social practice, but also how such entities are sustained temporally. Drawing on feminist analysis, it is possible to highlight the gendered temporality of the spatial structures of the public and private; in so doing, giving further critical substance to that which is often taken as either so central to human existence that it is seen as an unproblematic 'fact of life', or is marginalized by social theorists in favour of gender-invisible theories.

Gendered time

What might be regarded as gendered spatial relates to geographical location, organizational structure, movement within and across and access to these and, thus, what has come to be most valued and prized in the spatial domain, where material advantage and discursive power is most likely exercised (Hearn, 1992). By contrast, the concept of the gendered temporal domain encapsulates linear time consciousness (Davies, 1990; Young, 1988); time as commodity and clock time (Thompson, 1967); cyclical time (Young, 1988); and access to time and the labelling, valuing and legitimizing of (different) time(s). Despite increasingly sophisticated insights into temporality, time is commonly understood as 'natural' and given. Thus the significance of time is its apparent insignificance, its social character being subsumed under a discourse of naturalness (Adam, 1990).

I should emphasize that the temporal and spatial are not considered here as separate domains, but as interwoven and interacting within a complex social milieu. As such, both are informed by dominant and subordinated discourses, shaping opportunity and constraints for the subject. The temporal cannot, then, be considered neutral. The allocation and disposal of time across and between the public and private spheres has power dimensions. Following which, (free) time can be understood, in neo-Marxist terms, as a form of capital in so much as it can be deployed, accumulated, utilized, taken up and discharged as an exercise of power and, thus, to the material and emotional benefit or disadvantage of individuals. For example, in stressing the contradictory character of 'free' time, some commentators suggest that those forced into free time through eviction from the labour force will be an emergent 'passive class', subjected to the 'hell' of 'compulsory leisure' (Beck, 2000: 62).

Directly or indirectly, the social character of time has long been central to sociological enquiry, with such diverse theorists as Giddens, Adam, Durkheim, Mead, Schutz, Thompson and Gorz all making contributions to our understanding of how time is experienced and structured as an integral part of the social web (for elaboration, see Adam, 1990). In the context of an analysis of industrial capitalism, neo-Marxist theories of time and its control have been particularly influential, introducing concepts such as time as commodification (Thompson, 1967), and (free) time as resistance to capitalist alienation pressures (Gorz, 1985). However, it was not until feminists undertook empirical research into women's leisure experiences (how women come to use, get access to, are limited within free time) that time first came to be recognized as a problematic site of control and conflict within gender relations (see Deem, 1986; Green, Hebron and Woodward, 1990; Talbot and Wimbush, 1989). Prior to this, many of the studies into time and gender tended to be implicit, focusing rather on the consequences for men of long-term unemployment – time without paid work (Bakke, 1933; Jahoda, 1979; Komarovsky, 1940). Reflecting wider concerns at the social and economic costs of having large numbers of men 'idle' as a result of emergent pressures arising from post-industrialization and globalization (see Lash and Urry, 1987), such studies can now be seen to have had a major influence on the current 'crisis of masculinity' discourse at large in Western societies (and discussed in chapter 2).

Research into male long-term unemployment undertaken in the middle and latter part of the twentieth century revealed boredom, frustration, loss of self-respect and self-confidence for men. Juxtaposing these observations with the inexorable swing in Western societies towards post-industrialization (see Kumar, 1995), many commentators construed that generations of males were being rendered into 'crisis' as their primary identity as family breadwinner became redundant. Many feminists, not unreasonably, responded with the point that the changing nature of paid work, and the freeing up of some men's time, presented men with the opportunity to change their attitudes towards housework and childcare (Hewitt, 1993; Morris, 1990; also Morgan, 1992). It was also pointed out that unemployment was not solely a male experience (Walby, 1986).

Despite a continuing reluctance on the part of many men theorists to recognize the connection, the empirical evidence to show that (free) time, or the lack of it, is a crucial factor in the social organization of gender is now overwhelming (see Cohen, 1992; Crosby and Jasker, 1993; Davies, 1990; Deem, 1986; Forman and Sowton, 1989; Hantrais, 1993; Hood, 1993; Knights and Odih, 1995; Scraton, 1999; Seidler, 1994a, 1997; Shelton, 1992). As these and other writers have demonstrated, connecting men and time can reveal the complex dynamics of gender relations in interesting ways. For example, Davies's (1990) study of Swedish women suggested that the dominant social consciousness of time in Western society is linear, materializing as clock time. Davies argues that temporal consciousness – how we perceive time – has both linear and cyclical characteristics. However, she suggests that the dominance of linear time arises out of a combination of male interests, women's specific subordination in society and the material and power interests of capitalism and patriarchy. Cyclical time, by contrast, is considered by Davies to be 'associated with everyday life prior to or concurrent with industrialization [reflecting] seasonal, local and natural rhythms' (ibid: 19) and women's work and women's lives. Anxious to avoid 'naturalizing' time, Davies stresses that both time concepts exist in society, but that linear time and clock time dominate. While there are dangers in considering time to have some inherent, essential association with the female, Davies's critique is useful for exploring notions of 'balance', deconstructing temporality and exploring the masculinist character of work and leisure.

Gendered leisure

A feminist analysis of time reveals, then, how its gendered character and disposal informs not only work and family, but, importantly, also free time itself. For in as much as the exercise of free time requires a degree of agency by the subject, so one's engagement in the passive–active practices of leisure assumes a similar freedom to 'choose'. As has been discussed, any notions of agency need to be understood as problematized within various discursive regimes of (gendered) power/knowledge; that is, the discursive subject is not free in any pure ontological sense to 'choose' her or his free time and associated activities. Nevertheless, having stated this important qualification on the concept of free will and choice, the rhetorical and ideological importance attached to leisure concepts and activities in a post-industrial society is profound, as leisure theorists such as Rojek (1995) emphasize. However, despite their usefulness in illuminating, for example, power relationships in the family (Shaw, 1985) and resistance to gender stereotyping (Wearing, 1995), leisure studies remain an area of critical enquiry that has not always readily engaged with feminist theories, nor indeed been readily accepted as part of mainstream social science research (see Deem, 1999). Male writers such as Rojek (1985), Parker (1983), Veal (1987), Clarke and Critcher (1985) and Coalter (1998) are amongst those receiving criticism for failing to recognize the gendered character of leisure (for discussion, see Deem, 1999; Scraton and Talbot, 1989; Wearing, 1998).

Despite the opportunities for resistance to gender stereotyping that leisure affords, it remains an area of human activity that is significantly prescribed through dominant gender norms. In short, if we understand free time to be a form of capital, then it is apparent that women have less of it, have reduced access to it and are less able to negotiate their actions within it (Green, Hebron and Woodward, 1990). While a coming leisured Western society was much heralded in the 1980s by male sociologists such as Veal (1987), for most people, women especially, it has yet to materialize. Indeed, transformations in the nature of work have brought insecurity, work intensification and demands for flexibility, and have confined a large portion of the workforce to the periphery of organizations where non-unionized, casual and temporary work is the norm (Sennett, 1998; Beck, 2000). And it is in the periphery of organizations where most women work (Walby, 1988). Overlaid and cut by further divisions of class, ethnicity and age, many women's leisure time can often appear as merely a brief interlude in an otherwise endless cycle of multiple work and family responsibilities (for discussion, see Franks, 1999).

Directly or indirectly, many feminist studies into women's and men's experiences of leisure and work expose the gender of time. For example, in their study of women's family lives, Crosby and Jasker refer to 'acute and chronic time starvation' (1993: 153) for those women increasingly having to juggle paid work, leisure, family and rest needs. Similarly, Sullivan's (1997) research into women's domestic lives reveals their leisure time to be more fragmented than that of men and more pressured as a consequence of the intensity of domestic tasks facing married mothers in particular. Men, however, are not immune from the pressures that arise from having limited time to fulfil work–family roles. Cohen (1992), for example, reveals the competing demands on professional middle-class men's time for friendships and relationships as work pressures intensify, and the adverse consequences that can arise from being unable – or unwilling – to meet all these demands. Cross-cultural and cross-national research into patterns of family life reveals the extent to which dominant discourses of masculinity influence the temporal boundaries and possibilities for individuals and families in most societies and cultures. For example, Ishii-Kuntz (1993) discusses the consequences of the absent Japanese father in a society where men achieve most of their masculine authority through engagement in paid work. Shelton and John (1993) explore the direct effect of race/ethnicity on men's household labour time, concluding that Hispanic and black men spend more time in household labour than white men. Similarly, Coltrane and Valdez's research into Chicano couples (1993) concludes that changes in the nature of post-industrialization and associated work patterns are factors in encouraging more middle-class Chicano couples to share household duties. Research by Hantrais (1993) into women professionals shows how gendered conceptions of time conspire to exacerbate the process of segregation facing women in the professions, while the work of Knights and Odih (1995) makes important contributions to our understanding of linear temporal frameworks within organizations and the incongruence such frameworks have for many women's daily lives.

Finally, one area of leisure-time activities wherein masculinities become particularly vivid is sport. Since the landmark text by pro-feminist scholars Michael Messner and Donald Sabo (1990), which introduced the writings on sport and masculinity by, amongst others, Kidd (1990), Connell (1990) and Whitson (1990), increasing attention has been given to the relationships between sport, men and masculine performances. Examples are numerous and include Majors's (2001) consideration of black masculinity in sports as a limited 'creative agency' – an identity politics exercised by black males in response to institutionalized racism (see also Baker and Boyd, 1997; Jefferson, 1998); Messner's (1992) research into masculine relationships, bondings, exclusions and the (displaced) intimacies of males in sport (see also Harvey, 1999; McKay, Messner and Sabo, 2000); Davis's (1997) study into the validation of (white, heterosexual) hegemonic masculinity through US media representations of women in sport (see also McKay and Middlemiss, 1995); Wheaton's (2000) examination of masculinist windsurfing culture as a site for the construction of an 'ambivalent masculinity'; and Klein's (2000) exploration of Latino masculinity in Mexican baseball. Men's relationship to Association Football has attracted particular attention from feminist and profeminist scholars, with various studies looking at football and language (Johnson and Finlay, 1997; Kennedy, 2000), hooliganism (Bairner, 1999), fanzine culture (Haynes, 1993), new patterns of consumption (King, 1997) and the legitimization of bodily practice (Archetti, 1994).

In sum, with time increasingly being recognized as pivotal to how we perceive and experience public and private divisions, and with feminist studies of gender and time offering further insights into gender relations, the opportunities to explore in more depth the relationship between masculinities and temporality have never been better. Whether the focus be management, professionalism and organizational life (Hantrais, 1993; Knights and Odih, 1995), notions of 'male time' (Davies, 1990), time and gender ideologies (Hood, 1993) or time, masculinities and emotion (Seidler, 1994a, 1997), the sociology of masculinity is likely to see increasing attention being given to gendered temporality and its connection with how men experience work, family and leisure.

Summary

This chapter has explored some of the myths, mysteries and actualities surrounding the complex public world of men. It has been argued that the various expressions of manliness and masculinity that men's public endeavours draw on and, in turn, validate contribute to the public and private distinctions that permeate most societies. Despite challenges from new technology, changes to working patterns, the increasing movement of people and the twenty-four hour society, the public and private dualism remains an underpinning factor in gender relations, a dichotomy that is built into our lives both spatially and temporally. This dualism permeates all corners of the social web, impacting on how we experience not only work, but leisure and time itself. Yet despite this centrality, the public and private dualism is one founded largely on myth. Such mirages and legends surrounding men's public endeavours are potent and ubiquitous. Indeed, even to talk of public and private is to contribute to those myths that sustain gender divisions. For giving credence to the notion of a public and private dualism is to reify a state of being that presumes a separation between emotion and practice and between family and work. Such a separation is not only impossible; it has a political (gender) dimension. So there is here a word of warning in talking and writing of the gendered public world of men, for to engage in such a concept requires the taking up of those discourses and myths that validate it. And myths are not neutral. Indeed, in respect of men and masculinity, myths are highly dangerous. As Barthes puts it:

> Myth deprives the object of which it speaks of all History. In it, history evaporates. It is a kind of ideal servant: it prepares all things, brings them, lays them out, the master arrives, it silently disappears: all that is left for one to do is to enjoy this beautiful object without wondering where it comes from. Or even better: it can only come from eternity. (1982: 151)

Myths work for us but also against us. They lay out easy and often compelling 'truths' about 'reality'. However, we take them up at our peril. The public world of men, men's heroic projects, men's empires, men as (natural) managers and leaders, professional man, superman – these are all myths of (heterosexual) hyper-masculinity. Few men are empire-builders and even fewer are heroes; those that fall into these categories often remain outside the public gaze. Indeed, the notion of the heroic male is even more problematic in an age when would-be heroes are subjected to the utmost media scrutiny. A Warhol-inscribed fifteen minutes of fame is as much as most women and men may be allotted. But despite these discontinuities, myths of men and masculinity can easily inform a gendered actuality. For they underpin societal notions of empire, nationhood and the world of work, and in so doing create a fantastical masculine world that the Other (woman, gay man, ethnic minority men) can only enter into and prosper within under some sufferance and through the exercise of resistance.

As feminist research clearly reveals, to be accepted at a senior level in many male-dominated public sites women must, to some degree, subsume themselves to the prevailing masculine logic and dominant discourse of masculinism. Professionalism, management, work and leisure are arenas wherein males have historically sought, and been given, masculine validation. Consequently, that which defines the public domain comes also to define men's sense of themselves as masculine, a process that privileges the public over the private and the male over the female. Despite women's increasing visibility in the public sphere, for most men their self-validation as masculine subjects continues to take place in the pub, golf house, football ground, management meeting, corporate office or salesroom, not in the private world of home and family. It is a gender division that materially, spatially and temporally benefits men, and one that many women, for complex reasons, collude in sustaining. This gendered divide not only contributes to maintaining the importance and centrality of the public over the private, it also requires us to pay homage to the masculine performances of men and stay quiet about the much harder task of managing in the private sphere. In sum, the imagery and narrative of men's heroic projects may be compelling, but many more heroic projects occur quietly, and usually invisibly, at home.

FURTHER READING

Collinson, D. L. and Hearn, J. (eds) (1996) *Men as Managers, Managers as Men*. London: Sage.

Gherardi, S. (1995) *Gender, Symbolism and Organizational Cultures*. London: Sage.

Hearn, J. (1992) *Men in the Public Eye*. London: Routledge.

Hood, J. C. (ed.) (1993) *Men, Work, and Family*. Thousand Oaks, Calif.: Sage.

Wearing, B. (1998) *Leisure and Feminist Theory*. London: Sage.

5
Private Men

The private 'I'

If the public world of men is rooted in myth and mystery, then men's private lives can appear deep, dark, almost gothic in their impenetrableness. In writing this book, and coming ever more to recognize the complexities of gender (while trying to write them as accessible and open), a recurring question for me has been: 'Do we really know men?' Can we ever know in any full sense this gender category that is omnipresent yet distant and obfuscatory? Of course, in asking this question I am confronted with my own ambiguities and depth. As a man I am not removed from the category and the associated myths that nurture it. How can I write of men if I cannot know myself as man?

In a political sense I can come to know myself as a gendered being and thus part of the larger gender category of 'man'. And certainly, as a profeminist man writing of men and masculinities my political–public associations are explicit. But what of my private self, that which is less apparent to the social world? This is much more problematic. For to assume I can come to 'know myself' would require me to believe in the humanistic agent of modernism, the Cartesian founding subject; an authentic self which can, through some rational process, be reached, civilized, tamed, nursed, saved, in part through taking up the (masculinist) grand narratives of the Enlightenment (for discussion, see Seidler, 1994a). None of this feels true for me. Maybe once I held a belief in the rational, humanist project, but that seems long ago now, before I began my own particular intellectual and emotional exploration into the minds and ideas of others. As a post-structuralist I can derive no comfort from belief that 'I' exist as an ontologically grounded individual: having an inner core that exists prior to me here, now, writing this, to be ever present on some spiritual journey of self-knowing long after my body has become dust. But does this, then, preclude my reaching to a private, inner space, a place that exists behind my social performances – an 'apolitical' space?

This question cannot be answered in any simple, absolute way for I cannot know that which is beyond my knowledge. Moreover, I recognize that even to talk of the individual and society as separate entities is, like public and private, to reaffirm what is ultimately a false dualism. Yet the 'I' bedevils us in so much as it demands a sovereign place in our consciousness, while remaining elusive, conditional and ephemeral. The 'I' that writes this page believes in itself in part through the very act of writing its account, and through presenting this account of its understanding to an audience of similar 'I's 'out there'. Recognizing, then, the limits to my reflexivity, and in trying to map a route through the conundrum of self-knowledge, I consider my self to be 'complete' and 'coherent' only through the dynamics of narrative practice.[1] Thus, in speaking of men and narrating my self as man, an attempt is being made to find a self-referential place that locates 'me' in time (Ricoeur, 1980) and in so doing purports to form, simultaneously, a closure between and connection with my self and the rest of the social world. In so much as this is a 'reflexive project of self' (Giddens, 1991), it is, then, one that remains within the discursive world, not grounded or existing a priori to my subjectivity. This 'I' exists, in part, as a continuing narrative of self with agentic characteristics, possibilities and limitations (see also Usher, 1998; McNay, 2000). So in writing of men I come also to write of myself as man; a narrative of the (masculine) self which at times is explicit and at other times less evident. However, the account that arises from such a narrative should not be taken as self-knowledge or truth, for again, my postmodern inclinations suggest this to be elusive. Despite its claim to this status and the demands it makes to be understood as 'real', this 'I' is not sovereign which speaks to you, to me. As Nietzsche puts it:

In fact, the assertion 'I think' presupposes that to ascertain what my current state of mind is, I compare it with other states of mind which are familiar to me. . . . It is falsifying the facts to say that the subject 'I' is a condition of the predicate 'think'. A thought comes when 'it' wants, not when 'I' want. . . . 'It' thinks but that this 'it' is identical with the good old 'I' is at best only an assumption. (Nietzsche, 1973: 16–17)

This 'it' or 'I' which offers me a sense of location in the social world is not without social status, for it is gendered. In stating that, I am recognizing my sense of my 'private world' to be gendered to its core. There is no part of me that is not male/man for I cannot ontologically exist outside my gendered landscape. I am a masculine subject, for, like all before me, my gender was stamped on me at birth. Thus there is an embodiment to my gender that I cannot dispose of easily, if at all.

By being marked as gendered, this self which is 'I' cannot, then, be apolitical in the way suggested by Craib (1994: 134), who states: 'The argument that the personal is political is an invasion of the "private" world by the state. The question "Who am I?" gets caught up in political arguments.' Yes, indeed. The private lives of men and women are political. There is no aspect of our lives that is not 'caught up' by the political. How we spend and negotiate our time in relationships is political. How we exercise our power at work and home is political. How we exercise our sexuality is political. How we educate is political. How we contribute to the myths of gender is political. The very language we use is political. To be gendered is to be politicized. It is not necessary to be a feminist or a member of the Christian Promise Keepers to engage in this political condition. Such associations are simply a more direct expression of what goes on across all societies between all women and men in all cultures – daily. It is not a sex war, all conflict and contestation. To see it as such is just to slip into simplistic masculinist terminology. Rather, gender is a political condition experienced as a journey requiring constant negotiation between individuals, none of whom have access to maps (or if they have each reads them differently), and all of whom have slightly different destinations in mind. In short, we cannot remove ourselves from gender. The best we can hope for is a mutually satisfying, fair and equitable temporary settlement. Though for many, women especially, even temporary settlements remain elusive.

The point I am making here is that to explore the private world of men is not simply to look at men's practices at home or men's involvement in childcare. Certainly, there is all this and more to that which we understand constitutes the 'private' of the public–private dualism. But there is also the apparent 'inner' world of the male, the points of (inter)subjectivity, the ambiguities of the self, and the emotional depths to the masculine subject, all of which we need to have some purchase on; that is, if we are to have an understanding of men and masculinity beyond that which presents itself as both material and illusory. The emotional labours of men, their intimacies, sexualities, relationships – all that is private in the personal, individual sense – require unpacking and illuminating. The public and private may well be fundamental referents in the ordering of the social web, but they signal deeper meanings for individuals beyond specific arenas of everyday practice and experience (see also Bailey, 2000). Yet to talk of a private, inner world of the individual is to reify the dualistic thinking that pervades social intercourse and gender relations. In the final analysis there can be no complete separation of the individual and society. As Burkitt argues, emotions do not arise from the depths of the individual but are 'expressive of relations between people' (1997: 40). However, to ignore the 'inner world of men' (and I have no other phrase for it) is dangerous, for, as we have seen in the public world, that which is hidden from view can readily come to appear as mystery and myth – a process of 'truth'-making that is neither truthful nor neutral.

In this respect, all of this book is about 'private men', not just this chapter. Whether it be men's knowledges, sense of embodiment, responses to feminism, exercise of power, public–private practices, or sense of masculine self, that which is 'private' in men and masculinity is that which is ultimately most revealing. Being a powerful organizing principle across the social web, the public and private, as traditionally understood, have much to offer through careful study and interrogation. However, examinations of material divisions can only reveal so much, not least because, as I argued in chapter 3, they tend to posit a juridico-discursive model of power as a prior factor in inequality. Consequently, it is as part of a wider move to more nuanced sociological interrogations of power, self and practice in the 'private sphere' that this chapter, indeed the book, examines the private world of men. The rest of this chapter is divided into four sections: fathers and families; friendships and relationships; sexualities; trust, intimacy and emotion.

Fathers and families

'We cannot say we want a strong and secure society when we ignore its very foundations: family life.' So stated British Prime Minister Tony Blair in 1997 (quoted in Silva and Smart, 1999: 3). For Blair, this statement was part of a continuing strategy to affirm his government's commitment not only to family life but to a 'strong proper family' – by implication a married heterosexual couple in employment. There is little new in this rhetoric, indeed, it would be nigh impossible to find any leader of any Western government not declaring his/her belief in the family as the bedrock of a stable, flourishing society. Outside of party politics, few people would disagree with the central premise that a 'strong family life' makes for a healthy society. For at the level of rhetoric it works well: being difficult to argue against, easy to absorb and powerful in its affirmation of both society and the individual. In all, 'strong families' are understood as a 'good thing'. But in reality?

In reality the 'family' is highly problematic. For example, how do we define it? Should we subject it to clear definitions or is it a 'movable feast', being redefined by each new generation? Should we not challenge the reductionistic power assumptions that rest with notions of compulsory heterosexuality? In Western societies increasingly marked by atheist inclinations (Smith, 2000), what does a church wedding signify for many couples, beyond, that is, a form of consumerism? Where do lone parents fit into Blair's model of the family? What about the rights of gay and lesbian couples to marry, to have children? Is the right to choose an abortion incompatible with a traditional view of the family, as Christian fundamentalists argue? How do we square the high divorce rate with the sanctity of marriage? Why should the nuclear family be seen as a model when recent research indicates that an act of male domestic violence against women takes place every thirty seconds in the UK (Stanko, 2000)? Of what benefit is the nuclear family for those children abused by their parents? How secure is the nuclear family in a society where consumer values reign, and parents put in long, stressful hours at work to keep up? How untainted is the moral basis underpinning belief in the family, church and state (May, 1998)? And where, today, are the male breadwinners, the men who, in the past, achieved some sense of masculine validation through their ability to feed and support their family (Creighton, 1999)?

If the above questions are easy to ask, they are not easy to answer. Indeed, in any absolute sense they cannot be answered, and certainly not by the state. For at the very moment that governments exhort us to return 'back to the basics' of matrimony and coupledom, women and men are forging out new ways of living together – and apart – and in so doing transforming gender relations in the private sector in ways undreamed of only a few generations ago (see Gavron, 1966; Oakley, 1974; cf. Demos, 1986; Sullivan, 2000). In short, what government pronouncements speak to is a modern definition of the family in an age when the 'crisis of modernity' (Touraine, 1988) has rendered such a definition obsolete. As Boh (1989) argues, far from there being an evolutionary convergence of family life patterns, the culmination of wider social transformatory pressures is ushering in divergence across Western societies in particular. One important consequence of such shifts is that it is now more appropriate to talk of the postmodern than the modern family (Hohn and Luscher, 1988; for discussion, see also Cheal, 1999; Morgan, 2001). However, none of these changes proves that there is a crisis in the social fabric as governments are prone to suggesting. On the contrary, recent UK research indicates that the social fabric is alive and well, and this despite the so-called 'demise of the family' (NCSR, 2000).

Whatever one's view of postmodernity, it is apparent that while change has happened quickly over the past twenty years, transformations in the family have been occurring steadily for centuries. Without exception, Western women in the twenty-first century do not live out their lives in patriarchal families where a man's position as head of the household is *enshrined in law*, and where his wife and children are, as a consequence and for all intents and purposes, his property. This was the case for English, Welsh and Scottish women in the seventeenth century (Kent, 1999). It remains the case today for millions of women globally, but in the UK at least, some things have changed for the better. But where does that leave men?

When looking at the rapidity and depth of change to family life patterns it is tempting to see them as illustrative of a larger crisis for men and masculinity. Clare (2000), for example, draws on the UK's burgeoning divorce rate (the highest in Europe), the rise in lone women parents, the rise in post-divorce absent fathers, and the decline of the traditional family from 38 per cent of all households in 1961 to 23 per cent in 1998 (*Social Trends*, 1999) as evidence of men's increasing separation from fatherhood and family life in general. Clare concludes that men are in danger of being rendered redundant by these combined social changes, with women now exercising decisions over family life in the absence of feckless males. Avoidance of the dire consequences of many men's apparent indifference to family responsibilities can only come, Clare suggests, from men redefining their sense of masculinity and the male roles in relation to childcare and family life.

In chapter 2 I examined the discourses informing the crisis of masculinity debate and therefore do not intend to revisit them here, other than to point out that the concept of masculinity that notions of agentic redefinition speak to assumes a modernist core self existing as part of a larger community of (male) selves. From a post-structuralist perspective such an assumption is untenable. What is more realistic is the contingent, almost chaotic, character of social change, recognized to be outside direct social or individual manipulation. Aside from this, Clare's detailed thesis does introduce two common assumptions about men and fatherhood that require addressing. The first concerns the supposed decline of the family, the second concerns changing patterns of men's relationship to fatherhood and family life.

Despite what many conservative sociologists would have us believe (see, for example, Murray, 1990; Fukuyama, 1997), transformations and disruptions to traditional notions of the family do not automatically usher in social disorder. As numerous studies have revealed, both women and men are, in the main, committed to 'family life' and continue to define themselves, socially and ontologically, as members of a family (Finch and Mason, 1993; Morgan, 1996; Silva and Smart, 1999). The organizing principles behind family life patterns may well be increasingly diverse and fluid, but one should not take this as proof that the family is in decline, nor as evidence of a growing lack of care, commitment or investment by men (and women) in the maintenance of family bonds. Indeed, given the rigidly masculinist conditions of family life that have historically underpinned Western societies, one might conclude that many men are creating, through negotiation with children and partners, new and more positive ways of relating to families and fatherhood (see Silva and Smart, 1999). To be sure, there is much evidence to show that, worldwide, men spend less time in childcare than mothers (see Coltrane, 1996; Engle, 1997), while the rise in the percentage of female-headed households is as marked in developing countries as it is in the West (Bruce et al., 1995). Yet to correlate these shifts with some innate reluctance or inability on the part of men to be good fathers is not only reductionistic; it is overly simplistic for two reasons.

First, it is neither possible nor wise to disaggregate families from the wider social conditions within which they exist. Changing patterns of women's and men's employment, post-industrialization, women's increased education opportunities, urbanization, class, cultural capital and globalization are all factors that need to be recognized as influencing how women and men will respond to childcare and family responsibilities (Engle, 1997; Morris, 1999; Silva and Smart, 1999). Second, the sheer plurality of family forms means that men can and do experience family life in ways that are far removed from, and often far more healthy than, those experienced by their fathers and grandfathers. Supporting research undertaken in the UK and Europe (see Hohn and Luscher, 1988; Silva and Smart, 1999; Warin et al., 1999; Sullivan, 2000), research in the USA (Lewis and Salt, 1986; Levine, Murphy and Wilson, 1993), Latin America (Mirande, 1977, 1988), Brazil (Barker, Loewenstein and Riberio, 1995), the Caribbean (Fox, 1999), India, Bangladesh and Pakistan (Jahn and Aslam, 1995; Bhasin, 1997) and Australia (Smith, 1998) reveals that many men are reflecting on their gender roles and family responsibilities and engaging in parenting and domestic work in real, practical ways. In short, being fathers within and beyond the 'procreation realm' (see Marsiglio, 1998).

However, what these studies also reveal is that there is no single pattern at work here, any more than there is one easy or natural model of fatherhood for all men to follow. In Britain there are now estimated to be some 90,000 full-time 'at-home dads' (Summerskill, 2000). But as most full-time 'at-home mums' will attest, this role is no soft option and men's successful engagement with it requires consideration, effort and negotiation from all those involved. Moreover, such efforts are not aided by the paucity of maternity and paternity provision available to new mothers and fathers. Prosperous countries such as the USA, the UK, Italy, Belgium, Ireland, Spain, France and Denmark offer little or no paternity provision, and this at a time when work pressures and stresses are intensifying on parents (NFPI, 2000).

While being a 'new father' implies a break with increasingly dated ideas of traditional male roles, and therefore carries with it some cultural capital for men, in practice it can often mean little more than a symbolic attachment to the *idea of being father* rather than a full, equal, and unmitigated engagement in its harder practices (McMahon, 1999). For those men who are fully fledged househusbands, the role can engender feelings of illegitimacy (as a man), self-doubt and social isolation (see Smith, 1998). During the past three decades Western men's attendance at antenatal classes and childbirth has become de rigeur, yet most remain unsure about their subsequent role in and relationship to childcare work (Warin et al., 1999). And in a majority of societies any emergent nurturing patterns of (new) fatherhood are likely to remain in tension with conventional notions of the authoritarian, aloof, male provider (see Fox, 1999).

What complicates, then, any clear understanding of the relationship of men and masculinity to notions of family and fatherhood is the fact that while ideals of both fatherhood and motherhood changed dramatically during the twentieth century (Dally, 1982; Kent, 1999), traditional gender stereotypes remain resilient in many cultures. Thus we have to recognize that while there is some evidence of a shift in attitudes to family and domestic roles by some men, dominant discourses of masculinity do not sit easy with these practices. Moreover, men's relative absence from the private sphere is further embedded in and validated by a performative work culture and government policies. Few would argue against men being active fathers, not least because there is evidence that the quality of the father–child interaction is a good predictor of that child's subsequent emotional and cognitive development (Easterbrook and Goldberg, 1985). But 'new fathers' are not born; they are made – a process that is aided or hindered by larger social, political and economic conditions. Given the harsh and at times brutal character of many men's (fathers') involvement in the private sphere, and the compelling attraction the public realm holds for many men and their sense of masculinity, it is perhaps not surprising that, like the 'new man', the 'new father' remains a relatively rare species. Also, aside from any tensions over masculine identity, childcare is probably the hardest task that anyone can engage in, woman or man. However, unlike women, men have available to them, through dominant discourses of gender and the organizing principles of the public–private dualism, numerous opportunities to 'legitimize' their absence from childwork and domestic activities, a situation that serves to make it much easier for them to excuse themselves from caring, supportive roles than for women. It is also salutary to remind ourselves that the vast majority of those individuals authorized to formulate corporate policies over childcare and government policies over paternity/maternity leave are men.

In sum, like most aspects of gender relations in the twenty-first century, fathers and their relationship to families are likely to undergo yet more change, most of it unplanned and unpredictable. For many, such changes as may occur will, however, be caught in tension with residual attitudes surrounding women's and men's roles. Moreover, feminists and profeminists can expect any shifts in the public and private spheres that threaten men's material and cultural dominance to be resisted by, for example, the Christian Promise Keepers and the various men's movements. Ultimately, whether ensuing gender changes present exciting possibilities or a retreat to traditional values, much will rest on men's ability and willingness to (re)negotiate new and equitable relationships with partners and children.

Friendships and relationships

Men's relationships

In a fascinating if at times disturbing biographically informed exploration into men's loves and relationships, Jonathon Rutherford writes: 'When men fall in love we surrender our solitude and relinquish our masquerade of self-sufficiency. A new story of our lives is waiting to begin; a recognition that "I am no longer myself without you"' (1999: 3).

For those wishing to acquire insights into what is arguably the most dense and impenetrable of human emotions, Rutherford forewarns that: 'to write about men's love and relationships is like entering an uncharted territory and inventing its geography' (1999: 2).

This warning is apposite, reminding us that as men and families are seen as a problematic combination, so are men and relationships. There is a commonly held view in many societies that men 'cannot do' relationships as effectively as women. That is, men are seen to lack the emotional tools, empathy, sensitivity, (self-)understanding, indeed maturity, necessary to enable a committed relationship on equal terms with loved ones and friends. In sum, masculinity may be useful for hunting, competition and climbing the career ladder, but it falls short when it comes to facilitating and enabling the emotional labour required to sustain a relationship.

Like many stereotypes, there is a prevailing sense that this one has some roots in reality. Yet while there is research to suggest that men are more reticent than women when it comes to sharing their feelings with others (see Miller, 1983; Rubin, 1985; Swain, 1989), one needs to be aware that this is an area of research where ideology often gets confused with behaviour (for discussion, see Walker, 1994). Certainly, there is no shortage of anecdotal evidence to support the stereotype surrounding men's emotional illiteracy. For example, while preparing for this chapter I spoke to several women friends and colleagues about their immediate perceptions on men and relationships, and received, not surprisingly, overwhelming confirmation of men's inadequacies in this area. Similarly, my own experience as a man has involved being confronted numerous times by women loved ones and friends over my own evident propensity to 'close down' my feelings and miss the emotional 'clues' that are apparently so obvious to them. I can certainly see this to be a fairly accurate reflection of my behaviour, but I am also aware that it has changed for the better as I've got older. However, it has taken several decades of reflexivity to get to a stage where I do not *automatically* go into defence mode when faced with my own emotional inadequacies. So I am certainly not dismissive of this aspect of a prevailing form of masculine being, having lived, and still living, out this form of subjectivity throughout my life, and having seen it all too evidently in other men. Yet is it this straightforward? Are all men reducible to this stereotype?

Certainly there is evidence to indicate that not only women but also men share this stereotype of the emotionally restricted male (Walker, 1994), and many of the writings within the sociology of masculinity support the view that men's relationships are problematic, if not bordering on the dysfunctional. Victor Seidler (1992a, 1992b, 1994b, 1997) is one profeminist writer who has explored this aspect of male subjectivity and practice in some depth, relating men's propensity to display an apparent self-sufficiency with forms of upbringing that bring pressures on men to be independent beings:

> Men have grown up to identify with the public world of work. We have learned to be independent and self-sufficient. We have learned to go it alone and to do without the help of others. We have learned to identify with our work, even when it is not a matter of finding personal fulfilment but simply earning a wage. . . . Often there is little that prepares us for relationships, for in learning to be self-sufficient we learn to do without others. Often our very sense of male identity is sustained through our capacity for *not* needing the help of others. (Seidler, 1992a: 1; original emphasis)

Seidler's succinct description of one of the main travails of being a male – and the burdens it brings for women – neatly captures the sense of loss and emotional immaturity that pervades masculine subjectivities, together with the pervasiveness of the public–private dualism in sustaining this condition. Masculinity is presented here as a stunted form of socialization, inadequate in a world where gender identities are apparently converging and where women's new-found independence and freedom from traditional feminine models presents males with challenges, not least over their (in)ability to let go of dated, patriarchalist, ways of being (see also Rutherford, 1999). Whether it be fear of rejection, vulnerability, wariness, guilt, a lack of self-esteem or simply emotional illiteracy, many men appear unable to expose their inner selves to the outer world. In a later work Seidler considers whether or not improvements might be made in this regard if men took up the suggestion of Robert Bly (1990) in *Iron John* and got 'back in touch with their inner masculinity' through sharing experiences and intimacies with other men. Seidler concludes that while such actions may well benefit some men, they 'do little to change our relationships to women, or really help us to reflect upon ways male superiority is sustained' (1997: 181).

Seidler's detailed and insightful account of men's selves raises the question as to how we understand the processes of masculine subjectivity and identity. As was discussed in chapter 1, Robert Bly's work is unapologetically deterministic and reductionist, in so much as it assumes a simplistic Jungian model of male–female subjectivity.

So engaging with Bly's work on Bly's theoretical terms is to lock oneself into a dualistic theoretical equation with predictable results. In short, we are left looking for answers to the 'male dilemma' in terms of changing men, while holding on to the idea that men cannot change because their inner core of masculinity precludes it. This approach to men and masculinities is clearly paradoxical in that it presents itself with 'irresolvable solutions'. Moreover, as was discussed in chapter 2, the idea of men changing as a political category, let alone as individuals, is anything but straightforward. Men have an investment in masculinities which extends within and yet beyond the material, a factor further complicated by the diversity of individuals located within the political category of men. Does this, then, deny the potential for changes to men's subjectivities arising from their intimate and emotional engagements with others?

Men's friendships

Whenever attempting to look at men's possibilities and potential it is vital to recognize differences between men. What type of men are we discussing here – gay, straight, bi, black, Asian, Latino? Also, how do issues of age, class and culture play across these stereotypes? A related issue concerns men's friendships. Are they as problematic as men's relationships? Certainly one would find it difficult to argue that men cannot do friendships. Indeed, Messner notes that for most of the twentieth century it was a commonly held view that men – not women – tended to form 'deep and lasting friendships' (1992: 215). Research on the friendships of American Indian and Asian men (Williams, 1992) and on black American men (Franklin II, 1992) reveals the importance of friendship to men's lives and the capacity that exists for empathy, trust and intimacy between and across different ethnic groups of men. Similarly, the extensive research undertaken by Peter Nardi indicates that for gay men, friendships are a defining characteristic of their lives, 'providing important sites for gay men's development, for the maintenance of personal identity and for the reproduction of gay community and political identity' (1999: 9; see also Nardi, 1992a; 2000; Mirande, 1997).

Whether based around straight, gay, white or black identities, men's friendships with other men can be seen to be crucially important in sustaining masculine subjectivities and men's sense of identity as men. However, recognizing this does not take us very far from the earlier point made by Seidler that men's same-sex friendships very rarely provide the possibilities for social transformations *between women and men*. This is an aspect of the sociology of masculinity that requires further research, though there is some evidence to suggest that cross-sex friendships that do not lead to heterosexual coupling can 'act as a catalyst for social change' (Swain, 1992: 168), not least because for the friendship to work both parties must address, in some form, conflicting discourses of sexuality and codes of intimacy. In so far as men's same-sex friendships are concerned, they also are surrounded by conflicting tensions over sexuality: as Nardi observes, they 'inevitably introduce – in ways they have never done before – questions about homosexuality' (1992b: 1). To make this point, Nardi traces the historical shifts in the discourses surrounding same-sex friendships between men, noting how such friendships have changed over time from being 'highly revered in ancient Greece and during the European Renaissance' to being 'medicalized and stigmatized' as part of a larger homophobic discourse from the late nineteenth century onwards (1992b: 2).

In looking at friendships in the late twentieth century Pahl (2000) considers friendship to be 'quintessentially postmodern', in so much as it speaks of unities but with a subtext of difference, individuality and individualism. This point is useful for it indicates that, unlike relationships, friendships come with varying degrees of intimacy and are thus loose enough to accommodate the fluctuations of increasingly mobile, technologically supported communities and individuals existing within and beyond fixed geographical boundaries. By contrast, relationships assume a deeper commitment, less flexibility, constant engagement and effort, and an unchanging belief in their worth and truthfulness. In short, friendships appear less demanding than relationships, a point further underlined by the emergence of the 'pure relationship'.

Pure relationships

The notion of the 'pure relationship' arises from the work of Anthony Giddens (1991, 1992) and has been particularly influential in linking shifts in the postmodern age with the changing expectations of the individual in respect of intimacy and trust (see below). Giddens sug-

gests that late twentieth-century processes of change are ushering in
a desire for 'pure relationships', wherein lovers 'enter into a situation
for its own sake' and remain in the relationship 'only so far as it is
thought by both parties to deliver enough satisfaction for each individual to stay in it' (1992: 58). Despite the instrumental and sexual
assumptions informing his understanding of relationships, Giddens
does usefully capture the sense that the pursuit of personal happiness
by the individual has become a powerful discourse in the late twentieth century. In short, a belief that one should pursue one's own
heaven on earth has replaced the grand narratives of modernism,
which sold the idea of heaven in the hereafter. Or, as Beck and Beck-
Gernsheim (1995) put it, love is the 'new secular religion', and the
pursuit of pure relationships are the means by which we worship and
raise up to new and unprecedented heights the status of the individual. 'Real love' may not be any easier to come by or sustain than for
previous generations, and certainly not for those men locked into traditional masculinist ways of being (see Rutherford, 1999). But what
is different in the postmodern age is the importance given to the
pursuit of love. However, the 'pure relationship' can also be seen to
be less about relationships as such, and more about the need for the
ontologically insecure individual to mitigate the existential dilemmas
that arise for her/him in a contingent, fragmented, increasingly secu-
larized, 'risk' society (Beck, 1992; Beck and Beck-Gernsheim, 1995;
Giddens, 1991).

   Given the historical and continuing unequal balance in public–
private gender relations, the notion of a sudden emergence of equality between women and men, which the pure relationship demands,
seems somewhat naive. Unless, of course, men change. Indeed, I
would suggest that the concept of the 'pure (heterosexual) relationship' does not work, either as theory or practice, unless men change.
However, on this matter Giddens has little to say, other than to recognize that 'men are the laggards in the transitions now occurring in
gender relationships' (1992: 59). Therefore, while the pure relationship indicates, for Giddens, a 'generic restructuring of intimacy' (ibid:
58) between the sexes, one key element in this restructuring – dominant notions of masculinity – remains problematic. I would suggest
that an individual's desire for a pure relationship cannot, of itself,
usher in a transformation in gender relations. As Jamieson (1999)
argues, the pure relationship may be an ideal for many couples, gay,
straight or lesbian; however, the very fact of having to negotiate

mundane everyday domestic duties can get in the way of idealistic aspirations. This points to the realization that relationships are inevitably invested with a degree of conflict, uncertainty, insecurity and disappointment (Craib, 1994). In short, relationships are not easy. By definition, relationships are demanding, requiring, in Giddens's terms, a conscious 'effort bargain' by both parties. The pure relationship may well reflect the aspirations of many couples, but elevating relationships to new heights, if not unattainable forms of 'purity', can only result in disappointment for those many individuals who fail to achieve this 'model'. Recognizing this, I would suggest it more likely that the potent mix of postmodern fragmentation and disappointment, amidst unresolved gender expectations, will serve to increase rather than resolve existential angst.

A final point is that the concept of the pure relationship may well be a manifestation of the late twentieth century, but it is associated with the traditional ideologies/discourses surrounding the 'ideal family' discussed earlier. The notions of permanence that the pure relationship suggests can be aligned with those of (nuclear) family commitment. Yet there is evidence that commitment in the twenty-first century, for both women and men, is, paradoxically, likely to be increasingly temporary. With marriage in decline in the West and people choosing to stay single longer before committing to marriage, the trend appears to be against permanence and commitment (see ONS, 2001). Maybe, as Pahl and Nardi suggest, friendships will come to provide the most constancy for individuals and, thus, the possibilities for social change, particularly in an age when increasing numbers of women and men are choosing singledom not coupledom.

Sexualities

As many would concur, the complications already inherent in masculinity – and gender – reach new depths of obfuscation when attention is turned to males and their expressions of sexuality. And not only males' sexualities. For all sexual practice and sexuality is imagined, experienced and acted out in a mental–physical place where nature, power and pleasure entwine, interact and reinforce each other in ways largely, if not wholly, beyond human comprehension. Despite attempts by many 'experts' to present it as such, human sexuality is not easily reducible to simplistic sociological or psychological concepts. Maybe it is for this reason that sexuality, perhaps more so than even gender, is riven with powerful stereotypes and dominant discursive models. That which we least understand, but possibly most value and appreciate as central to our selves, lends itself readily to the fears and manipulations of individuals and societies.

Yet for some feminists there is little confusion about sexuality. For example, Catherine MacKinnon argues that 'feminism fundamentally identifies sexuality as the primary social sphere of male power' (MacKinnon, 1982: 529, quoted in Segal, 1997: 207). Radical feminists such as MacKinnon, Andrea Dworkin, Robin Morgan and Susan Griffin argue that male sexual dominance underpins or is the defining characteristic of all expressions of male power and oppression, from racism, class exploitation and Fascism through to imperialism and the nuclear arms race. As Segal (1997) notes, this raising of male sexuality to hitherto unparalleled heights of importance resonates with the views of (predominantly male) scientists such as Sigmund Freud, Richard von Krafft-Ebing and, more recently, Roger Scruton and Richard Dawkin, all of whom 'are repeating the dominant contemporary cultural discourses and iconographies surrounding sexuality' (Segal, 1997: 208; also Weeks, 1991); that is, that male sexuality is an 'overpowering instinct', barely controllable, and irreducibly sustained and necessarily validated by the centrality and functionalism of the gender order. In short, the male genital organ suggests not only a physical actuality and sexual potential, but, as phallus, symbolizes (the inevitability of) male power and dominance.

What is immediately evident from both radical feminist and conservative Darwinian views of sexuality is how power and, correspondingly, ideas around passivity and inevitability come to interrupt and disrupt the possibility of deeper understanding. In both perspectives we can see human sexuality being enlisted to a political cause. But, then, sexuality is so diverse, confusing and culturally informed that perhaps it is beyond any real understanding. Moreover, sexuality does have so many political dimensions and possibilities that need to be recognized as sustaining and validating gender political categories. Rape, coercion, abuse, paedophilia, slavery, oppression, violence, discrimination – these are all aspects of the sexual that can be seen to be the 'dark side' of human activity. To this list many women and men would add prostitution and pornography in all its forms (for discussion, see Barry, 1979; O'Connell Davidson and Layder, 1994; O'Neill, 2000; Pateman, 1988; Segal, 1997). To be sure, not only men use or financially benefit from prostitution and pornography, or abuse, enslave, oppress and discriminate through sexuality. Women also do this, and have done, one can presume, since the beginnings of human history. Yet by any measure, it is predominantly men who are involved in these aspects of sexuality. So despite skating on contradictions and flirting with determinism, what radical feminism does achieve so powerfully is to confront men with the personal/ political consequences of this 'dark side' of their sexuality.

But is there such a thing as 'male sexuality'? What do we mean by this term, one that is so loaded politically and ideologically? What form of sexuality is being presumed here – bisexual, homosexual, transsexual, heterosexual? Of what cultural origin is this sexuality – white/Western/Latino/Chicano/black/Oriental (for discussion, see *Sexualities*, 1998; also Mirande, 1997)? Invariably, the term 'male sexuality' assumes heterosexuality as the 'norm'. But, as with gender, what is considered 'normal' sexuality is not necessarily 'natural'. In speaking of a singular 'male sexuality', we immediately imply a gendered embeddedness to sexual practice. If we talk of male sexuality as something inherent and to be assumed in the male species, we tread the path towards establishing the related myth of male sexual prowess as an insatiable urge, one that compels men to act out fantasies of domination over women and others, all the while sustaining the power effects of 'compulsory heterosexuality' (Rich, 1980; also Brittan, 1989). Yet is it this straightforward? Lynne Segal thinks not:

> The point is that it seems wilfully blind for feminists to buy into the bravado behind many men's repression of their sexual anxieties and insecurities, by endorsing myths of the inevitable link between sexuality and male dominance. It becomes a way of women colluding in men's defensive denial of their own confusion and doubts about sexuality, concealing that which we most need to reveal and understand. Male sexuality is most certainly not any single shared experience for men. It is not any single or simple thing at all – but the site of any number of emotions of weakness and strength, pleasure and

pain, anxiety, conflict, tension and struggle, none of them mapped out
in such a way as to make the obliteration of the agency of women in
heterosexual engagements inevitable. (1997: 215)

Segal alerts us to the only inherent aspects of sexuality – its fraught
and multiple character – and she does this by explicating the tensions
beneath the surface of male banter, male fraternities and male sexual
swagger. Like gender, sexuality is not given, it is learnt, imposed,
acquired, worked at, experimented with, negotiated and, often with
difficulty, experienced. To even talk of such a thing as male sexuality is to collaborate in discursive 'sexist assumptions that the power
of the penis is uncontrollable' (Hollway, 1984, quoted in Segal, 1997:
215) and that women's vulnerability is self-evident and functional. In
short, a 'natural' male sexual dominance can too easily be equated
with a 'natural' male political and social dominance.

The understanding of sexuality elaborated by Wendy Hollway and
Lynne Segal owes much to poststructuralist thought, particularly the
work of Michel Foucault, who defines sexuality as:

The name that can be given to a historical construct: not just a fur-
tive reality that is difficult to grasp, but a great surface network in
which the stimulation of bodies, the intensification of pleasures, the
incitement to discourse, the formation of special knowledges, the
strengthening of controls and resistances, are linked to one another, in
accordance with a few major strategies of knowledge and power.
(Foucault, 1978: 105–6)

Foucault considers discourses of sexuality to have emerged and then
proliferated from the nineteenth century onwards, producing a field
of knowledge in which a 'formation of morality' (Nead, 1988) served
to define 'normal' sexual pleasure. In this respect, we can see how
discourses of sexuality are implicated in the exercise of power relations. However, such discourses should not be seen as simply or
only repressive in their effects, or as working for the hegemonic
advantage of a particular group. As discussed in chapters 2 and 3,
discourses are also enabling and productive, as well as serving to
define, regulate and label that which is understood as 'normal' or
'deviant'.

A recognition of sexuality as discursive opens up countless possibilities for understanding the complex relationship between sexu-

alities and identities and for tracing the historical shifts in the social regulations surrounding sexual practices (for example, see Weeks, 2000; Nead, 1988). However, as Segal (1997, 1999) argues, in undertaking such research it is necessary to have some perspective on masculinities, in particular how many men's sense of themselves as masculine comes to inform their sexual behaviour and attitudes (for example, see O'Neill, 2000). Failure to recognize the scripts of masculinity, and the related political dualisms at work within culturally specific notions of sexuality, merely serves to conceal the power effects of gendered sexualist discourse.

One central tenet of many men's sense of their masculinity is a desire to control both self and others, a condition that in terms of sexuality can manifest itself in the urge to 'master and possess the other while simultaneously seeming to yield, surrender, capitulate' (Clare, 2000: 201). Clare suggests that many men's 'preoccupation with being in control' is at the heart of male aggression, sexual and otherwise. Being 'in control' (or temporarily renouncing control so as to achieve an erotic state) can be a highly sexual experience for many men, not least because it momentarily allows them to dismiss the contingency at the heart of their maleness whilst positing them as potent. However, such control is always elusive, subject to disruption, and requires constant work by the individual. In short, many men's efforts at controlling (sexual) relationships would, perhaps, be better spent just 'being in' the relationship and accepting that attempts at control are not only futile, they are damaging.

As Seidler (1997) suggests, a key factor in men needing to control is a lack of confidence and inner security about their masculinity, maleness, sexuality. Following this point, a number of feminist and profeminist writers have noted the strong connections between an insecure male's sense of masculinity and sexuality, male bonding, and the universal physical and verbal oppression of women. Some feminists have referred to this as a 'rape culture' (Herman, 1984) at the heart of masculinity, a (hetero)sexist treatment of women that posits them as sexual objects to be used and abused for male gratification and power lust (see May, 1998). Michael Messner's research into US college 'locker room culture' supports this view. Messner reveals the fine line many male athletes tread between desiring to conform to a dominant 'heterosexist masculine culture', engaging in the 'highly sexualized views of women' that are central to this culture, and undertaking 'actual aggression against women' (1992: 101)[2] (see also for discussion, Messner and Sabo, 1990; Scully, 1990; Kimmel, 2000).

Michael Kimmel suggests that what lies behind such attitudes and practices is men's shame about their sexuality. He speculates that 'if masculinity is a homosocial enactment, its overriding emotion is fear' (1994: 129), not least a fear of one's own sexuality, manhood and *of other men*' (ibid: 131; original emphasis). Kimmel describes this as the 'secret' at the heart of American manhood, the fear that we as men will be 'exposed' as less than man (gay, cissy, unmanly and so on). The shame that men face in being 'unmasked' as unmanly provides the conditions for homophobia and the objectification of women. Kimmel quotes Leverenz (1986), who states that men's real fear 'is not of women but of being ashamed or humiliated in front of other men, or being dominated by stronger men' (Kimmel, 1994: 131). In this respect, men's complicity in sexist or homophobic behaviour arises not from their core sexuality, but from a desire not to be excluded from male groups; not to be cast out and declared 'not a male/man, like us' (Seidler, 1997).

Kimmel's thesis is supported by Larry May's recollection of his own experiences as a teenager, which reveal the ways in which discursive sexist language and male bonding patterns can come to create the conditions for actual sexual violence against women:

> As a teenager, I ran in a crowd that talked incessantly about sex. Since most of us were quite afraid of discovering our own sexual inadequacies, we were quite afraid of women's sexuality. To mask our fear, of which we were quite ashamed, we maintained a posture of bravado, which we were able to sustain through mutual reinforcement when in small groups or packs. Riding from shopping mall to fast food establishment, we would tell each other stories about our sexual exploits, stories we all secretly believed to be pure fiction. We drew strength from the camaraderie we felt during these experiences. Some members of our group would yell obscenities at women on the street as we drove by. Over time, conversations turned more and more to group sex, especially forced sex with women we passed on the road. To give it its proper name, our conversation increasingly turned to rape. . . . Only much later in life did I think that there was anything wrong – morally, socially, or politically – with what went on in that group of adolescents who seemed so ready to engage in rape. (May, 1998: 79–80)

In reflecting on his experiences, and the wider incidence of organized, mass rapes of women and children by men, May concludes that all men have a 'collective responsibility' to oppose rape and sexual harassment by men in their societies.

While there is nothing absolute, unchanging or inevitable about men and their sexuality, there is this disturbing connection between male sexual behaviour and many men's 'need' to exercise power and control over others. Under certain, usually restricted conditions, and in sites largely inhabited or dominated by males, this desire can manifest itself as an oppressive, violent and hierarchical hyper-masculine culture. The most obvious example is the prison (Toch, 1998), but to this one could add criminal gangs (Hagedorn, 1998; Newburn and Stanko, 1994), the school environment (Lesko, 2000; Mac an Ghaill, 1994), the uniform services (Barrett, 1996, 2001) and corporate sites (Chapple, 1998). Male rape by heterosexual male prisoners is an act that starkly illustrates the relationship between male insecurity, power and sexuality. Men who would, on the 'outside', presumably wish to deny any homosexual affiliations feel 'free' to engage in homosexual rape in total masculinist institutional environments, such as prisons, without fear of being labelled unmanly. Perversely, the act of rape (by men on women and other men) is not only often without shame for the male perpetrator; it can be seen to validate an insecure but oppressive form of masculinity and heterosexuality (for discussion, see Hearn, 1998b; Jackson, 1999; May, 1998).

Finally, how might we understand (male) sexualities in what Jeffrey Weeks (1995, also 2000) describes as 'the age of uncertainty': the postmodern era in which the inherent instability of the self, the multiplicity and fluidity of identities, and the dissipation of boundaries between peoples and cultures are so evident (see also Simon, 1996). Weeks suggests that the immensely significant social, political and cultural transformations now being visited across the world, not least driven by the impact of AIDS, create opportunities for individuals to construct new (sexual) narratives of self and belonging; a 'necessary fiction' of self, offering some stability in an increasingly complex social world. Weeks's emphasis is on the individual's pursuit of difference, but in a social milieu that still requires a caring, supportive communality – indeed, requires this even more so in the era of AIDS, when many communities are under threat.

Again, the central thesis is one of changing values, largely driven by massive, destabilizing, if not uncontrollable, social and cultural pressures. Weeks recognizes the changing expectations of women, new models of family life and a greater accommodation of diverse sexual expressions in Western societies in particular. However, the issue of men changing appears more complex, and on this Weeks has little to offer, other than to recognize that new expectations of women often result in a 'male backlash' and the 'flight from responsibility' exemplified by those in the various men's movements (see also Ehrenreich, 1983; Messner, 1997). In short, for many men their sense of sexuality remains a confusing, but self-sustaining mix of predatory behaviour and deep insecurity. Maybe, as Segal suggests, male sexuality becomes intelligible only when placed in the context of 'men's intimate relationships with others – or lack of them' (1997: 215).

Trust, intimacy and emotion

While much has been written by feminists and profeminists concerning men, masculinities and sexualities, the family and relationships, much less attention has been given to three elementary factors at the heart of the private domain: trust, intimacy and emotion. Yet, as has been discussed, any unpacking of the private world of men must at some point explore these dimensions of maleness (see Rutherford, 1992; Seidler, 1997). This relative omission within the sociology of masculinity may be a consequence of a concern by many writers to explore macro gender conditions, in particular larger patterns of power and domination by men, especially now in an era of globalization (for example, see Connell, 1998), rather than examine gender 'close-up', that is, at the level of (inter)subjectivities. Also, research into trust, intimacy and emotion does not, perhaps, lend itself well to quantitative research methods, to wholesale data collection through the application of 'objective', scientific systems of measurement and observation (for discussion, see Greenwood, 1994). Perhaps this is one reason why, as Ann Oakley puts it:

> [sociology] has catered more efficiently for social action and inaction in the public than in the private realm: it has favoured those structures, processes and interactions associated with the typically unselfconscious world-view of dominant groups. (1998: 22)

This point could certainly be argued to be a factor in the relative lack of sociological focus on intimacy, emotion and trust. Nevertheless, scholars such as Lynn Jamieson (1998), Anthony Giddens (1992) and Barbara Misztal (1998) are making important contributions to our understanding of how forms of intimacy and trust are experienced by individuals and played out across societies. This section is offered, then, as a brief indication of what is now a developing, but still undeveloped, area of the sociology of masculinity; as such, it does not seek to locate itself in an extensive literature, but rather signals new directions and opportunities for research into men and masculinities.

Trust

In sociological terms, trust can be understood to perform three functions. First, it reduces social complexity and potential frictions arising, in part, from diversity by enabling cooperation between individuals and communities. The presence of trust promotes communality, social cohesiveness, economic and cultural collaboration and communication (see Dunn, 1984; Luhmann, 1979). Second, the ability to trust others, systems and institutions appears central to our ontological security and, thus, our personality. As Misztal puts it: 'ontological security, as the most important psychological need, is founded upon the formation of trust relationships' (1998: 91). Thus, trust plays a key role in alleviating 'persistent existential anxiety' by providing a sense of security, constancy and continuity in an otherwise transient world (ibid; see also Beck, 1995; Giddens, 1990). Misztal argues that a third property of trust is its capacity to act as a form of 'social lubricant' or 'social capital', by providing some stability and predictability in a complex, contingent, social environment. In this regard, trust also exists as a form of 'habitus' (Bourdieu, 1977), a 'protective mechanism' (Misztal, 1998: 102) that works through the reproduction, remembering and following of daily rules and social interactions by the individual. As Hume (1985) puts it: 'habit makes us expect, for the future, a similar train of events which have appeared in the past' (quoted in Misztal, 1998: 102).

For scholars such as Giddens, Misztal and Beck, the increasing complexity and fragmentation at the heart of postmodern societies are paradoxical, being the consequence of 'the triumph of the instrumentally rational order', where the very 'intention of control ultimately ends up producing the opposite' (Beck, 1995: 9). To this can be added the declaration by Jean-François Lyotard (1994) that the aftermath of the modern industrial age has ushered in a 'post-modern condition' within which the grand narratives of modernity no longer hold sway. Under these combined historical conditions, trust assumes even greater importance. First, the privileging of scientific knowledge over narrative knowledge has questioned traditional forms of trust as we see new risks and threats emerging from our now shaken belief in the veracity of science (for example, ecological disasters, genetic engineering, over-reliance on unsustainable forms of energy, virulent diseases and the regular incidence of technological disasters). Second, with the breakdown of religious and communal bonds, and the rise in secularism and individualism, trust between persons must follow new forms, habits and rules, few of which are prescribed or invested in the expectations and narratives of the old order.

Gender adds a further twist to the issue of trust, for we must recognize that trust comes with a gendered script – it is not gender neutral. For example, it can be argued that the rise of individualism in Western societies, if not globally, puts under question the increasingly dated 'gender order'. The gender order, prior to, say, the 1980s, was certainly damaging, not least for women and 'others', yet, like all discursive regimes, it did offer the conditions of possibility for a form of communal stability or order. However, there can be little doubt that a combination of conditions is ushering in a challenge to traditional gender assumptions and divisions. New habits, bonds, rules – what Misztal terms 'trust systems' – are developing and informing new communities. In many such communities traditional gender values no longer have the influence they once had. Indeed, many communities and relationships are flourishing precisely because they have renounced traditional gender values and refashioned new ones (see Beck and Beck-Gernsheim, 1995; also Sweetman, 1997). Under these transformatory conditions all individuals are faced with change as old orders break down or just wither away from neglect or disinterest. Yet our trust in persons, what Giddens (1990) refers to as 'basic trust', remains an elementary aspect of our sense of self – our ontological grounding. So what do we come to trust in gendered individuals who are increasingly contingent and diverse? How do we measure or assess trust in individuals, between individuals and between communities which are constantly changing? In short, what part will gender play in facilitating or disrupting trust and, thus, ontological security and wider social mechanisms?

My next point concerns the concept of the 'pure relationship'. As was discussed above, a key problem with the concept of the 'pure relationship' is its reliance on trust between *equal* partners (Jamieson, 1999). Yet such equality, necessary as it might be, is not automatic in gender relationships. On the contrary, one could argue that few gender relationships are equal in every sense, though, to be sure, many individuals aspire to this. In suggesting that women and men are fashioning new, more equitable relationships, writers such as Beck and Beck-Gernsheim (1995) suggest that the breakdown of traditional values may well present opportunities for people. However, in displacing traditional values that often contained comforting 'trust systems', we must fashion new bonds of trust and intimacy, a necessary adaptation if we are to alleviate the physical and psychological consequences of existential disorientation. So we can see here two opposing pressures: the desire by many men to hold on to traditional values and, thus, material advantage over women; and the changed expectations of a new, increasingly powerful class of women, unimpressed by the traditional gendered narratives of the past. I would suggest that trust, or lack of it, will be a key factor in facilitating or disrupting the possibilities of negotiation between these gendered groups of individuals.

Masculinity and trust clearly present themselves as an interesting area for research within the sociology of masculinity. We have to look more closely at the discourses and narratives of masculinity under which trust flourishes or does not flourish. What role or function do discourses of masculinity play in facilitating trust between men as individuals and as groups, and between women and men? What displays of masculinity are most trusted in different environs, and how do these then come to cement male friendships, fraternities, organizational cultures and relationships? What are the signifying practices of masculinity that signal or disrupt trust for the masculine subject, and how do these then come to enable material advantage for men? And, in an age when traditional gender values are increasingly questioned, what new habits and regulations informing gendered trust systems are developing within communities and between individuals?

In sum, trust is highly problematic for men and masculinity, for before one can trust, one must let go of fear and of a desire to control.

One must accept one's inadequacies, limitations and needs, while being prepared to submit these needs to the hands of another. It is ironic that the very pursuit of scientific reason, as discussed by Lyotard, and the subsequent promotion of 'rational systems' – both highly masculinist modernist principles of being defining the nineteenth and twentieth centuries – have resulted in a breakdown of trust systems, not an increase. It is as if men, as the primary makers, holders and deployers of rational systems, have sought to control trust through so-called rational mechanistic 'order' rather than subjectively trust in each other as fellow human beings.

Intimacy

As with trust, so an exploration of intimacy reveals its multiple, diverse and contradictory character. Intimacy is not a single entity, only connected by some innate process to the body, sexuality or sexual desire. Reflecting this dynamic view of intimacy, Anthony Giddens (1992) suggests that a 'generic restructuring of intimacy' has taken place in modern societies. For Giddens, this 'transformation of intimacy' heralds the possibility of a radical democratization of gender relationships arising from women's emancipation from the nineteenth-century discourses on sexuality that located sexuality in the rule of the phallus. In contrast to discourses that centralized and privileged male sexual pleasure and experience, Giddens argues that 'plastic sexuality', that is sexual activity 'freed from the needs of reproduction' (ibid: 2), will be the basis and impetus for the pursuit of the 'pure relationship' discussed above. The pure relationship comes to exemplify women's and men's desire for emotional fulfilment and, thus, new forms of intimacy between equals. Mirroring the larger trends within Western societies for more democracy, autonomy and openness for individuals, this new form of intimacy signals a 'democratising of the interpersonal domain' (ibid: 3). In making his case, Giddens connects intimacy in modern societies with emergent forms of self-identity legitimation, enabled through the reflexive project of the self and made increasingly necessary as a consequence of the deep-rooted social transformations arising from 'high modernity' (Giddens, 1990, 1991). In short, the conditions of possibility in modern societies are such that both women and men will increasingly engage with each other on an equal basis. For both genders are now not only released from the rigid, disciplinary discourses of sexuality that emerged from the nineteenth century onwards; both genders are also rendered ontologically vulnerable through the historical shifts of the late twentieth century, which swept away those traditional values long anchoring women's and men's sense of self.

Intrigued by what she calls Giddens's 'optimism' towards gender relations, Lynn Jamieson (1998, 1999) considers the implications of his thesis for a radical transformation of intimacy and, by implication, gender politics and wider social relations. Jamieson argues that larger social and economic conditions, down to the practicalities of 'who last cleaned the toilet' (1999: 490), all serve to hinder and bedevil the possibilities for pure relationships and new forms of open, reflexive intimacies between women and men. In taking a feminist critique to Giddens's notion of intimacy as central to a 'meaningful life in contemporary society', Jamieson (1998: 1), while recognizing that change in gender relationships is occurring, argues that there is a lack of evidence to indicate that the pursuit of intimacy is now the 'organising principle' in women's and men's personal lives. Indeed, Jamieson goes on to suggest that consumerism and 'rampant' self-interest, as connected characteristics of modern societies, may have 'catastrophic consequences for personal and social life' (1998: 170). These factors, when aligned with the continuing multiple roles of women, dominance of gender stereotypes, and the capacity of couples to experience intimacy while living out unequal relationships, do not indicate the inevitability of intimate disclosures becoming the key basis for new, pure relationships.

A further dimension is that, as with trust, with intimacy one must let go of fear, insecurity and control tendencies if one is to experience it fully and without instrumentality. But, as with trust, intimacy is not ungendered. Ways of being a man and exhibiting masculinity intrude into men's experiences and displays of intimacy, potentially rendering it synthetic, strategic or to be avoided. Deborah Kerfoot (1999) draws on the work of Bologh (1990) to argue that emotional intimacy stands in contrast to instrumental intimacy, which she characterizes as a repression of the other in social relations. Kerfoot argues that masculine subjects are unable to 'let go' in their relationships, the result being that they come to deny the possibility for *jouissance* (Irigaray, 1980) – pleasure in its largest sense from engagement with others – and, thus, full connection with others:

Much in the manner of a child's skipping game, emotional intimacy presents a range of possibilities for subject/object positions: social encounters are thus characterized by movement – the to and fro – as participants in the social encounter move within and between subject/object positioning in playful fashion. This playful attitude to relationships stands in contrast to the discourses and practices of masculinity. In their representation of intimacy as amenable to instrumental control, such discourses are founded upon a denial of the very conditions that could make such alternative subjectivities possible. (Kerfoot, 1999: 198)

Kerfoot's feminist poststructuralist analysis alerts us to the discursive character of intimacy, and also to intimacy's gendered dimensions. Here we see intimacy not as something innate to the subject, but as something framed around and experienced within larger, but constantly shifting, social relations. To be sure, Giddens's notion of changes in intimacy and the growing importance given to self-reflexivity do resonate with the *Zeitgeist* of the postmodern age. But, as Jamieson argues, recognition must also be given to continuing gender inequalities, indeed to the deep-rootedness of gender divisions in society. And out of this deep-rootedness grow dominant understandings of masculinity. As Kerfoot and others have noted (see also Seidler, 1997; Kerfoot and Whitehead, 1998b), for many men it is the very spontaneity of intimacy – and trust – that is so threatening and precarious. It is the unscripted response, the unpredictable, uncontrollable situation, that many men avoid. In seeking to control the uncertainty that might be generated by emotional intimacy, many men – consciously or otherwise – reach for conventional practices and behaviours of stereotypical masculinity. Here, masculinity becomes a means of rendering social relations manageable, not a means for disclosing intimacies (Kerfoot and Whitehead, 1998b).

In order for the moment to be experienced as genuine, and thereby unscripted, emotional intimacy requires merely responding to the other, rather than drawing on a knowledge of *how to* respond. To script the encounter in order to provide the means by which it might be managed is at one and the same time to 'lose the moment' and for emotional intimacy to evaporate. Masculinity gives the appearance of providing masculine subjects with the knowledge of how to respond, and of how to manage – rather than experience – intimate situations.

In consequence, emotional intimacy remains ever on the horizon for masculine subjects, who are ever guarding against its possibility. (Kerfoot and Whitehead, 1998b: 15; original emphasis)

Emotions and feelings

Whatever one's view of Giddens's optimistic thesis, it is clear from the above discussion on intimacy that dominant discourses of masculinity do not sit easy with notions of emotional literacy and maturity. In this respect it becomes difficult for feminist and profeminist writers on the one hand to acknowledge that not all women and men are the same, while on the other recognizing that conventional, powerful discourses of masculinity, although stereotypical, do influence the behaviours and practices of countless women and men. Similarly, the idea that emotional maturity is the province of the female, and that men are emotionally incompetent, only serves to further rein force the gendered public and private dualism at the heart of most societies, modern or otherwise. As Jackson and Scott note, 'we should be wary of valorising what is symptomatic of subordination, however tempting it might be to deride men's emotional incompetence' (1997: 568, quoted in Jamieson, 1999: 490).

The concerted efforts by feminists to challenge the dualistic assumptions of male rationality and female irrationality inevitably have to confront the roots of philosophy and theology, that is, the oppositions of body and mind, and emotion and reason, that are embedded in Western thought (see Seidler, 1994a, 1994b; Peterson, 1998). As Genevieve Lloyd argues, the belief that emotions and feelings need to be managed, controlled and subdued, for to allow them free rein is to flirt with madness and hysteria, speaks to an understanding of the female as mysterious and dangerous: 'From the beginning of philosophical thought, femaleness was symbolically associated with what Reason supposedly left behind – the dark powers of the earth goddesses, immersion in unknown forces associated with mysterious female powers'. (1984: 2, quoted in Crawford et al., 1992: 17)

The relationship between masculinity and theology is further exposed in the writings of Max Weber, whose text *The Protestant Ethic and the Spirit of Capitalism* (1930) reveals the ways in which a powerful Protestant morality prepares individuals for the demands of work, particularly employment in capitalist work systems. In this study, men and their supposedly 'natural' instrumentalist masculinity are clearly associated with the rational, non-emotional decision-making that is seen as essential to progress and achievement within increasingly competitive nineteenth- and twentieth-century organizations and nation-states (for discussion, see Morgan, 1992; Seidler, 1994a, 1994b).

Yet, as writings within the sociology of masculinity reveal, despite the claims made by classic sociological and philosophical texts, masculinity is not a singular, cohesive entity. Similarly, as Lloyd (1984) argues, emotions are not simply the product of innate, gendered impulses, operating in some functional or sexually complementary fashion. There are numerous dimensions to emotionality, none of which is easily reducible to either simple moral attributes or biological distinctions. Crawford et al. (1992), for example, examine some of the numerous dimensions to emotion, all of which, they argue, are informed, in some way, through our sense of gender and the agentic processes of memory work.

The extent to which emotions are constructed agentically from the discourses at our disposal as Crawford et al. suggest (also Jackson, 1993), or are experienced as a separation from society, an inner psychoanalytical process (Craib, 1995), or exist 'only in the activities between interdependent people' (Burkitt, 1997: 53) and, thus, as the very basis of social life itself (Gergen, 1994) are debates that continue to run in sociology and psychology and are unlikely to be closed within either discipline. Nevertheless, what can be stated with some certainty is that common-sense understandings of emotion and feeling rely to a great extent on simplistic gendered dualisms and on the powerful discourses of theology and philosophy that inform them.

Within the sociology of masculinity, much of the discussion on masculinities and emotion has tended to emerge from profeminist men's accounts of being a man and the personal costs this has often elicited in respect of damaged relationships, expressions of violence and anger, repressed feelings and denial of emotions (see Jackson, 1990; Rutherford, 1999; Seidler, 1992b, 1997). The beginnings of men's excursion into the hitherto mysterious world of their own emotions began, for many, in the late 1970s with their participation in men's groups. Andrew Tolson was one such man, and he gives this account of his experience in such a group:

We began to discover that we had no language of feeling. We were trapped in public, specialised languages of work, learned in universities or factories, which acted as a shield against deeper emotional solidarities. When we talked about ourselves and our experiences these would be presented through the public languages in abstract formal ways. The factory manager actually talked about himself as if he functioned like a machine. The student-philosopher spoke about his 'bad faith' and his struggle to be 'authentic'. And the man on the dole, in this context kept silent – and was perceived to be incoherent, swept along by a fluid introspective experience. (1977: 135–6, quoted in Rutherford, 1992: 10)

Tolson expertly weaves into his account the ways in which these men appear to retreat to the comparatively comfortable, secure, 'known' world of the public sphere, and the class hierarchy it largely sustains, in their search for emotional expression and self-reflection. It is a Weberian world where work, organization and management define both self and other; a masculinist, instrumental place where bureaucracy, rules, order and, by implication, reason, rationality and progress appear to dominate. However, as Tolson notes, by the late 1970s it was a world undergoing profound change, buffeted not only by the impact of globalization and post-industrialization, but, increasingly, by feminism itself. Developing this thesis, Rutherford (1992) argues that one of the consequences of feminism, and women's changed expectations about work and home, has been to confront many men with the tenuousness at the heart of their sense of masculine self, an insecurity heightened by the emotional tensions, blockages and inarticulation at the root of many prevailing expressions of masculinity.

Endings and openings

Despite the overwhelming evidence of many men's emotional blockages, it would be both simplistic and misleading to assume that all men are either lacking the emotional depths apparently available to women or are overly emotional when it comes to aggressive and violent expression. In short, as Hearn (1993) puts it, we should not presume men to be either too much in control or too much out of control of themselves. Men are not biologically programmed to deny their emotions or to avoid intimacy. Yet there is this persistent and valid concern over men's propensity for instrumental engagements, a tendency that, as Kerfoot (1999) argues, ultimately serves to define the emotional dimensions of the masculine subject. And, certainly, there is much in male behaviour that corresponds to Kerfoot's thesis. In this respect, one has to doubt the veracity of Giddens's argument that postmodernity has rendered traditionally dominant representations of sexuality and intimacy redundant. Moreover, there are many dimensions to the postmodern era, many of which are only now beginning to emerge. To be sure, one of the more positive shifts concerns the increasing multiplicity of family life, and the ways in which the demise of traditional gender expectations comes to enable this diversity of being (a family). However, another intriguing development is the proliferation of Internet chatrooms and their capacity to produce intimate engagements between individuals. As Thomas's (1999) research reveals, once they are in the chatroom, both women and men are finding their inhibitions slipping away online, the medium creating, quite literally, a meeting of minds or 'mind meld'. Consequently, the Internet is proving to be a significant factor in contemporary divorce and the formation of off-line relationships. Yet again, we see in the postmodern, technological age some indication of how new masculinities and ways of being a man may come to be expressed, with men's emotional reticence possibly giving way to pseudo-intimate engagements online.

However, a more negative aspect concerns men and sexuality, at least in respect of the potential transformations in intimacy posited by Giddens. Prostitution, for example, does not appear to be on the decline in the postmodern age. Indeed, sex work is assuming a globalized character, with the sex tourist and the movement of women sex workers across national borders increasingly recognized as an international problem. Moreover, one of the common themes disclosed by the men users of prostitutes quoted in O'Neill's extensive research (2000) is a desire for a lack of intimacy in their habitual, sexualized commercial exchanges. Where intimacy is desired by these men, it emerges as a fleeting commercial exchange sustained by fantasy and financial negotiation (Frank, 1998). Similarly, the phenomenal use of pornography on the Internet, by far the most successful part of the e-economy, does not suggest the possibility of increased intimacies between individuals. Rather, this trend suggests a distorting of intimacy, the rendering of bodies and sexuality into plasticity and caricature, to be instrumentally used for distant relief and voyeuristic consumption. Likewise, the hyper-gendered and sexualized imagery of modern computer game characters does not promote, or even speak of, tenderness and love between women and men, but the opposite. In this respect, 'cyber-sexuality' (Wolmark, 1999) may be liberating for some, though just 'who or what gets constructed as the other' in cyberspace is, as Balsamo (1999: 153) argues, a feminist issue. In short, while there are undoubtedly some positive social transformations occurring in the postmodern age, the use of stereotypical male and female imagery to sell sexuality remains depressingly familiar, as does men's propensity to buy (into) them, not least as a form of emotion and intimacy management.

Trust, intimacy and emotion, if they are about anything, must be about letting go, being in the moment, renouncing control and renouncing attempts to manage situations and individuals. Yet masculinity, certainly as it has been commonly defined and understood, finds its roots, its discursive nourishment, in those philosophical and cultural beliefs that associate men with reason, rationality and emotional control. In the final analysis, it is this dualism, wrought in language, text and symbolism – and declaring the naturalness of the supposedly rational public world of men and the supposedly emotive private world of women – that is at the heart of contemporary definitions of gender. As such, all aspects of men and masculinities will ultimately come down to this simple but highly potent public and private dichotomy. Yet, as this chapter has sought to reveal, it is a dichotomy that is anything but simple and straightforward in practice. From the complexities of the private 'I', through the changing patterns of family life and relationships, to the falsity of a prevailing, given, male sexuality, there is little about 'private men' that is either singular or unambiguous.

FURTHER READING

Allan, G. (ed.) (1999) *The Sociology of the Family: A Reader*. Oxford: Blackwell.
McMahon, A. (1999) *Taking Care of Men: Sexual Politics in the Public Mind*. Cambridge: Cambridge University Press.

Nardi, P. M. (ed.) (1992) *Men's Friendships*. Thousand Oaks, Calif.: Sage.
Segal, L. (1997) *Slow Motion: Changing Masculinities, Changing Men.* London: Virago.
Seidler, V. J. (1994) *Unreasonable Men: Masculinity and Social Theory.* London: Routledge.

6
Materializing Male Bodies

Within the sociology of masculinity the male body is omnipresent yet relatively invisible; for although study is of the embodied category of men, theoretical and empirical examinations of men's embodiedness are few. Exceptions are the important contributions made by Connell (1987, 1995) and Petersen (1998), both of whom, though drawing on different theoretical perspectives, deconstruct any notion of givenness to the male body while highlighting the relationship between gendered bodies and gendered power (see also Morgan, 1993). Most critical gender perspectives on the male body have concerned themselves with the relationship between men's sense of embodiment, masculinities and sport (Messner, 1992; Messner and Sabo, 1990; McKay, Messner and Sabo, 2000). More specific studies include Kerfoot's (2000) examination of the relationship between the male body, masculinities and organizations; Jefferson's (1998) exploration of how notions of 'hardness' come to inform embodied masculinity; Cornwall and Lindisfarne's (1994) ethnographic research into the male body and cultural expressions of masculinity; Mosse's (1996) historical analysis of male physicality and the creation of modern masculinities; Silverman's (1992) discussion of symbolic castration and male subjectivity; and Sabo and Gordon's (1995) volume on men's health and illness.

For the most part it seems that the profeminist literature on men and masculinities has been unable or unwilling to grapple with the male body, other than to suggest, in social constructionist terms, that the body is 'a field on which social determination runs riot' (Connell, 1995: 50; also Shilling, 1993). To be sure, within sociology itself debates about the body have only a relatively recent history, being driven, particularly, by feminist scholarship (see Price and Shildrick, 1999; also Scott and Morgan, 1993) and cultural studies (Hall, 1997; also Featherstone, Hepworth and Turner, 1991).[1] Indeed, Frank goes so far as to suggest that 'in contemporary theory the body remains silent' (1991: 36). Yet, while recognizing this, one would still expect the body to have a much larger presence within critical debates on men and masculinities, not least because male physicality and masculinity seem symbiotically connected.

In contrast to academia, the media now endlessly pore over and scrutinize men's bodies. This is the case whether the male body undergoes very public symbolic castration (as happened to Bill Clinton during the Monica Lewinsky affair), actual castration (as in the case of John Wayne Bobbitt) or suffers economic emasculation and commodification as entertainingly portrayed in the film *The Full Monty* (see Goddard, 2000). Some might argue that the male body is now subject to objectification and (patterns of) consumption in a similar way to that which has long been experienced by female bodies. Though, to be sure, the 'beauty myths' (Chapkis, 1986) informing female embodiment arise from a quite different set of power equations to those informing male embodiment.

It is evident, then, that new discourses surrounding men's bodies have emerged into the public domain. In particular, they include growing concern about men's health and new scrutinies on men in terms of body shape, style and deportment. For example, those men in the public eye, such as politicians, find their dress, taste in fashion and physical form increasingly subject to comment and critique. In general terms, previous boundaries surrounding men's bodies appear to be eroding or changing, with increasing numbers of men, like women, pursuing a form of individual legitimation through body enhancement, whether this be an exercise regime, cosmetic surgery or the application of face creams. Some writers have termed this trend the 'Adonis complex' and connected it with the crisis of masculinity thesis. A theme of these works is that, in an age when women have 'invaded' all other male domains, 'the pursuit of muscle' remains the one avenue left open for men to exhibit their true masculine self (see Pope, Phillips and Olivardia, 2000).

This chapter aims to bring the male body more directly into the sociology of masculinity in several ways. First, the chapter takes as its primary theme the *materiality of masculinities* and the relationship this materiality has to the body. My concern here is to explore some of the ways in which men's sense of themselves as embodied agents serves to inform their physical presence in, and relationship to, the world and to others. Moreover, to recognize that male body existence, and the system of possibilities open to it, performs multiple projects wherein being and becoming (a male) carries with it the political (power) conditions and potentialities of gender identity. A second objective is to consider the notion that the material form of the male body is *inevitably* inscribed with masculinities; similarly, that masculinities, by definition, speak to and of the male (body). This argument is developed in the final chapter, notably in relation to subjectivity and ontology. The point that will be explored below concerns the importance of recognizing that males' sense of embodiment informs and shapes their multiple physical–discursive materializations and relationships – to their own bodies, to others' bodies (male and female), to the spatial field in which they find themselves. None of this is received or experienced unproblematically, and I recognize that placing male with masculinity in what might be seen as a predetermined manner is to place the body in the masculine–feminine binary that has been so effectively critiqued in third-wave feminist scholarship (see Butler, 1993). Nevertheless, the anatomical differences between the sexes make a powerful claim upon the body/subject for difference, and from that sense of difference so the discourses of gender go to work. The physicality that speaks of the male is discursively inscribed upon and located within an *embodied* political gender category, and, for most males, experienced as a physical if not emotional separation from the feminine throughout their lives. However, while recognizing the ontological connections between masculinities and male bodies, there are numerous points of disruption that serve to put men's sense of embodied masculinity under question. Drawing on the concept of the panoptic gaze, this chapter will conclude by discussing just a few of the ways in which male bodies are positioned as 'Other' and rendered insecure, notably through the cultural inscriptions and authoritative gazes surrounding race, sexuality, health and age.

Male bodies

In this section I will not describe in detail those idealizations of the male body circulating in image, text or symbolism across the social world. My reasoning is that, first, the reader will be able to identify numerous places within the book where these constitutions are evident, be it across the public or private spheres. Second, in so much as a central aim of this book is to draw attention to emergent themes within the sociology of masculinity, identified as a third wave of theorizing, I am more interested in the ways in which identity and materiality connect with the body, both to constitute it and to discursively exercise power and resistance upon and through it. Lastly, notions of the male body are historically differentiated, temporally and spatially located and highly specific to cultural sites. There is no singular male body from which we can ascertain a particular, singular masculinity, though dominant discourses surrounding the body are powerful in their persuasion of what counts as normal or natural and, thus, what is or is not valued in terms of male embodiment. My point is that all male bodies are places upon which masculinities become inscribed, but not in any predictable or linear fashion.

As numerous feminists have noted, there seems to have been no time or place when body evaluation and classification has not served to reinforce or write not only the masculine–feminine binary, but also racialist (Hall, 1997; hooks, 1981), sexualist (Petersen, 1998) and nationalist distinctions (Frank, 1991). The bifurcation of women and men as embodied beings took a particular turn during the period of the Western Enlightenment, when the belief in the Cartesian body–mind dualism served to reinforce the biological essentialism at the heart of male power, not least by depositing a 'universal voice of reason' (Seidler, 1994a: 31) on sex difference. Underpinned by a new class-based, philosophical and ethical order, the truths about women and men would be discovered, so it was believed by many, through rational scientific application (for discussion, see Petersen, 1998; Jordanova, 1999). As was discussed in chapter 1, the belief that science can rationally and finally 'know' the body and, thus, the human character continues to be no less apparent today. Yet it is clear that research into the body can no longer rely on sociobiological accounts, geneticism or evolutionary psychology, but must try to understand how patterns and pressures of capitalist, post-industrial production (Turner, 1984), and commodification and consumption (Bourdieu, 1984), combine with gendered, sexual (reproductive) experiences (O'Brien, 1983; Butler, 1993), cultural significations (Hill Collins, 1991) and psychoanalytical processes (Grosz, 1990) to produce a body in flux, frequently rendered anxious, yet always subject to some level of external regulation. Thus we can state with some confidence that bodies are not neutral or power-free, any more than the mind–body separation is tenable – though, as is discussed below, the extent to which individual (female) bodies are totally regulated or free and agentic continues to be a key debate in feminist theory. Nevertheless, it should be recognized that the structure/agency binary does not go to work on the body in any straightforward manner. The very diversity, multiplicity and contingency of bodies precludes closure of any sort. Bodies change within lifetimes, are changing as we live in them and are unique to the subject; bodies do not exist in some given, unchanging system. Yet, while we cannot achieve closure over the body, we can come to some appreciation of how dominant discourses act upon bodies in a performative yet material manner.

Male bodies in process

It is evident from the discussion in previous chapters that masculinity transcends its illusory, mythological foundations to emerge as a physical presence in the world in the shape of the male, his behaviour and expectations. The material actuality of masculinities extends beyond the particular conditions and constraints circulating in the public and private spheres. These spheres, in so much as they exist as distinct entities, become reified, in part, through the presence of male bodies and their fraternities. For Merleau-Ponty (1962), 'the body is the original subject that constitutes space; there would be no space without the body' (Young, 1990: 152). If this is the case, then there is no space within the public–private that is not already prefigured by (gendered) bodies, marking out territories for inclusion and exclusion of the female and male. At the same time, the public–private dualism is brought into existence only through the presence of embodied beings. This is not to determine or essentialize the capacities of the gendered, sexed body within any given sphere, but rather, following Irigaray (1985), it is to raise the status of the body to that place wherein the discursive possibilities open to the subject become inscribed, inculcated and enacted. Thus the body of which we speak is not a biologically programmed, predetermined entity, but a discursive constitution: a 'contested terrain [upon which] the interplay of text and physicality [render] a body in process, never fixed or solid, but always multiple and fluid' (Price and Shildrick, 1999: 4).

The male body can be understood, then, as the place from which masculinities appear both as illusion and as materiality. In appearing whole and complete, the body does emit a powerful semiotic presence in the social world (for example, Chapkis, 1986; for discussion, see Hall, 1997). However, as Foucault puts it, the body is not unified but is a site of struggle between opposing discursive power regimes:

> The body is the inscribed surface of events (traced by language and dissolved by ideas), the locus of a dissociated self (adopting the illusion of a substantial unity), and a volume in perpetual disintegration. Genealogy, as an analysis of descent, is thus situated within the articulation of the body and history. Its task is to expose a body totally imprinted by history and the processes of history's destruction of the body. (Foucault, 1984: 83)

For Foucault, the body is the ultimate surface upon which power and resistance operate. He uses genealogical analysis, the 'philosophy of the event',[2] to expose the haphazard yet powerful dynamics of change to which the (sexualized) body has been subject over recent history. Foucault's work stresses the absence of any cognitive, self-reflexive subject, working to enable her/his body in the social world in some rational, linear fashion. Rather, Foucault signals a complex process of movement, where discord rather than harmony rules. This point is an important one to make, for it challenges the idea that the male body, the vehicle for masculinities, is in any way singular, sovereign or complete. As a signifier of maleness it speaks to the gender category of (heterosexual) men and thus to a political configuration within which discursive power regimes exist. Yet at the same time it is itself subject to the microstrategies of power. The male body, like the masculinities it suggests, is always open to disruption and anxiety (see, for example, Jefferson, 1998).

What Foucault's work does so effectively is move us away from the Enlightenment, modernist notion of a mind–body split, while also providing us with the theoretical tools to question and deconstruct the modernist scientific forms of knowledge that have served to 'pathologize' bodies within particular power regimes (see McNay, 1992, 1994; Petersen, 1998). However, as was discussed in chapter 3, just how we use Foucault's theories, indeed which theories to use and which not to use, are significant questions for any social theorist. We can recognize from Foucauldian analysis the power/resistance dimensions to the mind–body relationship in so much as the materiality of the body takes place through regulated practices, which are not, however, applied to the body in any prior, cognitive fashion by knowing agents. Similarly, the body can be understood to be that final place wherein, in Merleau-Ponty's terms also, the subject comes to exist in space, while not being a body over which the discursive subject exerts sovereignty. However, a difficulty then arises for feminists in respect of how to theoretically connect the discursiveness of the body with the materiality of gender difference (Bordo, 1993). This is further complicated in terms of Foucauldian analysis as his genealogical method was concerned to highlight the ways in which the body was subject to the interests of capitalism and labour. While not dismissive of this connection, feminists have sought to take his model and also apply it to a critique of gender (for examples, see McNay, 1994; Ramazanoglu, 1993).

As has already been indicated, in respect of feminist theory a rich and dynamic debate has opened up on the body, though with few and notable exceptions little work has been undertaken within the sociology of masculinity that connects with these discussions. Given the limitations of space, I will concern myself here with the work of just two key feminist writers in this field, Iris Marion Young and Judith Butler. These feminist scholars have drawn on the works of, respectively, Merleau-Ponty and Foucault to provide insights into the gendered body in ways that introduce the body as a contested place, yet materialized in the social world through the dynamics of gender. I would argue that, in slightly different ways, Young and Butler provide us with important feminist theoretical tools with which to unpack the key issue surrounding the male body, that is, how to understand the relationship between the embodiedness of masculinities, the materiality of gender and the ways in which female and male bodies become subject to different technologies of power.

Throwing like a boy

Iris Marion Young's (1990) work, *Throwing Like a Girl*, is an insightful study into how feminine body comportment and movement arises
not from women's innate anatomy or biology, but from the 'structures of feminine existence' (ibid: 143) existing prior to the emergence
of the body into the social arena. Young's argument is that most
women experience their body as an object subjected to the gaze of
another, as a fragile 'thing' positioned in a gendered space, which
serves to inform the degree and extent to which she may use it, exercise it, express it and receive it:

> The modalities of feminine bodily existence have their root in the fact
> that feminine existence experiences the body as a mere thing – a fragile
> thing, which must be picked up and coaxed into movement, a thing
> that exists as *looked at and acted upon*. To be sure, any lived body
> exists as a material thing as well as a transcending subject. For femi-
> nine bodily existence, however, the body is often lived as a thing that
> is other than it, a thing like other things in the world. (ibid: 150;
> original emphasis)

Young goes on to discuss how women move, sit, stand, walk, engage
in sport and physical activities, how they experience their bodies and
feminine existence as an 'existential closure' in the space that surrounds them. The notion of space being used by Young is one that
owes much to Merleau-Ponty's (1962) notion of the lived body and
its relationship to the world in which it is placed and the world it
part constructs from its own physical presence. For Merleau-Ponty,
ontology and subjectivity are located in the body, primarily through
its orientation to the world:

> The body is the first locus of intentionality, as pure presence to the
> world and openness upon its possibilities. The primordial intentional
> act is the motion of the body orientating itself with respect to and
> moving within its surroundings. (Young, 1990: 148)

Young applies Beauvoir's (1973) existential feminism (for overview,
see Tong, 1993) to Merleau-Ponty's concepts in order to produce an
understanding of feminine bodily existence – woman's motility and
spatiality – as immanently positioned in a male-dominated culture,

where her very sense of being, self and subjectivity as 'Other' arises from the fact of her bodily presence and entity being subject to restrictions and inhibitions.

> There is a specific positive style of feminine body comportment – walking like a girl, tilting her head like a girl, standing and sitting like a girl, gesturing like a girl, and so on. The girl learns actively to hamper her movements. She is told that she must be careful not to get hurt, not to get dirty, not to tear her clothes, that the things she desires are dangerous to her. Thus she develops a bodily timidity that increases with age. In assuming to be a girl she takes herself to be fragile. (Young, 1990: 154)

I would suggest that most men do not experience their bodies in this way. Dominant masculinities, and the sense of bodily presence and existence they suggest, do not position the male/masculine subject as timid, careful, restricted; in assuming to be boy/man the male does not take himself to be fragile. On the contrary, dominant notions of embodied masculinity speak of force, hardness, toughness, physical competence (Connell, 1983; also Jefferson, 1998). Moreover, masculine bodily existence suggests the occupation of space, the capacity to define space, the ability to exercise control over space and a preparedness to put one's body at risk in order to achieve these expectations. The male/boy/man is *expected* to transcend space, or to place his body in aggressive motion within it, in so doing posturing to self and others the assuredness of his masculinity. Thus, the male's ontological security is part invested in his bodily presence and its relationship to the world. As is discussed in chapter 7, what emerges here is a gendered ontology; to be precise, a *masculine ontology*. However, this 'being in the world' is not simply about physical strength; it concerns the application of one's physicality to space. Masculinity suggests an approach to space and objects that is not preconditioned by hesitation but by confident expression and a purposeful, outward intentionality. Look at children playing in the school playground: the boy running headlong into space, creating space for himself and at the same time restricting space for others, especially girls; the girls together, huddled, talking, sharing, discussing, slower movements, more considered movements, their bodies occupying space on the perimeter of the primary or most visible field of play – usually a competitive sports activity involving boys. To be sure, there are numerous exceptions to these scenarios, but, as Young says, we should not allow the exceptions to deny the differing realities of the lived experiences of most women's and men's bodily existence. And this is not to suggest some feminine or masculine essence to behavioural differences between women and men, but to point out how gendered power relations come to inscribe themselves upon the body in ways that usher into existence the materialities of gendered being. As Young puts it:

> I take 'femininity' to designate not a mysterious quality or essence that all women have by virtue of their being biologically female. It is, rather, a set of structures and conditions that delimit the typical *situation* of being a woman in a particular society, as well as the typical way in which this situation is lived by the women themselves. This understanding of 'feminine' existence makes it possible to say that some women escape or transcend the typical situation and definition of women in various degrees and respects. (1990: 144; original emphasis)

Young's thesis describes a patriarchal state wherein femininity and masculinity are measured in deportment, posture, mobility, the differing performance of physical tasks by differentially gendered bodies. As discussed in chapter 3, I would argue that this social world is masculinist rather than patriarchal and, thus, discursive in its constitution and orientation. Nevertheless, it is, in the final reckoning, a spatiality wherein the male body is privileged and prominent. It is a world where masculine bodily performance is primarily, and often violently, expressed as occupation, control, objectification and subjugation (of others' bodies), competition (against others' bodies) and the willingness to expose, to risk and danger, one's own body. The masculine body is not one that is deemed to be rendered passive by its environment but one that seeks to render the environment passive to it, primarily by virtue of the male body's actions within, and transcendence of, its immediate space. In short, the male child bodily occupying space in the playground emerges as the male adult bodily occupying space, or seeking to, in the office meeting, in the sports ground, on the street, on the highways and, not least, through the entrepreneurial masculinity writ large in the corporations now straddling the globalized marketplace (Connell, 1998; also Hassard, Holliday and Willmott, 2000). To be sure, the masculinities, as bodily expressions, which accompany such displays are largely idealized, and many if not most men can sustain them only through effort, if at all. The point is not only that many men fail to achieve a seamless, constant, symbiotic relationship between their bodies and dominant discourses of masculinity, but that they attempt to; moreover, that their subjectivity and sense of masculine self is primarily invested in such attempts.

It is important to recognize that Young's analysis is not merely a description of feminine and masculine bodily existence in patriarchy, but a theoretical insight from which to understand how the gendered body brings into existence gendered practice while being subject to forms of regulation. Thus we have here a clear link with gendered subjectivity, power, embodiment and materiality. However, unlike Young, I would place these elements as discursive, for this then opens the theorist up to a rich source of theoretical positions from which to link power and identity to the material body. Arguably the most influential feminist theories in this regard have come from the pen of Judith Butler.

Materializing the discursive male body

Butler's work is extensive, deep and complex in its theoretical explorations, so what is offered here is an extremely partial overview of her important work on the body.

In establishing her theoretical position, Butler's first aim is to name the sex–gender distinction as an artifice. She argues that to understand gender as the cultural interpretation of sex is to fail to recognize that 'gender is also the discursive/cultural means by which "sexed nature" or "a natural sex" is produced and established as pre-discursive, prior to culture, a politically neutral surface *on which* culture acts' (1990: 7; original emphasis). For Butler, there is no pre-discursive sexed body, untrammelled by power relations. Indeed, to assume such is to be co-opted into the power effects of discursive production, whereby that which is culture appears as nature. To be sure, the binary gender system operates in such a way as to prefigure the sex–gender distinction in language and culture, thus suggesting stability. Nevertheless, in feminist poststructuralist terms, this binary operates in the service of a field of power relations through which is concealed the cultural invention of such 'truths' and knowledges.

From this position it becomes immediately apparent that the body is forever discursively inscribed, never to exist in any full sense beyond the cultural parameters that surround and reify it. In short, rather than seek out 'natural' explanations for bodies, we must recognize, from the first, the power/knowledge inventions that usher the sexed/gendered body into existence. This understanding brings us back to the question as to the extent the body is a passive medium of external power relations. Is woman forever destined to be the 'Other' upon which is inscribed a masculinist mark? Beauvoir's suggestion that 'one is not born a woman, but, rather, becomes one' (1973: 301) implies a degree of agency, wherein choice of gendered embodiedness is available. However, Beauvoir also considers that for women to transcend the immanence of the 'Other' imposed on them by men necessitates struggle and resistance, particularly against what Kaufmann McCall (1979) describes as the 'internalized' notion women have of themselves as 'inessential'. An equally paradoxical approach to women's agency is taken by Luce Irigaray (1985), who argues that the phallogocentric logic of a masculinist signifying economy, encompassing both ontological and epistemological structures, signals that woman is 'marked off' from the domain of the signifiable; her very existence is mediated through men whereby she emerges as 'masculine woman'. However, for Irigaray, there is a non-definable 'feminine feminine' representation, which offers women the opportunity to establish a discursive space outside the dominant phallic epistemology (for discussion, see Grosz, 1986).

Butler argues that both Beauvoir's and Irigaray's theses are reductive in that they posit a 'totalizing claim' that is itself rooted in a false notion of a 'primary condition of oppression' (1990: 14). Butler goes on to question the assumption of unity, stability and 'agreed upon identity' contained in these concepts, preferring to see gender (identity) as too momentary to be totalizing and absolute. Unlike modernist feminists (for example, Assiter, 1996), Butler questions any claim to a universal womanist epistemology. However, Butler is not dismissive of the power effects of gender on the body. On the contrary, she sees the body in Foucauldian terms, as regulated, enabled and materialized through power. This process is not, however, one of construction of the subject; rather it is:

> a process of reiteration by which both 'subjects' and 'acts' come to appear. . . . There is no power that acts, but only a reiterated acting

that is power in its persistence and instability. . . . What I would propose in place of these conceptions of construction is a return to the notion of matter, not as site or surface, but as *a process of material-ization that stabilizes over time to produce the effect of boundary, fixity, and surface we call matter*. (Butler, 1993: 9; original emphasis)

In this understanding, the sexed/gendered body materializes through the dynamics and processes of discourse. It is named in discourse and so comes to make its appearance as sovereign and given and thus, *apparently, outside discourse*. In the process, however, it conceals the means of its own invention:

> The body is not an independent materiality that is invested by power relations to it, but it is that for which materialization and investiture are coextensive. . . . 'Materiality' designates a certain effect of power or, rather, *is* power in its formative and constituting effects. (Butler, 1993: 34; original emphasis)

This concept of bodies as discursive materiality exposes not just the power effects of gender, but also the absence of any prediscursive 'I' or self to the body. As was discussed in chapter 5, in poststructural-ist terms the 'I' that speaks has no presence and is not knowing beyond its discursivity (Butler, 1993: 225). However, the 'I' that speaks does occupy a political position, for in speaking it makes claim to forms of knowledges that are themselves associated with particu-lar political categories (Hekman, 1990). Thus there remains the issue of male bodies and their association with the power regimes that serve to provide a material advantage to the masculine subject. In this respect, I would argue, as I did in chapter 2, that it is necessary to see the discursive subject as embodied within distinct gender cate-gories of female and male. In this case, the materiality is formed not just as bodies but as an embodied presence and signification that speaks to a particular form of knowing, knowledge and truth about the world. To be sure, these categories are discursive and, thus, enabling and not simply regulatory. And they are categories which, in extreme situations (for example, full gender reassignment), bodies can move across. But for the most part they are categories, or power regimes, into which discourses materialize an embodied entity, not a unity of identities and not a stable, constant sovereign subject, but a politicized physical presence nonetheless. As is discussed in chapter

7, in their operation as macro-discursive significations of sexed/ gendered subjects, these power regimes constitute political arenas from which bodies achieve some ontological comfort, presence and status.

In sum, I would argue that both Young and Butler provide us with the theoretical means by which to understand the power effects of male bodies, located as they are in a discursive regime and binary system that posits female and male as essentially different. Young's work takes the materiality of the body as a phenomenological and existential dynamic, which is then experienced as a differential power expression within space. Butler provides a set of theoretical tools by which to understand how all subjects, and the bodies upon which they are inscribed, arise not from any natural sex distinction, but from the regulatory enabling power effects manifest in discursive materiality. When we see men's bodies, no matter how diverse, we see not only the materiality of discourse; we observe a political presence whose association with the discursive category/regime of the male serves to delineate the boundaries, possibilities and conditions of the masculine subject – indeed, as is discussed in chapter 7, one that provides an ontological purchase for this otherwise fragmented entity. However, saying this is not to presume the limits on the male body, nor to apply to all male bodies a physical privilege and status that is inevitable. As will now be discussed, despite its existential status as 'Subject', the male body has other potential inscriptions, many of which render it precarious and serve to position it as 'Other'.

Gazing on the male body

The work by Butler and Young tells us that no bodies exist outside the cultural conditions of their own materialization. Thus no bodies are ungendered; all are subjected to a regime of truth about their sex/sexuality/genderedness. A further tool by which to understand the disciplinary or regulatory dimensions of this process is the *panoptic gaze*. The panopticon is a form of prison, designed in the eighteenth century in such a way as to ensure prisoners would always be open to observation by their jailors. Foucault took this physical model and used it to understand the power of the institutive/authoritative gaze on individuals, particularly in the fields of medicine and psychiatry (for elaboration, see Danaher, Schirato and Webb, 2000; Cousins and Houssain, 1984; Rabinow, 1991). In gender terms we can see the gaze applied to both women's and men's bodies, whereby the discursive subject comes to discipline and manage her/his body as self-surveillance. So the gaze is not simply directed at us; we regulate our own bodies in the knowledge and presence of the authoritative gaze. However, the gaze itself is not neutral but invested with powers, in so much as it comes with a set of moral, social and cultural codes or assumptions; an 'economy of looks' that places values on the body, and different values on different bodies. While accepting that for many feminists the authoritative gaze is male (Mulvey, 1989; for discussion, see Waterhouse, 1993; Shildrick and Price, 1999), it is also important to recognize that male bodies are not outside of the gaze, but, indeed, also subject to multiple gazes, including that of the female (Goddard, 2000). In this section I will briefly explore the notion of the authoritative gaze as deployed on black men, gay men and ageing men.

Race man

Black men's bodies constitute a highly contested arena. A complex interplay of powers impact on black male embodiedness in ways that have only recently begun to be understood and researched within the sociology of masculinity and elsewhere. In populist terms it is tempting to talk of a black masculinity, and to suggest that its expressions constitute a form of resistance to a racist system. And, certainly, there is research to suggest that some black males appropriate various social and cultural spaces and stylize their masculinities in such a way as to present themselves as a spectacle of self-expression and agency – adopting a 'cool pose' (for example, see Majors, 2001) and/or explicit 'hardness' (for example, see Jefferson, 1989). Thus, for black men, 'stylizing their bodies' (West, 1993) can be understood as the exercise of power and the practice of resistance. However, the notion of a singular black masculinity is problematic, not least because it can be used to 'naturalize' differences between black and white men (Hall, 1997). As with all subjects, black men materialize with multiple bodies, not one. The black male body may appear singular, as might its expression of masculinity. But the authoritative gaze on black men's bodies takes multiple forms. What we can discern through this complex process is a black–white dualism that prefigures a power relationship, not only between black and white, but also, for example, between woman and man. Thus the gaze is multiplied and embodiment complicated by gender, but not only by gender, also by class, age, sexuality, disability, history, nationhood and culture. In short, by being contested, black men's bodies become highly politicized. They are made visible precisely because, in stark and stereotypical terms, the black male body becomes racially and sexually symbolic of both power and resistance. Kobena Mercer describes the contesting powers surrounding the black body, and the ambivalence they suggest for the stereotypical 'white gaze', as follows:

> Blacks are looked down upon and despised as worthless, ugly and ultimately inhuman. But in the blink of an eye, whites look up to and revere black bodies, lost in awe and envy as the black subject is idealised as the embodiment of its aesthetic ideal. (1994: 201, quoted in Hall, 1997: 276)

The politicizing of the black male and 'his embodied masculinity' is well caught by Hazel Carby in her book *Race Men* (1998). Carby explores how different cultural idealizations of black men permeate Western societies generally and North America particularly, in so doing coming to shape paradigms of race and gender. In particular, Carby raises critical questions concerning the gendered processes by which modes of thought surrounding African American men acquire dominance. She sets about this process by deconstructing idealized depictions of black men, contained, for example, in W. E. B. du Bois's *The Souls of Black Folk* and in the work and lives of black male writers and artists such as Leadbelly (Huddie Ledbetter), Miles Davis, Danny Glover and Paul Robeson. Carby's aim is to expose how dominant definitions of black masculinity, while appearing real and potent, actually conceal the existential and political crisis at the heart of North American and European culture. 'Race man', Carby argues, becomes a black signifier or representation for black and white segments of American society, but it is a signifier constructed from male-centred assumptions leaving women, sexuality and gender as a 'decorative function' (1998: 5).

Carby applies a black feminist gaze to black men's bodies, and in so doing opens up a discursive space through what Irigaray (1985) terms the phallogocentric discourse reifying woman's Otherness. Yet black men are also located as 'Other', largely through the institutional and authoritative gaze of the white male. As Dyer notes, although white men's bodies may be rendered vulnerable and inadequate in certain situations, especially at a time when no singular white male-embodied representation dominates, the white male 'far from being displaced from the centre of discourse by a myriad of postmodern voices, continues to predominate in the control of the image. It is their bodily vulnerability that matters' (1997: 299–300). However, in discussing this very issue, McDowell captures the concern of feminists when she laments the trend in many of the writings on black men and masculinity to 'separate race from gender and gender from race [thereby creating] complex problems of exclusion and distortion for women of color' (1997: 381, quoted in Crenshaw, 1993). McDowell argues that it is now necessary to 'move beyond a focus on the artistic, sculptured body that "looks hard" and holds its "precious prescribed pose", to one less taut, one less muscle-bound' (1997: 381).

The ambivalence of the white gaze on 'muscle-bound' black bodies can probably best be seen in the unresolved relationship between black sports people and the white-dominated countries/cultures that many represent in the international arena. Sportsmen such as Linford Christie, Carl Lewis and Michael Jordan step into the arena to multiple gazes: as black icon, national icon, sexual icon, capitalist/consumerist icon. For the white spectator, just what does the black superstar's body represent in terms of cultural identity? For the black athlete, at what point does the personal/political investment of being black overcome the political/cultural investment of being British, French or American? As identities, the terms are not so discrete as they appear, and certainly cannot be lived out in compartmentalized fashion. Again, the power of the gaze lies in its multiplicity, for it is through these multiple authoritative gazes that the paradoxes of embodied masculinity become apparent, as much for those who gaze as for those who are gazed upon.

A gay body of men

While the panoptic gaze can be understood as a regulatory mechanism, disciplining otherwise 'unruly' bodies to cultural codes and social protocols, its existence has subversive potential. For example, gay men's bodies, as stereotype, may exist in some imaginary place within the social subconscious, and to this 'order' so a regulatory process operates. Yet the stereotype is not fact, but fiction. Thus it can be reformed, refigured, resymbolized in materiality. Gay men can occupy numerous materialities, some of which may, apparently, 'conform' to dominant understandings of how a gay man might position himself as an embodied presence in the world: through posture, movement, dress, style, manner and so on. However, gay men can also occupy materialities that challenge and displace such notions, resulting in the power of the gaze being reconverted on to the gazer, while also being internalized by the subject as an expression of power and resistance.

An example of such reconverting is evident in the work of the late gay, white American photographer Robert Mapplethorpe. Mapplethorpe produced outstanding and unforgettable studies of both women and men, but he is especially known for his evocative portrayals of black gay nude males (see Mapplethorpe, 1996). Technically brilliant, Mapplethorpe's photographs show black gay men in striking and unfamiliar poses, their bodies timelessly captured in intimate, sometimes sexually explicit, sometimes emotionally distant, disturbing poses. The imagery is almost impossible to categorize, for it depends on the gazer's subjectivity as to whether one sees the photographs as erotic, pornographic, aesthetic, emotive or simply beautiful. Similarly, the black male models can be understood to be both objectified and dignified by the process of being gazed upon. Mapplethorpe's images may elicit in the spectator (repressed) desire for the 'Other' and/or repulsion – a desire for avoidance (Phelan, 1993; Munoz, 1997). However, what is beyond question is that the black male body, gay or otherwise, cannot be avoided, for Mapplethorpe *demands* the gaze to be laid upon it, and in this process challenges the gazer to attempt to appropriate the imagery and performance into a conventional paradigm. The gazer is compelled to the imagery, to be repulsed and/or attracted, and in this act so the dominant (white, heterosexual, male) power position becomes disrupted and contested. The inherent instability of meaning becomes evident, whether it be invested in a racialized gaze, a homophobic gaze, or a compulsory-heterosexual gaze (Hall, 1997).[3] Through his photographic deployment of imagery, Mapplethorpe creates a site of struggle, the arena being dominant notions of representation and truth, the contestants being both the gazed upon and the gazing. Of course, Mapplethorpe himself is part of the contest. Indeed, he might be described as the joker, the white gay man who appropriates black bodies for exploitation. Whatever one's perspective, as Mercer argues, Mapplethorpe 'makes strange' black gay sexuality, thereby opening upon new terrains of truth and meaning:

> the textual ambivalence of the black nude photograph is strictly undecidable because Mapplethorpe's photographs do not provide an unequivocal yes/no answer to the question of whether they reinforce or undermine commonplace racist stereotypes – rather, he throws the binary structure of the question back at the spectator, where it is torn apart in the disruptive 'shock effect'. (Mercer, 1991: 189, quoted in Munoz, 1997: 351)

Mapplethorpe's work indicates something of the struggle that takes place over bodies. The struggle is not, however, simply one of power over bodies, but a struggle over dominant representation and meaning, a struggle for being in the world. In this process, all discursive subjects are both participants and investors. As participants they (you and I) cannot remove themselves from being both gazers (spectators) and the gazed upon (objectified). We are all, then, active participants in the endless quest for truth and meaning. As discursive subjects, our own self-representation and self-meaning is inevitably caught up in this act of materialization. In the very instant that the gaze embodies us and thus materializes us as individuals, so it positions us in multiple (political) categories, each of which is culturally invented through its own regimes of truth and knowledge.

Men's ageing bodies

A further regime of truth surrounding male embodiment concerns age. As men grow older the authoritative gaze on them changes, and they in turn internalize new subjectivities and sense of self as the years pass, their bodies alter, their health becomes more fragile, their place in the world as men shifts (Sabo and Gordon, 1995). There may, for some men, be dignity and opportunity in ageing, while for others the years from fifty onwards may signal a deep and lasting existential crisis, compounded by insecure work conditions, health problems, crisis of confidence over sexuality and relationships, and deepening recognition of their own mortality. Whatever men's responses to growing older, it can be stated with some confidence that if men's bodies and the masculinities inscribed upon them are made precarious by multiple gazes, then they are, like women's bodies, rendered particularly insecure through ageing. For if masculinity is about occupation, vigour, activity, mastery and overcoming space, then ageing is the inevitable process that puts under question such dominant representations of maleness. As Thompson says: 'the social construction maintains that "old men" are not men at all' (1994: 13). Yet despite these intriguing issues, men's ageing bodies have had little attention from gender theorists, the focus tending to be on young men, physically active men, men who appear to embody a dominant masculinity through their muscle and 'cool pose'. Therefore, it is, as Thompson notes, 'timely to look inside the elderly male population to appreciate the diversity among older men' (1994: 1).

In undertaking such an examination several questions present themselves. For example, what is the relationship between men's ageing bodies and men's changing masculine subjectivities? How do men 'become older'? What is now meant, for both women and men, by the label 'older man'? What issues arise for men and their sense of masculinity in terms of health and illness? These questions pose interesting areas for research into men and masculinities. Not least because they signal something of the fluidity and disruption that comes with constantly shifting notions of masculinity. Masculinity is not static and unchanging over a male's life; it changes just as the body moves in time and space. The masculinities that become inscribed on the youthful male body become transformed just as the body is transformed through ageing. Yet, despite its inevitability, such a process was perhaps more predictable for past generations of men than for present. For the dominant discourses around ageing appear to be undergoing some profound shift, ushering in new and possibly less restricted ways of thinking about age and the body, both women's and men's.

Such movements as there might be in older men's embodiment are not occurring by happenstance, but as a direct consequence of wider cultural, economic and social changes. In the UK the over-fifties account for a third of the population. By 2040 they will account for half. This group has an annual income of £166 billion and rising.

Not only are Western men living longer; they are more physically active than previous generations.[4] The male menopause is now recognized as a medical condition, with testosterone replacement therapy readily available in the UK to fifty-something men. Similarly, Viagra is helping eradicate that scourge of many older men's bodies – impotence.

Similar demographic and economic shifts are taking place in the US. Thirteen per cent of Americans are now aged sixty-five and older, and this will rise to an expected 20 per cent by 2030.[5] Life expectancy at birth for US white males has increased from 48.2 years in 1900 to 72.6 in 1990. For US black males the increase is from 32.5 in 1900 to 66.00 in 1990 (Thompson, 1994). Increasing numbers of older American males are benefiting from a general 'quality-of-life advantage' in terms of income. As a group, they have more disposable income than younger men, have fewer time/work demands on them than younger men and have greater autonomy than younger men (Lazer and Shaw, 1987). In both the US and the UK the over-fifties, at least those with the income and cultural capital, are increasingly being recognized as the main beneficiaries of a more relaxed if not hedonistic attitude to life; not growing old quietly and gracefully but as self-indulgent pleasure-seekers (ESRC, 2000; Thompson, 1994).

However, there are other sides to this equation. In the UK over a third of men over fifty, but below pension age, have no paid work. Men aged 50–64 are between two and three times as likely to die of a heart attack or stroke as are women of the same age (ONS, 1999). More men over fifty are living alone following divorce or separation, and, as a consequence, many of them suffer financial hardship, medical problems and loneliness (ONS, 1997; see also Sabo and Gordon, 1995). Recent research in the UK indicates that while those men in professions and management can generally look forward to an affluent early retirement, men outside this privileged cohort may experience growing social and psychological problems (ESRC, 2000; ONS, 1999). And in both the US and the UK older men of colour are particularly disadvantaged, lacking access to the medical, economic and social benefits enjoyed by most older white men (Staples, 1995; Thompson, 1994; ESRC, 2000).

The relationship between men, masculinities, health and illness connects directly with that of men and ageing. This is especially so in as much as men's health, both physical and mental, can undermine or reinforce their sense of being men. Deteriorating health can weaken men's association with dominant codes of masculinity, while robust health speaks of men's potency and mastery of situations. Similarly, men's expression of masculinity can have a direct influence on and correspondence with their health, ability to recover from illness, and, indeed, incidence of illness. In short, it is increasingly recognized that 'masculinity is among the more significant risk factors associated with men's illness' (Kimmel, 1995c: vii; see also Sabo and Gordon, 1995).

Apart from economics and health, a further and related key variable in the ability of older men to manage later life transformations appears to lie in their sense of masculinity. In the US, research indicates that the older man who has 'internalised traditional masculinity, creates stresses for himself by his inability to acknowledge dependency on the help of others' (Solomon and Szwabo, 1994: 56). Similarly, those men, of all ethnic groups, who are able and prepared to let go of a desire to master situations can derive enormous life satisfaction and positive morale from assuming more carefree nurturing roles, particularly as grandparents (Thomas, 1994). Although mortality rates for older men are higher than for older women across the Western world, there is evidence that older men's friendships with other men are one of the key factors in lowering the risk of mortality in all ethnic groups (Adams, 1994). It also appears, perhaps not as a surprise, that those men able and prepared to engage fully in relationships, either marital or otherwise, benefit from increased emotional well-being, experience less depression and enjoy higher self-esteem (Keith, 1994).

Macro changes within Western culture have helped trigger a new gaze on older men, and while very few can aspire to be, or wish to be, a Sean Connery or a David Bowie, more men are drawing on such media icons to challenge the stereotypes of ageing that have long held sway. The masculinities that ensue from such profound social transformations cannot be predicted. Nevertheless, as always, whatever ways of being a man and senses of masculinity do emerge will be heavily mitigated by factors of class, economics, culture, ethnicity and, not least, health. In sum, it is evident that older men are an important and emerging research focus within the sociology of masculinity, offering opportunities for better understanding the complex relationship between masculinities and embodiment.

Summary

This chapter has explored the male body as a critical, though contested, site for the inculcation and practice of masculinities. Recognizing that no male body exists in a singular, complete form, it is argued that in order to appreciate the centrality of the male body to masculine formations, it is necessary to understand the multiplicity of male embodiment and the complex ways in which masculinities come to materialize through men's physical presence in the world. A key aspect of this presence of the male body concerns how maleness relates to space, movement, posture and presentation. The male body can be understood as a fluid and shifting materiality, invested through numerous truths and knowledges, the most powerful of which purport to locate the male body as grounded in an unchanging biological essence. However, drawing on the work of Iris Marion Young and Judith Butler, it is argued that the male body, while symbolically located in the political category of men, is a discursive enterprise, made real only through the contested powers that mark it.

Of the numerous theoretical tools that theorists might usefully deploy in the pursuit of the male body, the concept of the panoptic or authoritative gaze, discussed here, is only one. Its deployment does, however, enable us to see the multiplicity of gazes, their different authorities, and how the exercise of power is partly legitimated through the gaze and its reconstitution by the discursive subject. Thus the gaze is not simply about reifying bodies; the gaze politicizes bodies, rendering them into numerous political fields of truth and knowledge, of which race, sexuality and age are but three.

FURTHER READING

Featherstone, M., Hepworth, M. and Turner, B. S. (eds) (1991) *The Body: Social Process and Cultural Theory*. London: Sage.

Hall, S. (ed.) (1997) *Representation: Cultural Representations and Signifying Practices*. London: Sage, in association with the Open University Press.

Messner, M. A. and Sabo, D. F. (eds) (1990) *Sport, Men, and the Gender Order*. Champaign, Ill.: Human Kinetics.

Price, J. and Shildrick, M. (eds) (1999) *Feminist Theory and the Body: A Reader*. Edinburgh: Edinburgh University Press.

Scott, S. and Morgan, D. (eds) (1993) *Body Matters*. London: The Falmer Press.

7

Desires of the Masculine Subject

The aim of this book has been to provide the reader with a comprehensive discussion of the key themes constituting the sociology of masculinity, while at the same time signalling new directions in the critical study of men. Throughout, I have been concerned to question not only essentialist accounts of men and masculinity, but also positivist, reductionist thinking within first- and second-wave writings of the sociology of masculinity. As I have tried to illustrate, since the late 1980s there have been profound and important developments in feminist scholarship, particularly in respect of poststructuralist and postmodernist theories. Yet too little of this work has permeated through to the sociology of masculinity. As a consequence one can concur with Petersen when he notes that 'the major challenges to thinking about the masculine have originated not with the cadres of "men's studies" scholars and "masculinity" researchers, but with those working in other areas' (1998: 125).

As Petersen indicates, if the sociology of masculinity is to become a fully fledged arm of feminist theory then it is now necessary to engage with the insights offered by poststructuralist thinkers such as Michel Foucault; moreover, to then move his theories forward as a (pro)feminist agenda in the forthright and imaginative way undertaken by feminists such as Judith Butler, Luce Irigaray, Susan Hekman, Jana Sawicki, Caroline Ramazanoglu, Nancy Fraser and Ann Game. Yet Foucault's work is not the last word in poststructuralist and postmodernist thinking. The works of writers such as

Jacques Lacan, Jacques Derrida, Paul Ricoeur, Pierre Bourdieu, Jean-François Lyotard, Gilles Deleuze and Felix Guattari present immense challenges to conventional understandings of power, identity and gender. Feminist theoreticans such as Chantal Mouffe (1996), Rosi Braidotti (1991), Julia Kristeva (1986), Elizabeth Grosz (1990), Lois McNay (2000), Chris Weedon (1991), Diane Elam (1994), Seyla Benhabib (1997) and Linda Nicholson (1990) are just a few of those who recognize the critical opportunities afforded by such scholarship (see also Buchanan and Colebrook, 2000). Consequently, in appropriating the often 'gender blind' theories of prominent male thinkers, and reforming them through a feminist/womanist scrutiny, these and other feminist scholars are sharpening the cutting edge of sociological enquiry. The challenge is now for 'masculinity researchers' to support such scholarship by doing the same.

This final chapter is offered, then, as a contribution to the debates instigated and under development by third-wave feminist scholars. However, it is not an attempt at closure, for if there is one insight we can draw from poststructuralism it is that knowledge and understanding, particularly about gender, cannot be ended, completed, concluded. Like identity, knowledge is always in process. It changes, almost inevitably without individuals being aware of it. Nevertheless, in sketching connections between men, masculinity and identity it is hoped that this chapter will make some contribution to third-wave profeminist scholarship, thereby opening up further avenues for research into the identity work of the masculine subject.

The chapter is structured so as to explore three key interrelated concepts that, it is suggested here, may be usefully deployed in further analysis of men's identity work and its relationship to being masculine. The first section provides a fuller conceptualization of the masculine subject (see chapter 3), notably in regard to Judith Butler's notion of performativity. Primarily drawing on the theories of Gilles Deleuze and Felix Guattari, the second section introduces the concept of a masculine ontology. The third section draws on the work of Lacan, Foucault, and Deleuze and Guattari to suggest that 'the desire to be' is the immanent condition of being (male and masculine). In concluding, the chapter considers the implications for feminist agendas of recognizing males as gendered, fluid, multiple, but ultimately political identities, rendered into being through the ontological desires of the masculine subject.

I recognize that many of the concepts under discussion in this chapter are less accessible than those arising from first- and second-wave feminist theories and explored earlier in this book. Nevertheless, like many who have grappled with poststructuralist analysis, I consider that the fruits of the labour significantly outweigh the cost. Therefore, I hope those readers less familiar with poststructuralist analysis not only achieve some purchase on the following debates, but also find the issues sufficiently stimulating to undertake further exploration.

The masculine subject

In poststructuralist terms there is no individual who exists outside of discourse. Yet discourses are not benign. They speak of privileged knowledges and ways of thinking about the world. So although the individual is a discursive subject, it cannot be a neutral one. For in taking up discourses as 'practices of self-signification', acts of performativity are undertaken (Butler, 1993, 1999). These acts posit not only a series of identities on the subject; they serve to locate that subject in associated regimes of power/knowledge. Through the 'repetition, sometimes ritualistic repetition, of normalized codes' (Bell, 1999: 3), identity emerges from abstraction into the social world, thus enabling the subject (man, woman) to take their place in a given 'community'. For example, when the pregnant woman undergoes an ultrasound scan to reveal the sex and well-being of the unborn child, she is subjecting the foetus to a process of identity work. It is not so much that the sex of the child is revealed; it is that the child is positioned in a discursive power regime as soon as the term 'male' or 'female' is pronounced upon it. From the moment of birth at least, the sexed child is then rendered unto a gender, albeit one that is largely conditional upon the prevailing discourses circulating the cultural and social spaces into which the child is born.

Such knowledges and 'truths' as surround the growing child are not fixed and secure; they are under constant movement, particularly in the postmodern age when all that once appeared solid increasingly appears contingent. Yet the child, as with all discursive subjects, must emerge into the world and take his/her place as an individual. He/she must take up an identity/identities, but cannot do this with absolute choice; they must take up those ways of being that are readily available, indeed which inculcate their very sense of self as being a sexual–gendered person. For those subjects rendered male, the discourses most likely to be placed at their disposal are masculine in their signification. In this way, a masculine subject emerges into the world. For as we assume the male/boy/man (discursive subject) to be masculine, so the discursive subject (male/boy/man) assumes themselves to be masculine. It is in this moment of assumption, and the circulatory arrangement that configures it, that the masculine subject is ushered into existence.

I suggest that it is the paradoxical 'persistence and instability' (Butler, 1993) of this arrangement that is at the heart of gender power and being. For the masculine subject has materialized from what was, prior to the scan in the example given, an 'it', an apolitical, neutral, disembodied presence. At the moment the 'it' is gazed upon, so a set of knowledges, codes and protocols are placed upon it, bringing forth a sexed–gendered being. From this moment onwards dominant cultural knowledges and truths come into play, not least concerning how to live and perform as a (heterosexual) male. To be sure, the masculine subject has the capacity to reconstitute itself in various forms and, as most parents know, it is impossible to predict the adult from the child. Nevertheless, without undertaking the physical and legal transformation of gender reassignment (see chapter 1), the discursive subject remains, fundamentally, male/man, a masculine subject.

The concept of the masculine subject is useful, then, for two reasons. First, it highlights the multiple discursivity that posits individuality on the subject, while also acknowledging the performative character of this constitution. There is no individuality prior to the discourses of sex and gender going to work on the subject and being taken up by the subject. Whatever is meant by the term 'masculine', in any cultural–social setting, is spoken of in terms of the male. The connection is made for us, it is assumed. It is presented as given. The dualistic ordering of Western thought and language underpins this association, in the process positing essential differences upon male and female (Lloyd, 1984; Petersen, 1998). Such knowledge formations have a powerful conditioning effect on the subjectivity of the individual, indeed on the embodied materiality of the individual, with the result that, in most societies, male/man/masculinity inevitably connects to ways of talking about males and males talking (for examples, see Johnson and Meinhof, 1997; also Cornwall and Lindisfarne, 1994).[1] Thus, the subjectivity of the male is lived out through a masculine gauze/gaze, a way of being in and seeing the world which, at its most fundamental, is not female/girl/woman. For the researcher into gender and masculinity it is necessary, then, to enter those places inhabited by men to discover how masculinities are acted out and understood in particular localized settings; but in so doing, remaining cognizant of the fact that what one is 'seeing' is only a small part of a masculine subject's repertoire of masculinities – not to assume, for example, that the form of masculinity on display at a football match inevitably and directly correlates to the forms of masculinity displayed, by the same subject, at work or in the family setting.

The second benefit associated with the concept of the masculine subject is that it critically connects 'man' as a political category with masculine identity work. In so doing, this connection exposes the political implications of masculine-orientated performativity. To be sure, the self is fragmented, multiple and contingent, our identities being processual within subject positions rather than being singular and accomplishable in any final, closed sense (see Mouffe, 1992; Hollway, 1989; also Gutterman, 2001). Nevertheless, it has been a clear theme of this book that masculinities are not simply myths or illusions, but discourses invested with political dimensions, not least in respect of the different materialities that arise for most women and men across virtually all social arenas. The material actuality of masculinities emerges from the presence of the political categories of woman and man. In turn, the presence of these political categories sustains their materiality. However, the power that configures these categories is not structural and unchanging but circulatory and discursive (see chapter 3). Following Assiter (1996) there is, then, the recognition that woman and man exist as embodied politicized categories, or, in Foucauldian terms, as sites of power/knowledge relations (also Bailey, 1993; Francis, forthcoming).

The use of the term 'masculine subject' enables us to interrogate the practices of identity work that arise from the category 'men' without reducing men to a prediscursive, essential identity. We can speak of masculinity in a particular locale; we can recognize its character and form. Moreover, we can do this without positing biologically essential differences to woman and man. In this way it becomes possible to explore masculinities as a constantly moving array of discursive practices, languages, behaviours, while also understanding 'men' as a more stable political category. By using the term 'masculine subject' neither man nor masculinity are (unintentionally) reified through critique; yet neither is the political significance of man (and woman) lost within a relativistic fudge. What is put under scrutiny is the material and power consequences arising from the practices of gender signification undertaken by discursive subjects.

Moreover, in identifying the practices of the masculine subject we do not confuse them with the practices of the feminine subject. For women cannot be masculine in any essential sense. Certainly, they can take up those practices, languages and behaviours that are considered masculine, but that is not the same as being a masculine subject. As feminine subject, girl/woman exists in a different political category to boy/man and, as such, is invested with a different set of knowledges and truths. As has been discussed, such epistemologies are formed out of the *lived experience* of being a discursive feminine subject; it is not essentially given, nor is it predictable. Woman's knowledge of the world is not ingrained through them by nature, and such knowledges/practices are not taken up by an, a priori knowing, sovereign subject – woman. Women (like men) are part of an 'epistemic community', grounded not in biology but in universalism; the universal experiences of being a feminine subject in a configuration of political categories (Assiter, 1996). Consequently, it is more accurate to say that 'being masculine' is, for women, a form of femininity. The discursive subject may take up multiple forms of self-expression, but such expressions, no matter how much they may contraindicate dominant gender stereotypes, do not, in themselves, remove the individual from a political category.

Masculine ontology

Masculine ontology is described herein as the pursuit of being and becoming masculine by the masculine subject. The search for ontological security is not confined to men but is a necessary aspect of being and becoming in the world for all subjects. However, as will now be discussed, it is possible to conceptualize the pursuit of masculine identification by males as a gendered quest, in which case it becomes more appropriate to term it a masculine ontology.

It is taken as given that the self is multiple, unstable and contingent, that is non-authentic. Yet the sense that subjects have of being whole and grounded in their identity is strong. Drawing on the work of Harold Garfinkel, Giddens examines this phenomenon, in so doing identifying ontological security as the most important psychological tool for 'managing' the disorganization and disorder lurking beyond the 'trivial aspects of day-to-day action and discourse' (1991: 36). In this regard, the search for ontological security, and the subsequent minimization of existential anxiety that goes with it, becomes a driving force for all subjects as they work at 'going on' in social life (for examples and discussion, see Collier, 1998; MacInnes, 1998; Misztal, 1998). The absence of any biological root or inner self creates the conditions of possibility for dread and anxiety arising from the recognition of unpredictability and tenuous existence, conditions that can never be totally removed, only assuaged. In Nietzschean terms, the world of the self is in a 'constant state of flux and change in which no entities preserve a stable entity' (Bogue, 1996: 20). In such contingent circumstances all is relational and momentary, nothing is absolute. Yet it is precisely within such uncertainty that the subject is required to seek an 'authentic self'.

Developing this idea, Gilles Deleuze explores these ambiguities of being. Deleuze (1983) describes the Nietzschean 'will to power' as a will to become, an 'inner centre' of force that enables the body to be both differentiated and linked, spatially and temporally, to the social web. The central force being described here is one that drives and enables the 'eternal return' required in being and becoming an individual – male/boy/man. This never-ending process serves to affirm the body's entry into and place within the social (see also Deleuze and Guattari, 1977). However, this is not a prediscursive position, but a state only made coherent and concrete in the act itself, a continual act of becoming. It is through this non-cognizant pursuit of a coherent, authentic self that the subject achieves the sense of ontological security necessary for continued individualization. In Foucauldian terms, this identity work recognizes the capacity of the subject to 'act upon himself, in the technology of self' (Foucault, 1988b: 19). Thus the self is not seen as totally subsumed under external hegemonic pressures or ideologies, but comes to fashion an existence and being as a 'coherent entity', albeit in an otherwise incoherent landscape.

In this understanding of self and identity processes, man is no more and no less than the universal embodied differentiation that prefigures a political category and its related knowledges and myths. For man to be and become that very category of being requires, then, constant engagement in those discursive practices of signification that suggest masculinity. These practices are both extensive and symbolically connected. As this book has discussed, they will include, amongst others, embodiment, language, sexual practice, emotional expression, bondings, work and leisure practices, intimate engagements and ways of relating – violently and non-violently – to loved ones and others. The force that drives this psychological need for ontological security is the desire to minimize existential anxiety – what Weber describes as the 'unprecedented inner loneliness' surrounding us all (quoted in MacInnes, 1998: 13).

Unlike Giddens and Deleuze, neither of whom recognize the centrality of gender to this identity work, I suggest that ontology can usefully be prefixed by gender identification. Thus what is under discussion here is masculine ontology. The point is that the masculine subject is not innately male/man, it can only *become* this through being positioned in and positioning itself within those discourses that speak of and suggest maleness/masculinity. It is in the process of doing this that ontological insecurity is relieved. As was discussed above, the body is sexed and gendered at point of entry into the social. Thus gender remains the primary identification of the discursive subject, and 'man' remains the prior politicized category that the masculine subject, through practices of self-signification, calls into existence (*pace* Winnicott, 1974). 'Man' should be understood, then, as the central, possibly most stable, reference point for the masculine subject as it seeks to create and realize its own existence in an otherwise transient and unstable social milieu.

Desire to be (a man)

What follows is a very selective appropriation of the complex works of Deleuze, Guattari, Lacan and Foucault. The aim is to sketch some connections between masculine ontology and the desire to be in the world by the masculine subject. The emphasis is on recognizing the centrality of desire for the masculine subject as it pursues 'ideal' representations of masculinity.

The concept of desire being discussed here is not primarily one of libido and sexuality, but rather production (of self). Desire, in this context, is understood as a primary force, an unconscious activity that is independent of linguistic expression or interpretation (Bogue, 1996). Thus desire is not simply a discursively anchored need or lack, but a requirement *to be* in the social world, to become an individual, or male/man (Deleuze and Guattari, 1988). This interpretation of desire emphasizes the positive productive dynamics fundamental to being and becoming. Thus the desire to be that drives this is a drive beyond the unconscious. As Deleuze describes it:

> Desire, in short, shares many of the characteristics of the nomadic and anonymous singularities ... which traverse 'men, plants and animals independently of the matter of their individualization and form of their personality'. (Deleuze, 1969: 61, quoted in Bogue, 1996: 89)

This understanding places desire as an instinct, beyond the social, as the 'immanent plane of existence' (Deleuze, 1990: 95). This removes the dichotomies between essence and existence, and between cognitive intent and the 'free-floating subject'. For desire can be understood as both a precondition of existence and as mediated by the conditions of its own production. In Butler's terms, desire can be understood as 'the drive [which is] indissociable from its cultural articulation' (1995: 248). A way of appreciating what is meant here is to see desire as the force that drives a baby to crawl/ walk, communicate, and from there on to apply such actions in increasingly sophisticated, yet learnt, fashion. These are fundamental aspects of being. However, they are always undertaken in particular social and cultural environments. And it is this specificity that serves to convert the 'desire to be' into 'social being'. As an 'ontological effect' desire is the point at which a sense of wholeness is made possible; the endless experiencing of events, relations and becomings, all requiring a degree of negotiation, re-referencing and accommodating by the discursive subject (for elaboration, see Goodchild, 1996).

If the work of Deleuze and Guattari has been useful in helping to illuminate the complexities of identity as 'desiring production', the writings of Lacan and Foucault stress the importance of recognition and reflection in self-production. For Lacan, meaning and subjectivity emerge only through discourse, being dependent on language and the 'chains of signification' that define reality for the subject (Lacan, 1977). Again, the question emerges, 'How can I know myself?' For Lacan, this question cannot be answered through recourse to an inner quest, but can be explored only through the subject's immersion and interaction in the social. Particularly important here is Lacan's concept of 'dialectic of recognition' (1977). Lacan argues that we can only obtain some sense of ourselves as coherent entities and identities in the gaze of others, how others respond to us, and in our perceptions of how we think others see us (for discussion, see Sarup, 1993). Thus desire arises as a condition and consequence of non-being; 'desire desires the recognition of another individual in order to know himself' (Leather, 1983: 109). In this pursuit of being and becoming, desire becomes mediated by the ideal(ized) representations of gender that gravitate towards the discursive subject. In sum, for the masculine subject to become a man, it must appropriate the 'ideal' meanings of manhood circulating within that subject's particular cultural setting and 'communities'.[2]

While there are important differences between the works of Deleuze and Lacan in respect of an understanding of desire, there are commonalities. The one that concerns us here is the recognition that the individual is an illusion, reified and reifiable only in social immersion and representation. As Sarup describes it: 'I can never be totally defined nor can I escape all definition. I am the quest for myself' (1993: 13). The emptiness and absence implied by this statement also resonate with the work of Nietzsche and Foucault, both of whom considered the individual to be lacking any underlying truth. From this we can see that the individual's very presence in the social is both a condition and a consequence of the social, a point that problematizes any idea that the individual and the social are separate entities (see chapter 5). What Deleuze and Lacan are stressing is the symbiosis of the subject–social, and the centrality of desire to this – a force beyond cognition, reason, rationality.

Similarly, for Foucault, the possibilities for self-creation are, in part, enabled by the desire of the subject to fashion and create their own selves. In this reading, desire is understood to be simultaneously an internal and external effect of discipline and the knowledge formations that create meaning for individuals. So although man exists in a political category of powerful knowledges purporting to give him meaning, he is not an entirely empty vessel for submersion in

restricted discourses. As Foucault argues, the self 'is not given to us
... we have to create ourselves as a work of art' (1991: 351).

As numerous feminist scholars have noted, the specific insights of
Lacan, Foucault and Deleuze can be most useful for feminist scholarship. Recognizing this, I would suggest that they also have particular insights to offer in terms of understanding men and
masculinities. As discussed, Lacan, Foucault and Deleuze all posit an
ontological dimension to desire: a desire to be, to become, to exist as
a social actor. Clearly, this concept connects with the notion of a masculine ontology. For the desire of the otherwise transient discursive
subject is a desire to be an individual, to be recognized, emergent in
the social world. Yet this individual is not ungendered; it has a sex
and gender posited on to it at entry into the social space. The taking
up of the practices of masculinity subsequently made available to the
emergent masculine subject becomes the 'fashioning of self' described
by Foucault. Thus the question is not whether this is a masculine
subject, but what form the masculine subject takes in the social
world, which discourses will be engaged in, inculcated, taken up by
the subject in its pursuit of identity validation and individualization.
This process is undoubtedly eased and facilitated by language and the
linguistic strategies available to the masculine subject in its pursuit of
identity (see Kiesling, 2001).

In no sense are 'man', 'masculine subject' or 'masculine ontology'
grounded or foundational. They are, I suggest, coexisting and self-
sustaining elements in the subject's endless cycle of construction and
maintenance of its gender identity. The one element of constancy is
in the term 'man', which, it is argued, exists as a product of historically specific power/knowledge relations; an embodied political category, signified by the dualistic ordering of knowledge that permeates
the social world.

Masculinity, then, is indivisible from the category man. One sustains the other; masculinity being the discursive framework that man
inhabits and from which he subjectively engages the social. As man
does not exist as a foundational entity, he can only be made real
through discursive expression and through engaging in the cultural
practices that suggest manhood. This is the ontological quest of the
masculine subject. As Sarup puts it: 'discourse is the agency whereby
the subject is produced and the existing order sustained' (1993: 24).
Thus, following Lacan and Foucault, for the subject to 'create itself
as a (masculine) work of art' it must reach for those ideal(ized) rep-

resentations of gender that surround it. These idealized expressions will remain just that: ideal, largely symbolic and out of permanent grasp. Consequently, despite its importance for the subject's ontology, being masculine must be constantly engaged with, worked at and explored. As a fundamental yet illusory presence, masculinity remains momentary, relational, elusive and open to disruption. The subject can never know oneself as a man, nor indeed feel masculine, other than through the gaze and reception of the Other and through its own narratives of self, which serve to render it individualized (Ricoeur, 1992). This process has profound consequences for the subjectivity of the individual and for the political dimensions of being male, not least because, as McNay succinctly puts it; *'individuals act in certain ways because it would violate their sense of being to do otherwise'* (2000: 80; my emphasis).

Implications and conclusion

Drawing on third-wave feminist and poststructuralist perspectives, this chapter has argued for an understanding of men and masculinities as non-divisible factors in a self-sustaining cycle of gender individualization. The entry of the subject into the social marks the point at which the prior codes of sex and gender signification 'go to work'. It is through the inculcation of multiple discourses across subject positions that the subject becomes aligned within a prior politicized category: male/man. At this point the subject can be identified as a masculine subject. That is, through the immanent search for existence and being (male/man), the subject engages with and works on the historically and culturally mediated codes of masculinity that prevail around it. As these codes are already placed at the disposal of the subject, they offer a ready means of identity signification. This search for being (male/man) is termed herein as masculinist ontology. My argument is that this identity work, in turn, sustains the political category man. The subject is not in any foundational sense man or masculine. It can only come to some sense of being man through masculine identity work: masculinist ontology.

In order to understand the inner force that drives the ontological search of the otherwise transient and amorphous self, this chapter has briefly discussed the works of Lacan, Foucault and Deleuze and

Guattari, in particular their privileging of desire as a fundamental element of self creation. In the absence of any biological anchor, desire is understood to exist as the internal engine of the discursive subject. Thus desire is elementary to each subject's identity work. However, it is work that is already largely predicated and prefigured by the fact of gender being impelled upon the subject from first exposure to the social.

A number of implications arise from the understanding of men and masculinities elaborated here. In terms of any feminist agenda of changing men there appear to be both possibilities and problematics. Possibilities clearly exist in respect of the social being a discursive environment, across which play contesting and contrasting regimes of power/knowledge. These are under constant shift as subjects contribute in knowing and unknowing ways to the discursive constitution of these regimes. While this is intersubjective micro-negotiation, the consequence is, as Foucault argues, to create the conditions under which the macro comes to be. Thus change is not only possible; it is inevitable, mainly through the sheer dynamic of this process. In this respect, masculinity, while it may be identifiable through certain patterns of behaviour, attitudes and practices, is always subject to change and subjective appropriation. In Butler's terms (1990) there is always the potential for disruption and subversion of 'normative ideals' (Petersen, 1998: 130), discursive identity work being the fulcrum through which this resistance is exercised. Moreover, despite the prevailing knowledge dualism, meanings associated with masculinity will continue to be specific to times and spaces.

The problematic lies in the universality of gender identity. As Assiter argues, to ignore the universality of women and men is to deny a fundamental reality. Despite the absence of any biological grounding to people's identities, the categories woman and man are too accessible, powerful and seductive to be removed by the political will of any group or social movement. Feminists have to live with these categories, and live them out as gendered individuals. It is a personal/political tension that many women, and some men, are only too familiar with. Gherardi (1995) describes it as a 'schizogenic' existence.

It is possible, then, to envisage future men adopting new behaviours and practices, but not to stop being men – though, as was discussed in chapter 2, some profeminist men do claim this as an aspiration. Nevertheless, the reality is that other than recourse to surgery for those few who wish it, men will remain. Indeed, so long as 'woman' remains a political category, so will 'man', and vice versa. As numerous feminist scholars have indicated, this embodied dualism is reinforced in language, philosophy, thought and practice. There can be no possibility of the sex/gender dichotomy disappearing, though the ideal representations that configure it are under constant movement and (re)negotiation across countless cultural sites.

The point remains, then, to what extent can men engage in 'alternative' practices (of self), especially those that might be considered less problematic for women, for society as a whole and, not least, for themselves? While it is clearly impossible to predict individual change, the desire to be male/man is not going to disappear. The vast majority of those subjects identified a priori as males will, with some inevitability, pursue an 'authentic' male self. As this chapter has suggested, this desire to be, which is immanent to the subject's existence, emerges as a search for a masculinist ontology. Thus the masculine subject is, by definition, engaged in the reification of 'man', moving man from abstraction to reality – making man real. In the pursuit of this aim, those gendered, idealized (masculine) codes of being that the subject finds at its disposal are likely to be taken up as practices of self-signification. It is in the inculcation and rearticulation of these codes that the masculine subject can be identified and man is brought forth into the world. This is the eternal being and becoming that Deleuze and Guattari describe.

To expect the masculine subject to knowingly engage in contraindicators, or 'feminine' codes of being, is, then, problematic. While a fundamental element of the masculine subject's desire for being (a man) is to have this identity validated by the gaze and reception of others, this process of self validation should *not be seen as solely a desire for approval*. On the contrary, the gender dichotomy is founded on simultaneous acceptance/rejection. One begets the other. Rejection or negation of the masculine by feminists, for example, may, somewhat perversely, further polarize many men's behaviour. As Lacan argues, to be accepted as masculine/male/man involves rejection as feminine/female/woman. Not only is (female) disapproval not necessarily a threat to the masculine subject's sense of self; it may, in some situations, actually strengthen it. This process of individualization can be understood, then, to invoke, if not the flight from, certainly the avoidance of the feminine for many males.

At the very least there is ambiguity in respect of sexuality and gender, if only because ideal representations of man/masculinity are not grounded and inevitable. The identity work of the masculine subject requires them to learn, assimilate and perform that which is fundamentally illusory, but which ultimately rests on the approving-disapproving gaze of the Other.

Clearly not all masculine subjects will relate to gender codes in identical ways. Other variables will operate here, particularly around cultural capital, ethnicity, race, age and sexual orientation. Therefore, the subject's engagement with ideal representations will inevitably be mediated by the interpretation brought to bear on this exercise. Of equal consideration will be the various public and private sites within which masculine subjects perform and 'find' themselves, together with the contrasting subject positions that constitute their larger frame of reference. For many masculine subjects any flight from the feminine is immanent to their existence as men and can be 'safely' expressed as such in their particular public and private realms. An example would be those men existing in cultural sites where a traditional sexual division of labour prevails, and/or where misogyny and possibly violence towards women are considered acceptable behaviours. For other men, any avoidance of the feminine will be touched with ambivalence and ambiguity, a situation that may require 'resolving' through reflexive negotiation within work and relationship settings (for similar discussion, see Beck and Beck-Gernsheim, 1995). An example here would be those men who are househusbands, or similar men adopting less rigid, less traditional codes of masculine behaviour.

Of further consideration are the multiple expressions of masculinity now present in this postmodern age. In all Western countries any metanarratives of masculinity that once prevailed have been put under question by feminism, leading to contrasting responses by men (see chapter 2). While this offers opportunities for increasing numbers of masculine subjects to acquire ontological purchase and gender validation through 'non-traditional' gender performativities, for others such explicit multiplicity is profoundly threatening. It may produce in some masculine subjects a sense of being under 'siege', a condition that many men now appear to express through membership of antifeminist political movements such as the Promise Keepers and the mythopoetic men's movement. Such masculinist polarization is also apparent in the intransigent behaviour of young (insecure) males (Mac an Ghaill, 1994) and in the proliferation of a laddish youth culture (see, for example, Gouch and Edwards, 1998). However, it should be noted that in all these radicalized expressions of masculinity, as in others, there is invariably some element of approving female gaze. In this respect, forms of femininity can be seen to collude in the reification of masculinities, reminding us that the conditions of gendered ontological quest are not confined to men.

While there are political dimensions to all forms of masculine expression, I have argued that these expressions cannot simply be understood as a cognitive search for material advantage. Indeed, the likelihood is that males' extreme 'flight from the feminine' is increasingly disadvantageous materially, certainly in education terms (see, for example, Connell, 2000; Francis, 1998; Whitehead, 1998). One can conclude from this that while there is no singular crisis of masculinity, being a man is perhaps more complicated now; certainly there appear to be more ways of being (a man). Moreover, emergent discourses of gender increasingly pressure the masculine subject to negotiate, reflect and consider his position as man, and to be more aware of how one's masculinist practices and assumptions might impact on others and self. In saying this, the concept of the masculine subject does not in any way excuse, or attempt to 'justify', men's oppressive, violent behaviours. Indeed, with the 'natural' explanations for men's practices now clearly dismissed as simplistic (see chapter 1), poststructuralist theory offers the way forward, I suggest, for connecting the personal to the political in ways that, up until now, only feminists have really tackled (for example, see Butler and Scott, 1992; Elam, 1994; Mouffe, 1996). Nevertheless, in endeavouring to understand often inexplicable (male) behaviour, it is necessary to recognize that the Promise Keepers (Messner, 1997), the 'macho lads' (Mac an Ghaill, 1994), the 'iron man' (Connell, 1990), the 'rugged individualist' (Roper, 1994) and the 'wild boys' (Collier, 1998) exist on an ontological plane as well as on an embodied one. Indeed, the two are irrevocably entwined.

To conclude, it would seem that change in men's subjectivities and practices is fraught with uncertainty and unpredictability. However, possibilities for positive change are apparent, not least because discourses of gender are under constant revision. The very work of feminist scholarship can be seen, then, to go a significant way to questioning, (re)forming and interrogating dominant gendered meanings and associations, in the process disrupting that which is largely performed by individuals, and understood by society, as natural, absolute and true.

FURTHER READING

Buchanan, I. and Colebrook, C. (eds) (2000) *Deleuze and Feminist Theory*. Edinburgh: Edinburgh University Press.

Grosz, E. (1990) *Jacques Lacan: A Feminist Introduction*. London: Routledge.

Hall, S. and du Gay, P. (eds) (2000) *Questions of Cultural Identity*. London: Sage.

Petersen, A. (1998) *Unmasking the Masculine: 'Men' and 'Identity' in a Sceptical Age*. London: Sage.

Weedon, C. (1991) *Feminist Practice and Poststructuralist Theory*. Oxford: Blackwell.

Notes

INTRODUCTION

1 The term postmodernity is used throughout the book to signal that, in Western countries, the prevailing social, philosophical, religious and cultural discourses have moved on from Enlightenment-inspired modernity. Thus, postmodernity identifies a historical shift, not a complete division or separation of philosophies and ideas, but sufficient distinction to justify the term 'post-'. In the West, the postmodern age can be seen in the promotion of multiplicity, individualism and secularism, and in an ironic, even cynical, approach towards ideologies. Replacing belief in the inevitability of God-given linear social progress and the universality of peoples, postmodernity opens up differences and exposes contingency. One of the key writers on postmodernity is Jean-François Lyotard. Charles Lemert sums up Lyotard's concept of postmodernity, as follows:

> Modernity is that culture which believes certain *metanarratives*, or widely shared stories, about the value and 'truth' of science, and truth itself . . . postmodernity is that culture in which those metanarratives are no longer considered completely legitimate and, thus, are not universally held to be completely credible. (Lemert, 1997: 39; original emphasis)

In this understanding, masculinities might be considered postmodern, not least because the prevailing discourses informing them are no longer rooted in the historical period of modernity. Moreover, as many feminists have noted (for example, Nicholson, 1990; also Nicholson and Seidman, 1996), it is one of the characteristics of the postmodern that what were previously understood to be unshakable belief systems and 'truths' are now rendered contingent and open to scrutiny; in which case, contemporary understandings of men and masculinities, indeed the scrutiny brought to bear by feminist/profeminist scholarship, certainly fits in this perspective.

CHAPTER 1 MASCULINITY – ILLUSION OR REALITY?

1 Gender or sex reassignment denotes the surgical changing of a transsexual's biological sex. A transsexual is a person who experiences their gender identity as incongruous with the anatomical reality and seeks to resolve this conflict through reassignment surgery. This treatment is highly successful. The term transsexual can refer to pre- and postoperative men and women, though once surgery is completed the identity of male and female is preferred. In the US, a legal change of sex involves chiefly a change in the birth certificate. In Europe, the process is more complicated, though under European Law discrimination on the grounds of gender reassignment is now illegal. See *www.pfc.org.uk* for detailed information concerning sex reassignment together with legal implications. For discussion, see Bornstein (1995); More and Whittle (1999).

2 For detailed discussion of the Human Genome Project, see *Nature* (2001); *Science Magazine* (2001); also *www.nature.com* and *www.sciencemag.org*.

3 Throughout the book the term 'Western' denotes North American, European and Australasian countries.

4 Brannon (1976) described 'our culture's blueprint of manhood' as: The Big Wheel, Give 'em Hell, The Sturdy Oak and No Sissy Stuff.

5 In the 1960s Robert J. Stoller and his colleagues established the UCLA (University of California at Los Angeles) Gender Identity Research Clinic in order to establish the precise formation of 'core gender identity'. In a challenge to the then dominance of Freudian theory, Stoller et al. concluded that an infant's perception of themselves as boy or girl was established between one and two years of age (for discussion, see Buhle, 1998).

6 Sandra Bem (1974) established the two-scale Bem Sex Role Inventory (BSRI) questionnaire to divide US students into four groups: masculine only, feminine only, androgynous (scoring both masculine and feminine) and undifferentiated (scoring neither) (for recent discussion, see Hofsted, 1998).

7 David Tacey, in his 1997 book *Remaking Men: Jung, Spirituality and Social Change*, provides an important, sophisticated Jungian analysis of men and masculinity.

8 See *www.gendercide.org/case_infanticide.html* for information on female infanticide.

CHAPTER 2   THE PERSONAL AND THE POLITICAL

1 I also recognize that many countries and peoples actively supported the regimes of Nazi Germany and Afrikaner-led South Africa.
2 It was at Columbine High School, Littleton, Denver, that one of the worst 'rage crimes' by males took place. On Tuesday, 20 April, 2000, two 18-year-old male students shot dead fifteen schoolmates and teachers, before killing themselves. This crime followed previous US school shootings by young males at Jonesboro, Arkansas; West Paducah, Kentucky; Pearl, Mississippi; and Springfield, Oregon.
3 Despite the prominence of the simplistic 'male crisis' thesis, there is an extensive and excellent literature that examines, in detail, gender 'power plays' (Francis, 1998) in the classroom and how these come to inform boys' and girls' approaches to and experiences of education and schooling. For example: Arnot, David and Weiner (1999); Askew and Ross (1988); Epstein et al. (1999); Francis (1998, 2000); Lingard and Douglas (1999); Salisbury and Jackson (1996).
4 See Newburn and Stanko (1994) for an examination of the relationship between men, masculinities and crime.
5 For an example of antifeminist rhetoric, see *www.ihatefeminism.com*.
6 For details of profeminist groups and organizations, see Sweetman (1997). For profeminist information resources, research and networking, see CROME: *Critical Research on Men in Europe*, *www.cromenet.org*.

CHAPTER 3   POWER AND RESISTANCE

1 At this point the inherent tension between (feminist) poststructuralist and (feminist) structuralist notions becomes apparent; that is, how to retain a modernist feminist understanding of women as an oppressed group, with a postmodernist/poststructuralist recognition that there is no founding subject, merely a fragmented, contingent, multiple, differentiated discursive self, signified and enabled precisely through the exercise of power and resistance. For examples and discussion of this complex, but key, feminist debate, see Assiter (1996); Butler and Scott (1992); Game (1991); Hekman (1990, 1999); Francis (2000); Ramazanoglu (1993); Segal (1999); Stanley (1997); Weedon (1991).

2 For elaboration and discussion of theories of the postmodern see Bauman
   (1994, 1997); Good and Velody (1998); Kumar (1995); Lemert (1997);
   Nicholson and Seidman (1996); Seidman (1996). For elaboration of
   feminist postmodernism, see Nicholson (1990). For elaboration and discussion of poststructuralist theory, see Sarup (1993); Weedon (1991);
   Game (1991).

CHAPTER 4   PUBLIC MEN

1 Lyotard's concept of 'performativity' refers to the postmodern condition
   within which the pursuit of, and belief in, 'efficiency' assumes its status
   as the single legitimizing measure of value and human worth, in the
   process taking precedence over subjective narratives. Thus the question
   is no longer asked, 'Is it true?', but, rather, 'What use is it?' Performativity encapsulates the functional and instrumental in an age when the
   pursuit of knowledge for its own sake is being displaced by the mercan-
   talization of knowledge – knowledge as a commercial/saleable commodity (for discussion, see Usher and Edwards, 1994).
2 I am pleased to record that an exception to this rule is the MBA offered
   in the management department at Keele University.

CHAPTER 5   PRIVATE MEN

1 Drawing on Ricoeur's analysis, Lois McNay summarizes the relationship
   between the self and narrative in the following way: 'The self has unity,
   but it is the dynamic unity of narrative which attempts to integrate permanence in time with its contrary, namely diverse, variability, disconti-
   nuity and instability. . . . Identity is neither completely in flux nor static:
   it has the dynamic unity of narrative configuration' (2000: 89).
2 Messner notes the high incidence of sexual assault by college males on
   women, quoting a report in the *Philadelphia Daily News* which stated
   that 'between 1983 and 1986, a US college athlete was reported for
   sexual assault an average of once every eighteen days' (1992: 101).

CHAPTER 6   MATERIALIZING MALE BODIES

1 Two of the earliest and most influential books to apply a sociological
   examination to the body are those by Turner (1984) and O'Neill (1985).
   See also Turner 1992.

2   Foucault defines genealogy as:

> a form of history which can account for the constitution of knowledges, discourses, domains of objects, etc., without having to make reference to a subject which is either transcendental in relation to the field of events or runs its empty sameness throughout the course of history. (1980: 117)

3   See Constantine-Simms (2001) for discussion of the 'greatest taboo' in black communities – homosexuality.
4   For example, 22 per cent of the 21,041 male finishers in the 1999 New York Marathon were aged over fifty, the eldest being ninety years old. Similarly, over 1,300 people over 60, most of them men, entered the 2000 London Marathon.
5   For details of American demographics for older people, see the Administration of Ageing website: *www.aoa.gov/aoa/STATS/profile/default.htm*

CHAPTER 7   DESIRES OF THE MASCULINE SUBJECT

1   As Scott Fabius Kiesling observes, 'comparatively little work has been published that focuses specifically on men's gender identity and the role of language in those identities' (2000: 1). However, the language males use is central to masculinities, not least because it provides a framework of understanding and connection for the masculine subject, thereby substantiating both individual and fraternal identities. Thus, men 'do gender' in part through taking up and reconstituting the language, vernacular and linguistic strategies that are seen to denote their membership of a given community of males (a political category). For further discussion, see Kiesling, 1998, 2000, 2001.
2   Like the work of Freud and Jung (see chapter 1), the work of Lacan has been both employed and dismissed by feminist scholars. Kristeva and Irigaray, for example, draw on Lacanian insights, particularly in respect of the 'interlocking domains of subjectivity, sexuality and language' (Grosz, 1990: 148). However, as Grosz goes on to discuss, there are important differences between those feminists who adhere to a Lacanian framework. Moreover, the possibilities of feminists utilizing Lacanian perspectives are clearly circumscribed by the phallocentric reductionism that pervades his understanding of a (masculinist) symbolic order.

Bibliography

Abdo, G. (2000) Hardline crackdown grips Iran, *The Guardian*, 1 May, p. 9.

Adam, B. (1990) *Time and Social Theory*. Cambridge: Polity.

Adam, B. D. (1977) A social history of gay politics, in: M. P. Levine (ed.), *Gay Men: The Sociology of Male Homosexuality*. New York: Harper & Row.

Adams, R. G. (1994) Older men's friendship patterns, in: E. H. Thompson, Jr (ed.), *Older Men's Lives*. Thousand Oaks, Calif.: Sage.

Afshar, H. (1998) *Islam and Feminisms: An Iranian Case Study*. London: Macmillan.

Allan, G. (ed.) (1999) *The Sociology of the Family: A Reader*. Oxford: Blackwell.

Almaguer, T. (1989) Chicano men: A cartography of homosexual identity and behaviour, in: M. S. Kimmel and M. A. Messner (eds), *Men's Lives*. Boston: Allyn and Bacon.

Altman, D. (1982) *The Homosexualisation of America*. Boston: Beacon.

Alumnajjed, M. (1998) *Women in Saudi Arabia Today*. London: Macmillan.

Amnesty International (1998a) *The International Criminal Court: Ensuring Justice for Women*. Amnesty International: London.

Amnesty International (1998b) *Annual Report: 1998*. Amnesty International: London.

Amnesty International (2000) *Annual Report: 2000*. Amnesty International: London.

Anthony, P. (1994) *Managing Culture*. Buckingham: Open University Press.

Archer, J. (ed.) (1994) *Male Violence*. London: Routledge.

Archer, J. and Lloyd, B. B. (1985) *Sex and Gender*. Cambridge: Cambridge University Press.

Archetti, E. (1994) Masculinity and football: The formation of national identity in Argentina, in: R. Giulianotti and J. Williams (eds), *Game without Frontiers: Football, Identity and Modernity*. Aldershot: Arena.

Armitage, J. (1977) *Man at Play: Nine Centuries of Pleasure Making*. London: Frederick Warner.

Arnot, M., David, M. and Weiner, G. (1999) *Closing the Gender Gap: Postwar Education and Social Change*. Cambridge: Polity.

Askew, S. and Ross, C. (1988) *Boys Don't Cry: Boys and Sexism in Education*. Milton Keynes: Open University Press.

Assiter, A. (1996) *Enlightened Women: Modernist Feminism in a Postmodern Age*. London: Routledge.

Baca-Zinn, M. (1982) Chicano men and masculinity, *The Journal of Ethnic Studies*, 10:2, pp. 29–44.

Bailey, J. (2000) Some meanings of 'the private' in sociological thought, *Sociology*, 34:3, pp. 381–401.

Bailey, M. E. (1993) Foucauldian feminism: contesting bodies, sexuality and identity, in: C. Ramazanoglu (ed.), *Up Against Foucault*. London: Routledge.

Bairner, A. (1999) Soccer, masculinity and violence in Northern Ireland: between hooliganism and terrorism, *Men and Masculinities*, 1:3, pp. 284–301.

Baker, A. and Boyd, T. (eds) (1997) *Out of Bounds: Sports, Media and the Politics of Identity*. Bloomington: Indiana University Press.

Baker, R. (1996) *Sperm Wars: The Science of the Sexes*. New York: BasicBooks.

Bakke, E. W. (1933) *The Unemployed Man*. London: Nisbet.

Ball, S. J. (ed.) (1990) *Foucault and Education: Disciplines and Knowledge*. London: Routledge.

Balsamo, A. (1999) Reading Cyborgs writing feminism, in: J. Wolmark (ed.), *Cybersexualities*. Edinburgh: Edinburgh University Press.

Barker, G., Loewenstein, I. and Riberio, M. (1995) Where the boys are: attitudes related to masculinity, fatherhood and violence toward women among low income adolescent males in Rio de Janeiro, Brazil. Mimeographed.

Barrett, F. J. (1996) The organizational construction of hegemonic masculinity: the case of the U.S. Navy, *Gender, Work and Organization*, 3:3, pp. 129–42.

Barrett, F. J. (2001) Gender strategies of women professionals: the case of the U.S. Navy, in: M. Dent and S. Whitehead (eds), *Managing Professional Identities*. London: Routledge.

Barrett, M. (1980) *Women's Oppression Today: Problems in Marxist Feminist Analysis.* London: Verso.

Barry, K. (1979) *Female Sexual Slavery.* Englewood Cliffs, NJ: Prentice Hall.

Barthes, R. (1982) *Mythologies.* Trans. A. Lavers. London: Paladin.

Bateson, P. and Martin, P. (2000) *Design for Life: How Behaviour Develops.* London: Jonathan Cape.

Bauman, Z. (1994) *Intimations of Postmodernity.* London: Routledge.

Bauman, Z. (1997) *Postmodernity and its Discontents.* Cambridge: Polity.

Beasley, C. (1999) *What is Feminism? An Introduction to Feminist Theory.* London: Sage.

Beauvoir, S. de (1973) [1953] *The Second Sex.* Trans. and ed. E. M. Parshley. New York: Vintage.

Beck, U. (1992) *The Risk Society: Towards a New Modernity.* London: Sage.

Beck, U. (1995) The reinvention of politics: towards a theory of reflexive modernization, in: U. Beck, A. Giddens and S. Lash, *Reflexive Modernization.* Cambridge: Polity.

Beck, U. (2000) *The Brave New World of Work.* Cambridge: Polity.

Beck, U. and Beck-Gernsheim, E. (1995) *The Normal Chaos of Love.* Cambridge: Polity.

Beechey, V. (1987) *Unequal Work.* London: Verso.

Bell, V. (1999) Performativity and belonging: an introduction, *Theory, Culture and Society,* 16:2, pp. 1–10.

Bem, S. L. (1974) The measurement of psychological androgyny, *Journal of Consulting and Clinical Psychology,* 42, pp. 155–62.

Benhabib, S. (1997) *Situating the Self.* Cambridge: Polity.

Benschop, Y. and Dooreward, H. (1998) Six of one and half a dozen of the other: the gender subtext of Taylorism and team-based work, *Gender, Work and Organization,* 5:1, pp. 5–18.

Berger, M., Wallis, B. and Watson, S. (eds) (1995) *Constructing Masculinity.* New York: Routledge.

Berry, C. and Jagose, A. (1996) Australian queer: editors' introduction, *Meanjin,* 55:1, pp. 5–11.

Bhabha, H. (1986) The other question, in: F. Barker (ed.), *Literature, Politics and Theory.* London: Methuen.

Bhasin, K. (1997) Gender workshops with men: experiences and reflections, in: C. Sweetman (ed.), *Men and Masculinities.* Oxford: Oxfam.

Biddulph, S. (1994) *Manhood: A Book About Setting Men Free.* Sydney: Finch.

Blackmore, J. (1997) Disciplining feminism: a look at gender-equity struggles in Australian higher education, in: L. Roman and L. Eyre (eds), *Dangerous Territories: Struggles for Difference and Equality.* New York: Routledge.

Blackmore, J. (1999) *Troubling Women: Feminism, Leadership and Educational Change*. Buckingham: Open University Press.

Bleys, R. C. (1996) *The Geography of Perversion: Male-to-Male Sexual Behaviour outside the West and the Ethnographic Imagination*. New York: New York University Press.

Blumer, H. (1969) *Symbolic Interactionism: Perspective and Method*. Englewood Cliffs, NJ: Prentice Hall.

Bly, R. (1990) *Iron John*. New York: Addison-Wesley.

Bogue, R. (1996) *Deleuze and Guattari*. London: Routledge.

Boh, K. (1989) European family life patterns – a reappraisal, in: K. Boh, M. Bak, C. Clason, M. Pankratova, J. Qvortrup, G. Sgritta and K. Waerness (eds), *Changing Patterns of European Family Life*. London: Routledge.

Bologh, R.W. (1990) *Love or Greatness: Max Weber and Masculine Thinking – A Feminist Inquiry*. London: Unwin Hyman.

Bordo, S. (1993) Feminism, Foucault and the politics of the body, in: C. Ramazanoglu (ed.), *Up Against Foucault*. London: Routledge.

Bornstein, K. (1995) *Gender Outlaws: On Men, Women, and the Rest of Us*. London: Vintage.

Bourdieu, P. (1977) *Outline of a Theory of Practice*. Trans. R. Nice. Cambridge: Cambridge University Press.

Bourdieu, P. (1984) *Distinction: A Social Critique of the Judgement of Taste*. Cambridge, Mass.: Harvard University Press.

Bowker, L. H. (ed.) (1998) *Masculinities and Violence*. Thousand Oaks, Calif.: Sage.

Braidotti, R. (1991) *Patterns of Dissonance*. Cambridge: Polity.

Brand, C. (1996) The colour of intelligence, *Times Higher Education Supplement*, 26 April, p. 19.

Brannon, R. (1976) The male sex role: our culture's blueprint for manhood and what it's done for us lately, in: D. David and R. Brannon (eds), *The Forty-Nine Percent Majority: The Male Sex Role*. Reading, Mass.: Addison-Wesley.

Brittan, A. (1989) *Masculinity and Power*. Oxford: Basil Blackwell.

Brod, H. (ed.) (1987) *The Making of Masculinities: The New Men's Studies*. Winchester, Mass.: Allen & Unwin.

Brod, H. (1994) Some thoughts on some histories of some masculinities: Jews and other others, in: H. Brod and M. Kaufman (eds), *Theorizing Masculinities*. Thousand Oaks, Calif.: Sage.

Brod, H. and Kaufman, M. (eds) (1994) *Theorizing Masculinities*. Thousand Oaks, Calif.: Sage.

Bruce, J., Lloyd, C. B. and Leonard, A., with Engle, P. L. and Duffy, N. (1995) *Families in Focus: New Perspectives on Mothers, Fathers and Children*. New York: Population Council.

Bruni, A. and Gherardi, S. (2001) Omega's story: the heterogeneous engineering of a gendered professional self, in: M. Dent and S. Whitehead (eds), *Managing Professional Identities*. London: Routledge.

Buchanan, I. and Colebrook, C. (eds) (2000) *Deleuze and Feminist Theory*. Edinburgh: Edinburgh University Press.

Buhle, M. J. (1998) *Feminism and its Discontents*. Cambridge, Mass.: Harvard University Press.

Burke, J. (2000) Love, honour and obey – or die, *The Observer*, 8 October, p. 10.

Burkitt, I. (1997) Social relationships and emotions, *Sociology*, 31:1, pp. 37–55.

Burris, B. H. (1996) Technocracy, patriarchy and management, in: D. L. Collinson and J. Hearn (eds), *Men as Managers, Managers as Men*. London: Sage.

Butler, J. (1990) *Gender Trouble: Feminism and the Subversion of Identity*. New York: Routledge.

Butler, J. (1993) *Bodies That Matter: The Discursive Limits of 'Sex'*. New York: Routledge.

Butler, J. (1995) Subjection, resistance, resignification: between Freud and Foucault, in: J. Rajchman (ed.), *The Identity in Question*. London: Routledge.

Butler, J. (1999) Revisiting bodies and pleasures, *Theory, Culture and Society* (special issue on 'Performativity and Belonging'), 16:2, pp. 11–20.

Butler, J. and Scott, J. W. (eds) (1992) *Feminists Theorize the Political*. New York: Routledge.

Cabinet Office (Women's Unit) (2000) *Women's Incomes over the Lifetime*. London: The Stationery Office.

Calas, M. and Smircich, L. (1992) Using the 'F' word: feminist theories and the social consequences of organizational research, in: A. Mills and P. Tancred (eds), *Gendering Organizational Analysis*. London: Sage.

Canaan, J. E. and Griffin, C. (1990) The new men's studies: part of the problem or part of the solution?, in: J. Hearn and D. H. J. Morgan (eds), *Men, Masculinities and Social Theory*. London: Routledge.

Carby, H. V. (1998) *Race Men*. Cambridge, Mass.: Harvard University Press.

Carrier, J. M. (1976) Cultural factors affecting urban Mexican male homosexual behaviour, *The Archives of Sexual Behaviour: An Interdisciplinary Research Journal*, 5:2, pp. 103–24.

Carrigan, T., Connell, R. W. and Lee, J. (1985) Toward a new sociology of masculinity, *Theory and Society*, 14, pp. 551–604.

Carrigan, T., Connell, B. and Lee, J. (1987) Hard and heavy: toward a new sociology of masculinity, in: M. Kaufman (ed.), *Beyond Patriarchy: Essays by Men on Pleasure, Power, and Change*. Toronto: Oxford University Press.

Casey, C. (1995) *Work, Self and Society: After Industrialism*. London: Routledge.

Castells, M. (1998) *The Information Age, Volume III: End of Millennium*. Oxford: Blackwell.

Chapkis, W. (1986) *Beauty Secrets*. London: Women's Press.

Chapple, C. L. (1998) Dow Corning and the silicone breast implant debacle: a case of corporate crime against women, in L. H. Bowker (ed.), *Masculinities and Violence*. Thousand Oaks, Calif.: Sage.

Charles, N. and Hughes-Freeland, F. (eds) (1996) *Practising Feminism: Identity, Difference, Power*. London: Routledge.

Cheal, D. (1999) The one and the many: modernity and postmodernity, in: G. Allan (ed.), *The Sociology of the Family: A Reader*. Oxford: Blackwell.

Cheng, C. (ed.) (1996) *Masculinities in Organizations*. Thousand Oaks, CA: Sage.

Cherrie, M. and Anzaldua, G. (eds) (1981) *This Bridge Called My Back: Writings by Radical Women of Color*. Watertown, Mass.: Persephone.

Chodorow, N. (1978) *The Reproduction of Mothering: Psychoanalysis and the Sociology of Gender*. Berkeley, Calif.: University of California Press.

Christian, H. (1994) *The Making of Anti-Sexist Men*. London: Routledge.

Christie, A. (ed.) (2001) *Men and Social Work*. Basingstoke: Palgrave.

Clare, A. (2000) *On Men: Masculinity in Crisis*. London: Chatto & Windus.

Clarke, J. and Critcher, C. (1985) *The Devil Makes Work: Leisure in Capitalist Britain*. London: Macmillan.

Clarke, J. and Newman, J. (1997) *The Managerial State*. London: Sage.

Clatterbaugh, K. (1990) *Contemporary Perspectives on Masculinity: Men, Women, and Politics in Modern Society*. Boulder, Col.: Westview Press.

Clegg, S. (1998) Foucault, power and organizations, in: A. McKinlay and K. Starkey (eds), *Foucault, Management and Organization Theory*. London: Sage.

Clifton, T. (1999) Fight Club. *http://reviews.imdb.com/Reviews/215/21530.`*

Coalter, F. (1998) Leisure studies, leisure policy and social citizenship: the failure of welfare or the limits of welfare? *Leisure Studies*, 17:1, pp. 21–36.

Cockburn, A. and Cockburn, P. (2000) *Out of the Ashes: The Resurrection of Saddam Hussein*. New York: Harper Perennial.

Cockburn, C. (1983) *Brothers: Male Dominance and Technological Change*. London: Pluto Press.

Cockburn, C. (1991) *In the Way of Women: Men's Resistance to Sex Equality in Organizations*. London: Macmillan.

Cohen, A. (1955) *Delinquent Boys: The Culture of the Gang*. New York: Free Press.

Cohen, J. (1997) Rethinking privacy: autonomy, identity and the abortion controversy, in: J. A. Weintraub and K. Kumar (eds), *Public and Private in Thought and Practice: Perspectives on a Grand Dichotomy.* London: University of Chicago Press.

Cohen, T. F. (1992) Men's families, men's friends, in: P. M. Nardi (ed.), *Men's Friendships.* Thousand Oaks, Calif.: Sage.

Collier, R. (1998) *Masculinities, Crime and Criminology.* London: Sage.

Collins, R. (1979) *The Credential Society.* Orlando, Fla.: Academic Press.

Collinson, D. and Hearn, J. (eds) (1996) *Men as Managers, Managers as Men.* London: Sage.

Collinson, D. and Hearn, J. (2001) Naming men as men: implications for work, organization and management, in: S. M. Whitehead and F. J. Barrett (eds), *The Masculinities Reader.* Cambridge: Polity Press.

Collinson, D. L., Knights, D. and Collinson, M. (1990) *Managing To Discriminate.* London: Routledge.

Coltrane, S. (1996) *Family Man: Fatherhood, Housework and Gender Equity.* New York: Oxford University Press.

Coltrane, S. and Valdez, E. O. (1993) Reluctant compliance: work–family role allocation in dual-earner Chicano families, in: J. C. Hood (ed.), *Men, Work, and Family.* Thousand Oaks, Calif.: Sage.

Connell, R. W. (1983) *Which Way is Up? Essays on Sex, Class and Culture.* London: Allen and Unwin.

Connell, R. W. (1987) *Gender and Power.* Cambridge: Polity.

Connell, R. W. (1990) An iron man: the body and some contradictions of hegemonic masculinity, in: M. A. Messner and D. Sabo (eds), *Sport, Men, and the Gender Order.* Champaign, Ill.: Human Kinetics.

Connell, R. W. (1994) Psychoanalysis on masculinity, in: H. Brod and M. Kaufman (eds), *Theorizing Masculinities.* Thousand Oaks, Calif.: Sage.

Connell, R. W. (1995) *Masculinities.* Cambridge: Polity.

Connell, R. W. (1998) Masculinities and globalization, *Men and Masculinities*, 1:1, pp. 3–23.

Connell, R. W. (2000) *The Men and the Boys.* Cambridge: Polity.

Constantine-Simms, D. (ed.) (2001) *The Greatest Taboo: Homosexuality in Black Communities.* Los Angeles: Alyson Books.

Cooper, D. (1994) Productive, relational and ubiquitous: conceptualising power within Foucauldian feminism, *Sociology*, 28:2, pp. 435–54.

Cornwall, A. and Lindisfarne, N. (eds) (1994) *Dislocating Masculinities: Comparative Ethnographies.* London: Routledge.

Cousins, M. and Houssain, A. (1984) *Michel Foucault.* London: Macmillan.

Coward, R. (1983) *Patriarchal Precedents: Sexuality and Social Relations.* London: Routledge & Kegan Paul.

Coyne, M. (1997) *The Crowded Prairie: American National Identity in the Hollywood Western.* New York: I. B. Tauris.

Craib, I. (1987) Masculinity and male dominance, *The Sociological Review*, 35:4, pp. 721–43.

Craib, I. (1994) *The Importance of Disappointment*. London: Routledge.

Craib, I. (1995) Some comments on the sociology of the emotions, *Sociology*, 29, pp. 151–8.

Craig, S. (ed.) (1992) *Men, Masculinity and the Media*. Thousand Oaks, Calif.: Sage.

Crawford, J., Kippax, S., Onyx, J., Gault, U. and Benton, P. (1992) *Emotion and Gender: Constructing Meaning from Memory*. London: Sage.

Creese, G. (1999) *Contracting Masculinity: Gender, Class, and Race in a White-Collar Union, 1944–1994*. New York: Oxford University Press.

Creighton, C. (1999) The rise and decline of the 'male breadwinner family' in Britain, *Cambridge Journal of Economics*, 23:5, pp. 519–41.

Crenshaw, K. (1993) Beyond racism and misogyny: black feminism and 2 Live Crew, in: M. J. Matsuda et al., *Words That Wound: Critical Race Theory, Assaultive Speech, and the First Amendment*. Boulder, Col.: Westview.

Crompton, R. (1987) Gender, status and professionalism, *Sociology*, 21, pp. 413–28.

Crosby, F. J. and Jasker, K. L. (1993) Women and men at home and at work: realities and illusions, in: S. Oskamp and M. Costango (eds), *Gender Issues in Contemporary Society*. Thousand Oaks, Calif.: Sage.

Dahrendorf, R. (1973) *Homo Sociologus*. London: Routledge & Kegan Paul.

Dally, A. (1982) *Inventing Motherhood: The Consequences of an Ideal*. London: Burnett Books.

Danaher, G., Schirato, T. and Webb, J. (2000) *Understanding Foucault*. London: Sage.

David, D. S. and Brannon, R. (eds) (1976) *The Male Sex Role*. London: Addison-Wesley.

Davidoff, L. and Hall, C. (1987) *Family Fortunes: Women and Men of the English Middle Class 1780–1850*. London: Routledge.

Davidson, M. J. (1997) *The Black and Ethnic Minority Woman Manager*. London: Paul Chapman.

Davidson, M. J. and Cooper, C. L. (1992) *Shattering the Glass Ceiling: The Woman Manager*. London: Paul Chapman.

Davies, D. (1996) The sociology of professions and the profession of gender, *Sociology*, 30:4, pp. 661–78.

Davies, K. (1990) *Women, Time and the Weaving of the Strands of Everyday Life*. Aldershot: Avebury.

Davis, A. (1983) *Women, Race and Class*. New York: Random House.

Davis, K. and Moore, W. E. (1967) Some principles of stratification, in: R. Bendix and S. M. Lipset (eds), *Class, Status, and Power*, 2nd edn. London: Routledge & Kegan Paul.

Davis, L. (1997) *The Swimsuit Issue and Sport: Hegemonic Masculinity in Sports Illustrated*. Albany: University of New York Press.

Dawkins, R. (1976) *The Selfish Gene*. Oxford: Oxford University Press.

Dawson, G. (1991) The blond Beduin: Lawrence of Arabia – imperial adventure and the imagining of English-British masculinity, in: M. Roper and J. Tosh (eds), *Manful Assertions*. London: Routledge.

Dawson, G. (1994) *Soldier Heroes: British Adventure, Empire and the Imagining of Masculinities*. London: Routledge.

Deem, R. (1986) *All Work and No Play*. Milton Keynes: Open University Press.

Deem, R. (1999) How do we get out of the ghetto? Strategies for research on gender and leisure for the twenty-first century, *Leisure Studies*, 18:3, pp. 161–77.

Deleuze, G. (1969) *The Logic of Sense*. Trans. M. Lester and C. Stivale. London: Athlone.

Deleuze, G. (1983) *Nietzsche and Philosophy*. Trans. H. Tomlinson. Minneapolis: University of Minnesota Press.

Deleuze, G. (1990) *Expressionism in Philosophy: Spinoza*. Trans. M. Joughin. New York: Zone.

Deleuze, G. and Guattari, F. (1977) *Anti-Oedipus*. Trans. R. Hurley, M. Seem and H. R. Lane. Minneapolis: University of Minnesota Press.

Deleuze, G. and Guattari, F. (1988) *A Thousand Plateaus*. Trans. B. Massumi. London: Athlone.

Delphy, C. (1977) *The Main Enemy*. London: Women's Research and Resource Centre.

Demos, J. (1986) *Past, Present and Personal: The Family and Life Course in American History*. New York: Oxford University Press.

Dent, M. (1993) Professionalism, educated labour and the state: hospital medicine and the new managerialism, *Sociological Review*, 41, pp. 244–73.

Dent, M. and Whitehead, S. (eds) (2001) *Managing Professional Identities: Knowledge, Performativity and the 'New' Professional*. London: Routledge.

Department for Education and Employment (DfEE) (2000) *Work–Life Balance 2000 Survey*. London: The Stationery Office.

Derrida, J. (1972) *Positions*. Chicago, Ill.: University of Chicago Press.

Dex, S. (1985) *The Sexual Division of Work*. Brighton: Wheatsheaf.

Dinnerstein, D. (1976) *The Mermaid and the Minotaur: Sexual Arrangements and Human Malaise*. New York: Harper & Row.

Dobash, R. E. and Dobash, R. P. (1992) *Women, Violence and Social Change*. London and New York: Routledge.

Dobash, R. E., Dobash, R. P., Cavanagh, K. and Lewis, R. (2000) *Changing Violent Men*. London: Sage.

Donald, R. R. (1992) Masculinity and machismo in Hollywood's war films, in: S. Craig (ed.), *Men, Masculinity, and the Media*. Thousand Oaks, Calif.: Sage.

Donaldson, M. (1993) What is hegemonic masculinity?, *Theory and Society*, 22, pp. 643–57.

Duke, J. T. (1976) *Conflict and Power in Social Theory*. New York: Brigham Young University Press.

Dunn, J. (1984) The concept of 'trust' in the politics of John Locke, in: R. Rorty, J. B. Schneewind and Q. Skinner (eds), *Philosophy in History*. Cambridge: Cambridge University Press.

Durkheim, E. (1957) *Professional Ethics and Civic Morals*. London: Routledge & Kegan Paul.

Durkheim, E. (1961) *Moral Education*. Glencoe, Ill.: The Free Press.

Dutton, K. R. (1995) *The Perfectible Body: The Western Idea of Physical Development*. London: Cassell.

Dworkin, A. (1981) *Our Blood: Prophecies and Discourses on Sexual Politics*. New York: G. P. Putnam.

Dwyer, C. (1999) Negotiations of femininity and identity for young British Muslim women, in: N. Laurie, C. Dwyer, S. Holloway and F. Smith, *Geographies of New Femininities*. London: Pearson Education.

Dyer, R. (1986) *Heavenly Bodies*. Basingstoke: Macmillan.

Dyer, R. (1997) The white man's Muscles, in: H. Stecopoulos and M. Uebel (eds), *Race and the Subject of Masculinities*. Durham, NC: Duke University Press.

Easterbrook, M. A. and Goldberg, W. A. (1985) Effects of early maternal employment on toddlers, mothers, and fathers, *Developmental Psychology*, 21, pp. 774–848.

Economic Social Research Council (ESRC) (2000) *Britain Towards 2010: The Changing Business Environment*. Swindon: ESRC.

Edley, N. and Wetherall, M. (1995) *Men in Perspective: Practice, Power and Identity*. London: Prentice Hall/Harvester Wheatsheaf.

Edmonds, C. (1999) Fight Club. *http://reviews.imdb.com/Reviews/214/21463*.

Edwards, S. (1989) *Policing Domestic Violence*. London: Sage.

Edwards, T. (1994) *Erotics and Politics: Gay Male Sexuality, Masculinity and Feminism*. London: Routledge.

Ehrenreich, B. (1983) *The Hearts of Men: American Dreams and the Flight from Commitment*. London: Pluto Press.

Eisenstein, H. (1985) *Contemporary Feminist Thought*. London: Unwin.

Elam, D. (1994) *Feminism and Deconstruction*. London: Routledge.

Elliott-Major, L. (2000) Ladies first, *The Guardian Education*, 16 January, p. 9.

Elshtain, J. B. (1981) *Public Man, Private Woman*. Princeton, NJ: Princeton University Press.

Eltahawy, M. (2000) Egypt's sexist divorce laws blamed not on Islam, but on men, *The Guardian*, 23 February.

Engle, P. L. (1997) The role of men in families: achieving gender equity and supporting children, in: C. Sweetman (ed.), *Men and Masculinity*. Oxford: Oxfam.

Epstein, D., Elwood, J., Hey, V. and Maw, J. (eds) (1999) *Failing Boys: Issues in Gender and Achievement*. Buckingham: Open University Press.

Equal Opportunities Commission (EOC) (1999) *Facts about Women and Men in Great Britain*. Manchester: EOC.

Equal Opportunities Commission (EOC) (2000) *Women and Men in Britain, 1999/2000*. Manchester: EOC.

European Commission (EC) (1998) *Equal Opportunities for Women and Men in the European Union (Annual Report 1997)*. Luxembourg: EC Publications.

Evans, T. (1994) Spiritual purity, in: *Seven Promises of a Promise Keeper*. Colorado Springs, Colo.: Focus on the Family.

Falabella, G. G. (1997) New masculinity: a different route, in: C. Sweetman (ed.), *Men and Masculinity*. Oxford: Oxfam.

Faludi, S. (1991) *Backlash: The Undeclared War Against Women*. London: Vintage.

Faludi, S. (1999) *Stiffed: The Betrayal of the Modern Man*. London: Chatto & Windus.

Fanon, F. (1986) *Black Skin, White Masks*. London: Pluto Press.

Fargamos, S. (1994) *Situating Feminism: From Thought to Action*. London: Sage.

Farrell, W. (1993) *The Myth of Male Power: Why Men Are The Disposable Sex*. New York: Simon & Schuster.

Fasteau, M. F. (1974) *The Male Machine*. New York: McGraw-Hill.

Faubion, J. D. (ed.) (1994) *Michel Foucault: Power. The Essential Works 3*. London: Allen Lane/The Penguin Press.

Fawcett Society Report (1997) *Fawcett Survey of Women MPs*. London: Fawcett Society.

Featherstone, M., Hepworth, M. and Turner, B. S. (eds) (1991) *The Body: Social Process and Cultural Theory*. London: Sage.

Fein, R. (1978) Research on fathering: social policy and an emergent perspective, *Journal of Social Issues*, 1:34, pp. 122–35.

Ferber, A. L. (2000) Racial warriors and weekend warriors: the construction of masculinity in mythopoetic and white supremacist discourse, *Men and Masculinities*, 3:1, pp. 30–56.

Ferree, M. M., Lorber, J. and Hess, B.B. (eds) (1999) *Revisioning Gender*. Thousand Oaks, Calif.: Sage.

Ferudi, F. (2000) An unsuitable man for a job, *The Independent (Education)*, 12 October, p. 5.

Finch, J. and Mason, J. (1993) *Negotiating Family Responsibilities*. London: Routledge.

Fineman, S. (ed.) (1993) *Emotion in Organizations*. London: Sage.

Firestone, S. (1970) *The Dialectic of Sex*. New York: Bantam Books.

Fisher, J. (1993) *The Road from Rio: Sustainable Development and the Non-Governmental Movements in the Third World*. Westport, Conn.: Praeger.

Flanders, M. L. (1994) *Breakthrough: The Career Woman's Guide to Shattering the Glass Ceiling*. London: Paul Chapman.

Fletcher, J. K. (1999) *Disappearing Acts: Gender, Power, and Relational Practice at Work*. Cambridge, Mass.: MIT Press.

Foley, P. X. (1999) Fight Club. *http:reviews.imdb.com/Reviews/213/21313*.

Forman, F. and Sowton, C. (eds) (1989) *Taking Our Time: Feminist Perspectives on Temporality*. Oxford: Pergamon Press.

Foucault, M. (1965) *Madness and Civilization: A History of Insanity in the Age of Reason*. Trans. R. Howard. London: Tavistock.

Foucault, M. (1970) *The Order of Things*. New York: Random House.

Foucault, M. (1972) *The Archeology of Knowledge*. Trans. A. M. Sheridan-Smith. London: Tavistock.

Foucault, M. (1973) *The Birth of the Clinic: An Archeology of Medical Perception*. Trans. of *Naissance de la clinique* (1963) by A. M. Sheridan-Smith. London: Tavistock.

Foucault, M. (1975) *Discipline and Punish: The Birth of the Prison*. Trans. A. M. Sheridan-Smith. Harmondsworth: Penguin.

Foucault, M. (1978) *The History of Sexuality, Volume 1: An Introduction*. Trans. R. Hurley. Harmondsworth: Penguin.

Foucault, M. (1980) *Power/Knowledge: Selected Interviews and Other Writings, 1972–1977*. Ed. C. Gordon. New York: Pantheon Press.

Foucault, M. (1983) The subject and power. Afterword to H. Dreyfus and P. Rabinow, *Michel Foucault: Beyond Structuralism and Hermeneutics*. Chicago, Ill.: University of Chicago Press.

Foucault, M. (1984) Nietzsche, genealogy, history, in: P. Rabinow (ed.), *The Foucault Reader*. London: Penguin.

Foucault, M. (1988a) The ethic of care for the self as a practice of freedom, in: J. Bernauer and D. Rasmussen (eds), *The Final Foucault*. Cambridge, Mass: MIT Press.

Foucault, M. (1988b) Technologies of self, in: L. H. Martin, J. Gutman and P. Hutton (eds), *Technologies of the Self: A Seminar with Michel Foucault*. London: Tavistock.

Foucault, M. (1991) On the genealogy of ethics: an overview of work in progress, in: P. Rabinow (ed.), *The Foucault Reader*. London: Penguin.

Foucault, M. (1994) *Power: The Essential Works 3*. Ed. J. D. Faubion. Trans. R. Hurley. London: Allen Lane and Penguin Press.

Fox, D. J. (1999) Masculinity and fatherhood reexamined: an ethnographic account of the contradictions of manhood in a rural Jamaican town, *Men and Masculinities*, 2:1, pp. 66–86.

Francis, B. (1998) *Power Plays: Primary School Children's Constructions of Gender, Power and Adult Work*. Stoke on Trent: Trentham Books.

Francis, B. (2000) *Boys, Girls and Achievement: Addressing the Classroom Issues*. London: Routledge.

Francis, B. (forthcoming) Modernist reductionism or poststructuralist relativism: Can we move on? an evaluation of the arguments in relation to feminist educational research, *Journal of Gender Studies*.

Frank, A. W. (1991) For a sociology of the body: an analytical review, in: M. Featherstone et al. (eds), *The Body*. London: Sage.

Frank, K. (1998) The production of identity and the negotiation of intimacy in a 'gentleman's club', *Sexualities*, 1:2, pp. 175–201.

Franklin II, C. W. (1992) 'Hey, Home – Yo, Bro': Friendship among black men, in: P. M. Nardi (ed.), *Men's Friendships*. Thousand Oaks, Calif.: Sage.

Franklin II, C. W. (1989) Black male – black female conflict: individually caused and culturally nurtured, in: M. S. Kimmel and M. A. Messner (eds), *Men's Lives*. Boston, Mass.: Allyn and Bacon.

Franks, S. (1999) *Having None of It: Women, Men and the Future of Work*. London: Granta Books.

Fraser, N. and Nicholson, L. J. (1990) Social criticism without philosophy: an encounter between feminism and postmodernism, in: L. J. Nicholson (ed.), *Feminism/Postmodernism*. New York: Routledge.

Freud, S. (1953) *Three Essays on the Theory of Sexuality: Complete Psychological Works, Standard Edition, Vol. 7*. London: Hogarth.

Freud, S. (1966) *Sigmund Freud: The Complete Introductory Lectures on Psychoanalysis*. Trans. and ed. J. Strachey. New York: W. W. Norton.

Freud, S. (1968) *Sexuality and the Psychology of Love*. New York: Collier Books.

Friedan, B. (1974) *The Feminine Mystique*. New York: Dell.

Frosh, S. (1994) *Sexual Difference: Masculinity and Psychoanalysis*. London: Routledge.

Fukuyama, F. (1997) *The End of Order*. London: Social Market Foundation.

Game, A. (1991) *Undoing the Social: Towards a Deconstructive Sociology*. Milton Keynes: Open University Press.

Game, A. and Pringle, R. (1984) *Gender at Work*. London: Pluto Press.

Gavron, H. (1966) *The Captive Wife*. London: Routledge & Kegan Paul.

Gay, P. du (1996) *Consumption and Identity at Work*. London: Sage.

George, N. (1998) *Hip Hop America*. New York: Viking.

Gergen, K. (1994) *Realities and Relationships: Soundings in Social Construction*. Cambridge, Mass.: Harvard University Press.

Gherardi, S. (1995) *Gender, Symbolism and Organizational Cultures.* London: Sage.

Giddens, A. (1990) *The Consquences of Modernity.* Cambridge: Polity.

Giddens, A. (1991) *Modernity and Self-Identity: Self and Society in the Late Modern Age.* Cambridge: Polity.

Giddens, A. (1992) *The Transformation of Intimacy.* Cambridge: Polity.

Giddens, A. (2000) In conversation, in: W. Hutton and A. Giddens (eds), *On the Edge: Living with Global Capitalism.* London: Jonathan Cape.

Gilder, G. (1973) *Sexual Suicide.* New York: Bantam.

Gilligan, C. (1982) *In a Different Voice.* Cambridge, Mass.: Harvard University Press.

Gilmore, D. G. (1990) *Manhood in the Making: Cultural Concepts of Masculinity.* New Haven, Conn.: Yale University Press.

Ginn, J. et al. (1996) Feminist fallacies: a reply to Hakim on women's employment, *British Journal of Sociology,* 47:1, pp. 167–74.

Goddard, K. (2000) 'Looks maketh the man': the female gaze and the construction of masculinity, *The Journal of Men's Studies,* 9:1, pp. 23–39.

Godenzi, A. (1999) Style or substance: men's response to feminist challenge, *Men and Masculinities,* 1:4, pp. 385–92.

Goffman, I. (1959) *The Presentation of Self in Everyday Life.* Harmondsworth: Penguin.

Goffman, I. (1970) *Strategic Interaction.* Oxford: Basil Blackwell.

Goldberg, H. (1976) *The Hazards of Being Male.* New York: Signet.

Goldhagen, D. (1996) *Hitler's Willing Executioners: Ordinary Germans and the Holocaust.* London: Little, Brown & Company.

Good, J. and Velody, I. (eds) (1998) *The Politics of Postmodernity.* Cambridge: Cambridge University Press.

Goodchild, P. (1996) *Deleuze and Guattari: An Introduction to the Politics of Desire.* London: Sage.

Gorz, A. (1985) *Paths to Paradise.* London: Pluto.

Gouch, B. and Edwards, G. (1998) The beer talking: four lads, a carry out and the reproduction of masculinities, *The Sociological Review,* 26:3, pp. 409–35.

Gramsci, A. (1971) *Selections from Prison Notebooks.* London: Lawrence & Wishart.

Gray, J. (1999) *Men are from Mars, Women are from Venus.* London: Vintage/Ebury.

Green, D. (1999) *Gender Violence in Africa.* London: Macmillan.

Green, E., Hebron, S. and Woodward, D. (1990) *Women's Leisure, What Leisure?* London: Macmillan.

Greenwood, J. D. (1994) *Realism, Identity and Emotion: Reclaiming Social Psychology.* London: Sage.

Greer, G. (1970) *The Female Eunuch.* London: Book Club Associates.

Griffin, C. (1996) Experiencing power: dimensions of gender, 'race' and class, in: N. Charles and F. Hughes-Freeland (eds), *Practising Feminism: Identity, Difference, Power*. London: Routledge.

Grimshaw, J. (1993) Practices of freedom, in: C. Ramazanoglu (ed.), *Up Against Foucault*. London: Routledge.

Grosz, E. (1986) Philosophy, subjectivity and the body: Kristeva and Irigaray, in: C. Patemen and E. Grosz (eds), *Feminist Challenges, Social and Political Theory*. Sydney: Allen and Unwin.

Grosz, E. (1990) *Jacques Lacan: A Feminist Introduction*. London: Routledge.

Guggenbuhl, A. (1997) *Men, Power and Myths: The Quest for Male Identity*. Trans. G. V. Hartman. New York: Continuum.

Gutterman, D. S. (2001) Postmodernism and the interrogation of masculinity, in: S. M. Whitehead and F. J. Barrett (eds), *The Masculinities Reader*. Cambridge: Polity.

Hacker, H. M. (1957) The new burdens of masculinity, *Marriage and Family Living*, 3, pp. 227–33.

Hagedorn, J. M. (1998) Frat boys, bossmen, studs, and gentlemen: a typology of gang masculinities, in: L. H. Bowker (ed.), *Masculinities and Violence*. Thousand Oaks, Calif.: Sage.

Hakim, C. (1996) *Key Issues in Women's Work: Female Heterogeneity and the Polarization of Women's Employment*. London: Athlone Press.

Halford, S., Savage, M. and Witz, A. (1997) *Gender, Careers and Organisations: Current Developments in Banking, Nursing and Local Government*. Basingstoke: Macmillan.

Hall, M. A. (1990) How should we theorize gender in the context of sport?, in: M. A. Messner and D. F. Sabo (eds), *Sport, Men and the Gender Order*. Champaign, Ill: Human Kinetics.

Hall, S. (1996) The after-life of Frantz Fanon, in: A. Read (ed.), *The Fact of Blackness: Frantz Fanon and Visual Representation*. Seattle, Wash.: Bay Press.

Hall, S. (ed.) (1997) *Representation: Cultural Representations and Signifying Practices*. London: Sage, in association with Open University Press.

Hall, S. and du Gay, P. (eds) (2000) *Questions of Cultural Identity*. London: Sage.

Hanmer, J. (1990) Men, power and the exploitation of women, in: J. Hearn and D. Morgan (eds), *Men, Masculinities and Social Theory*. London: Allen & Unwin.

Hantrais, L. (1993) The gender of time in professional occupations, *Time and Society*, 2:2, pp. 139–57.

Harding, S. (1991) *Whose Science? Whose Knowledge? Thinking from Women's Lives*. Ithaca, NY: Cornell University Press.

Hargreaves, D. H. (1967) *Social Relations in a Secondary School*. London: Routledge & Kegan Paul.

Hargreaves, J. A. (ed.) (1982) *Sport, Culture and Ideology*. London: Routledge & Kegan Paul.

Hartley, R. E. (1959) Sex-role pressures and the socialization of the male child, *Psychological Reports*, 5, pp. 457–68.

Hartmann, H. (1981) The unhappy marriage of marxism and feminism: towards a more progressive union, in: L. Sargent (ed.), *Women and Revolution*. Boston, Mass.: South End.

Hartsock, N. C. M. (1983) The feminist standpoint: developing the ground for a specifically feminist historical materialism, in: S. Harding and M. B. Hintikka (eds), *Discovering Reality*. Dordrecht, Netherlands: Reidel.

Harvey, S. J. (1999) Hegemonic masculinity, friendship, and group formation in an athletic subculture, *The Journal of Men's Studies*, 8:1, pp. 91–108.

Hassard, J., Holliday, R. and Willmott, H. (eds) (2000) *Body and Organization*. London: Sage.

Hatty, S. E. (2000) *Masculinities, Violence, and Culture*. Thousand Oaks, Calif.: Sage.

Hawkes, G. (1996) *A Sociology of Sex and Sexuality*. Buckingham: Open University Press.

Haynes, R. (1993) Every man (?) a football artist: football writing and masculinity, in: S. Redhead (ed.), *The Passion and the Fashion: Football Fandom in the New Europe*. Aldershot: Avebury.

Hearn, J. (1987) *The Gender of Oppression: Men, Masculinity and the Critique of Marxism*. Brighton: Wheatsheaf.

Hearn, J. (1992) *Men in the Public Eye*. London: Routledge.

Hearn, J. (1993) Emotive subjects: organizational men, organizational masculinities and the (de)construction of 'emotions', in: S. Fineman (ed.), *Emotions in Organizations*. London: Sage.

Hearn, J. (1994) Research in men and masculinities: some sociological issues and possibilities, *The Australian and New Zealand Journal of Sociology*, 30:1, pp. 47–70.

Hearn, J. (1998a) Theorizing men and men's theorizing: varieties of discursive practices in men's theorizing of men, *Theory and Society*, 27, pp. 781–816.

Hearn, J. (1998b) *The Violences of Men*. London: Sage.

Hearn, J. (1999) A crisis in masculinity, or new agendas for men?, in: S. Walby (ed.), *New Agendas for Women*. London: Macmillan.

Hearn, J. and Melechi, A. (1992) The transatlantic gaze: masculinities, youth and the American imaginary, in: S. Craig (ed.), *Men, Masculinity, and the Media*. Thousand Oaks, Calif.: Sage.

Hearn, J. and Parkin, W. (1988) Women, men and leadership: a critical review of assumptions, practices and change in industrialized nations, in: N. J. Adler and D. Izraeli (eds), *Women in Management Worldwide*. New York: M. E. Sharpe.

Hearn, J., Sheppard, D. L., Tancred-Sheriff, P. and Burrell, G. (eds) (1989) *The Sexuality of Organization*. London: Sage.

Heath, S. (1987) Male feminism, in: A. Jardine and P. Smith (eds), *Men in Feminism*. London: Methuen.

Hekman, S. J. (1990) *Gender and Knowledge: Elements of a Postmodern Feminism*. Cambridge: Polity.

Hekman, S. J. (1999) *The Future of Differences*. Cambridge: Polity.

Henriques, J., Hollway, W., Urwin, C., Venn, C. and Walkerdine, V. (eds) (1984) *Changing the Subject: Psychology, Social Regulation and Subjectivity*. London: Methuen.

Hensman, R. (ed.) (1992) Special issue on Gender and Nationalism, *Journal of Gender Studies*, 4:1.

Herman, D. (1984) The rape culture, in: J. Freeman (ed.), *Women: A Feminist Perspective*. Mountain View, Calif.: Mayfield.

Hess, B. B. and Ferree, M. M. (eds) (1987) *Analyzing Gender*. London: Sage.

Hewitt, P. (1993) *About Time: The Revolution in Work and Family Life*. London: Rivers Oram Press.

Hill Collins, P. (1991) *Black Feminist Thought. Knowledge, Consciousness and the Politics of Empowerment*. New York: Routledge.

Hochschild, A. R. (1989) *The Second Shift*. New York: Avon Books.

Hochschild, A. R. (1997) *The Time Bind*. New York: Metropolitan Books.

Hodson, P. (1984) *Men: An Investigation into the Emotional Male*. London: British Broadcasting Corporation.

Hofsted, G. (and associates) (1998) *Masculinity and Femininity: The Taboo Dimension of National Cultures*. Thousand Oaks, Calif.: Sage.

Hohn, C. and Luscher, K. (1988) The changing family in the Federal Republic of Germany, *Journal of Family Issues*, 9, pp. 317–35.

Hollway, W. (1984) Women's power in heterosexual sex, *Women's Studies International Forum*, 7:1, pp. 63–8.

Hollway, W. (1984) Gender difference and the production of subjectivity, in: I. Henriques, W. Hollway, C. Urwin, C. Venn and V. Walkerdine (eds), *Changing the Subject*. London: Methuen.

Holmwood, J. (1995) Feminism and epistemology: what kind of successor science?, *Sociology*, 29:3, pp. 411–28.

Hondagneu-Sotelo, P. and Messner, M. A. (1994) Gender displays and men's power: the 'new man' and the Mexican immigrant man, in: H. Brod and M. Kaufman (eds), *Theorizing Masculinities*. Thousand Oaks, Calif.: Sage.

Hood, J. C. (ed.) (1993) *Men, Work, and Family*. Thousand Oaks, Calif.: Sage.

hooks, b. (1981) *Ain't I a Woman: Black Women and Feminism*. Boston, Mass.: South End Press.

hooks, b. (1984) *Feminist Theory: From Margin to Center*. Boston, Mass.: South End Press.

hooks, b. (1991) *Yearning: Race, Gender and Cultural Politics*. London: Turnaround.

hooks, b. (1989) Men: comrades in struggle, in: M. S. Kimmel and M. A. Messner (eds), *Men's Lives*. Boston, Mass.: Allyn and Bacon.

Horrocks, R. (1994) *Masculinity in Crisis: Myths, Fantasies and Realities*. London: Macmillan.

Hughes, C. (2000) Is it possible to be a feminist manager in the 'real world' of further education?, *Journal of Further and Higher Education*, 21:2, pp. 251–60.

Hume, D. (1985) *Enquiries Concering Human Understanding and Concerning the Principles of Morals*. Oxford: Clarendon Press.

Humm, M. (ed.) (1992) *Feminisms: A Reader*. Hemel Hempstead: Harvester Wheatsheaf.

Hutton, W. (1996) *The State We're In*. London: Vintage.

Institute of Management (IoM) (1995 and 1998) *National Management Salary Survey*. Kingston upon Thames: Institute of Management.

Irigaray, L. (1980) When our lips speak together, *Signs*, 6:1, pp. 69–79.

Irigaray, L. (1985) *The Sex Which Is Not One*. Trans. C. Porter with C. Burke. Ithaca, NY: Cornell University Press.

Irwin, S. (1999) Resourcing the family: gendered claims and obligations and issues of explanation, in: E. B. Silva and C. Smart (eds), *The New Family?* London: Sage.

Ishii-Kuntz, M. (1993) Japanese fathers: work demands and family roles, in: J. C. Hood (ed.), *Men, Work, and Family*. Thousand Oaks, Calif.: Sage.

Jackson, D. (1990) *Unmasking Masculinity: A Critical Autobiography*. London: Unwin Hyman.

Jackson, S. (1993) Even sociologists fall in love: an exploration in the sociology of emotions, *Sociology*, 27, pp. 210–20.

Jackson, S. (1999) *Heterosexuality in Question*. London: Sage.

Jackson, S. and Scott, S. (1997) Gut reactions to matters of the heart: reflections on rationality, irrationality and sexuality, *The Sociological Review*, 45, pp. 551–75.

Jahn, A. and Aslam, A. (1995) Fathers' perception of child health: a case study in a squatter settlement of Karachi, Pakistan, *Health Transition Review*, 5:2, pp. 191–206.

Jahoda, M. (1979) The impact of unemployment in the 1930s and 1970s, *Bulletin of British Psychological Society*, 32, pp. 432–41.

Jamieson, L. (1998) *Intimacy: Personal Relationships in Modern Societies*. Cambridge: Polity.

Jamieson, L. (1999) Intimacy transformed? A critical look at the 'pure relationship', *Sociology*, 33:3, pp. 477–94.

Jefferson, T. (1994) Theorising masculine subjectivity, in: T. Newburn and E. A. Stanko (eds), *Just Boys Doing Business? Men, Masculinities and Crime*. London: Routledge.

Jefferson, T. (1998) Muscle, 'hard men' and 'Iron' Mike Tyson: reflections on desire, anxiety and the embodiment of masculinity, *Body and Society*, 4:1, pp. 77–98.

Johnson, S. and Finlay, F. (1997) Do men gossip? An analysis of football talk on television, in: S. Johnson and U. H. Meinhof (eds), *Language and Masculinity*. Oxford: Blackwell.

Johnson, S. and Meinhof, U. H. (eds) (1997) *Language and Masculinity*. Oxford: Blackwell.

Jordanova, L. (1999) Natural facts: a historical perspective on science and sexuality, in: J. Price and M. Shildrick (eds), *Feminist Theory and the Body*. Edinburgh: Edinburgh University Press.

Jung, C. G. (1928/1953) The relations between the ego and the unconscious, in: *Collected Works, Volume 7: Two Essays on Analytical Psychology*. London: Routledge & Kegan Paul.

Kandiyoti, D. (1988) Bargaining with patriarchy, *Gender and Society*, 2:3, pp. 274–329.

Kanter, R. M. (1977) *Men and Women of the Corporation*. New York: BasicBooks.

Karam, A. M. (1998) *Women, Islamisms, and the State: Contemporary Feminisms in Egypt*. London: Macmillan.

Kaufman, M. (1987) *Beyond Patriarchy*. Toronto: Oxford University Press.

Kaufmann McCall, K. (1979) Simone de Beauvoir, *The Second Sex*, and Jean-Paul Sartre, *Signs: Journal of Women in Culture and Society*, 5:2.

Keith, P. M. (1994) A typology of orientations toward household and marital roles of older men and women, in: E. H. Thompson, Jr (ed.), *Older Men's Lives*. Thousand Oaks, Calif.: Sage.

Kennedy, E. (2000) 'You talk a good game': football and masculine style on British Television, *Men and Masculinities*, 3:1, pp. 57–84.

Kent, K. S. (1999) *Gender and Power in Britain, 1640–1990*. London: Routledge.

Kenway, J. (1995) Masculinities in schools: under siege, on the defensive and under reconstruction?, *Discourse: Studies in the Cultural Politics of Education*, 16:1, pp. 59–80.

Kerfoot, D. (1999) The organization of intimacy: managerialism, masculinity and the masculine subject, in: S. Whitehead and R. Moodley (eds), *Transforming Managers: Gendering Change in the Public Sector*. London: UCL Press.

Kerfoot, D. (2000) Body work: estrangement, disembodiment and the organizational 'other', in: J. Hassard, R. Holliday and II. Willmott (eds), *Body and Organization*. London: Sage.

Kerfoot, D. (2001) Managing the 'professional' man, in: M. Dent and S. Whitehead (eds), *Managing Professional Identities: Knowledge, Performativity and the 'New' Professional*. London: Routledge.

Kerfoot, D. and Knights, D. (1993) Management, masculinity and manipulation: from paternalism to corporate strategy in financial services, *Journal of Management Studies*, 30:41, pp. 659–977.

Kerfoot, D. and Knights, D. (1996) The best is yet to come? The quest for embodiment in managerial work, in: D. L. Collinson and J. Hearn (eds), *Men as Managers, Managers as Men*. London: Sage.

Kerfoot, D. and Whitehead, S. (1998a) 'Boys Own' stuff: masculinity and the management of further education, *The Sociological Review*, 46:3, pp. 436–57.

Kerfoot, D. and Whitehead, S. (1998b) Can trust be trusted? Dilemmas for managers, management and organisation. Paper presented at the 14 Biennial EGOS Colloquium, University of Maastricht, The Netherlands, 9–11 July.

Kerfoot, D. and Whitehead, S. (2000) Keeping all the balls in the air: further education and the masculine/managerial subject, *Journal of Further and Higher Education*, 24:2, pp. 183–202.

Kerouac, J. (1957) *On the Road*. New York: Viking Press.

Kidd, B. (1990) The men's cultural centre: sports and the dynamic of women's oppression/men's oppression, in: M. A. Messner and D. Sabo (eds), *Sport, Men, and the Gender Order*. Champaign, Ill.: Human Kinetics.

Kiesling, S. F. (1998) Men's identities and sociolinguistic variation: the case of fraternity men, *Journal of Sociolinguistics*, 2:1, pp. 69–99.

Kiesling, S. F. (2000) 'Now I gotta watch what I say': shifting constructions of masculinity in discourse. Unpublished paper.

Kiesling, S. F. (2001) Power and the language of men, in: S. M. Whitehead and F. J. Barrett (eds), *The Masculinities Reader*. Cambridge: Polity.

Kilduff, M. and Mehra, A. (1996) Hegemonic masculinity among the elite: power, identity and homophily in social networks, in: C. Cheng (ed.), *Masculinities in Organizations*. Thousand Oaks, Calif.: Sage.

Kimmel, M. S. (1987a) Rethinking 'Masculinity': new directions in research, in: M. S. Kimmel (ed.), *Changing Men: New Directions in Research on Men and Masculinity*. Newbury Park, Calif.: Sage.

Kimmel, M. S. (1987b) The contemporary 'crisis' of masculinity in historical perspective, in: H. Brod (ed.), *The Making of Masculinities: The New Men's Studies*. Boston, Mass.: Unwin & Hyman.

Kimmel, M. S. (1994) Masculinity as homophobia: fear, shame and silence in the construction of gender identity', in: H. Brod and M. Kaufman (eds), *Theorizing Masculinities*. Thousand Oaks, Calif.: Sage.

Kimmel, M. S. (ed.) (1995a) *The Politics of Manhood*. Philadelphia, Pa.: Temple University Press.

Kimmel, M. S. (1995b) 'Born to Run': nineteenth-century fantasies of masculine retreat and re-creation (*or* The historical rust on Iron John), in: M. S. Kimmel (ed.), *The Politics of Manhood*. Philadelphia, Pa.: Temple University Press.

Kimmel, M. S. (1995c) Series editor's introduction, in: D. Sabo and D. F. Gordon (eds), *Men's Health and Illness*. Thousand Oaks, Calif.: Sage.

Kimmel, M. S. (1996) *Manhood in America: A Cultural History*. New York: Free Press.

Kimmel, M. S. (2000) *The Gendered Society*. Oxford: Oxford University Press.

Kimmel, M. S. and Messner, M. (1989) Introduction, in: M. S. Kimmel and M. Messner (eds), *Men's Lives*. Boston, Mass.: Allyn and Bacon.

King, A. (1997) The lads: masculinity and the new consumption of football, *Sociology*, 31:2, pp. 329–46.

Klein, A. M. (2000) Dueling machos: masculinity and sport in Mexican baseball, in: J. McKay, M. A. Messner and D. Sabo (eds), *Masculinities, Gender Relations, and Sport*. Thousand Oaks, Calif.: Sage.

Knights, D. and Odih, P. (1995) 'It's about time!': The significance of gendered time for financial services consumption, *Time and Society*, 4:2, pp. 205–31.

Knights, D. and Willmott, H. (1999) *Management Lives: Power and Identity in Work Organizations*. London: Sage.

Komarovsky, M. (1940) *The Unemployed Man and His Family*. New York: Dryden.

Komarovsky, M. (1950) Functional analysis of sex roles, *American Sociological Review*, 15, pp. 508–16.

Kristeva, J. (1986) A new type of intellectual: the dissident, in: T. Moi (ed.), *The Kristeva Reader*. New York: Columbia University Press.

Kumar, K. (1995) *From Post-Industrial to Post-Modern Society*. Oxford: Blackwell.

LaBier, D. (1986) *Modern Madness: The Hidden Link Between Work and Emotional Conflict*. New York: Simon and Schuster.

Lacan, J. (1977) *Ecrits: A Selection*. London: Tavistock.

Lahn, B. T. and Jegalian, S. (1999) The key to masculinity, *Scientific American*, 10:2, pp. 20–5.

Lancaster, R. (1998) Transgenderism in Latin America: some critical introductory remarks on identities and practices, *Sexualities*, 1:3, pp. 261–74.

Lash, S. and Urry, J. (1987) *The End of Organised Capitalism*. Cambridge: Polity.

Laurentis, T. de (1991) Queer theory: lesbian and gay sexualities: an introduction, *Differences: A Journal of Feminist Cultural Studies*, 3:2, pp. iii–xviii.

Laurie, N., Dwyer, C., Holloway, S. and Smith, F. (1999) *Geographies of New Femininities*. New York: Pearson Education.

Lazer, W. and Shaw, E. H. (1987) How older Americans spend their money, *American Demographics*, 9, pp. 36–41.

Leather, P. (1983) Desire: a structural model of motivation, *Human Relations*, 36, pp. 109–22.

Lee, D. and Newby, H. (1984) *The Problem of Sociology: An Introduction to the Discipline*. London: Hutchinson.

Leeper, M. R. (1999) Fight Club. *http://reviews.imdb.com/Reviews/212/21241*.

Legge, K. (1995) *Human Resource Management: Rhetorics and Realities*. London: Macmillan.

Leibowitz, E. (1996) Million man mea culpa: the promise keepers' plan for Christian male redemption, *LA Weekly*, 31 May–6 June, pp. 22–5.

Lemert, C. (1997) *Postmodernism Is Not What You Think*. Oxford: Blackwell.

Lennon, K. (1995) Gender and knowledge, *Journal of Gender Studies*, 4:2, pp. 133–43.

Lennon, K. and Whitford, M. (eds) (1994) *Knowing the Difference: Feminist Perspectives on Epistemology*. London: Routledge.

Lesko, N. (ed.) (2000) *Masculinities at School*. Thousand Oaks, Calif.: Sage.

Levant, R. F. and Pollack, W. S. (eds) (1995) *A New Psychology of Men*. New York: BasicBooks.

Leverenz, D. (1986) Manhood, humiliation and public life: some stories, *Southwest Review*, 71, Fall.

Levine, J. A., Murphy, D. T. and Wilson, S. (1993) *Getting Men Involved*. New York: Scholastic.

Lewis, R. A. and Salt, R. E. (eds) (1986) *Men in Families*. Beverly Hills, Calif.: Sage.

Lingard, B. and Douglas, P. (1999) *Men Engaging Feminisms: Pro-feminism, Backlashes and Schooling*. Buckingham: Open University Press.

Linton, R. (ed.) (1945) *The Science of Man in World Crisis*. New York: Columbia University Press.

Lloyd, G. (1984) *Man of Reason: 'Male' and 'Female' in Western Philosophy*. London: Methuen.

Luhman, N. (1979) *Trust and Power*. Chichester: Wiley.

Lyndon, N. (1992) *No More Sex War: The Failures of Feminism*. London: Sinclair Stevenson.

Lyotard, J-F. (1994) *The Postmodern Condition: A Report on Knowledge*. Manchester: Manchester University Press.

McAulay, G. (2000) No more Mr Nice Guy, *Counterblast, BBC2 Television*, British Broadcasting Corporation, 24 January.

McDowell, D. E. (1997) Pecs and reps: muscling in on race and the subject of masculinities, in: H. Stecopoulos and M. Uebel (eds), *Race and the Subject of Masculinities*. Durham, NC: Duke University Press.

Mac an Ghaill, M. (1994) *The Making of Men: Masculinities, Sexualities and Schooling*. Buckingham: Open University Press.

Mac an Ghaill, M. (ed.) (1996) *Understanding Masculinities*. Buckingham: Open University Press.

MacInnes, J. (1998) *The End of Masculinity*. Buckingham: Open University Press.

McKay, J. and Middlemiss, I. (1995) 'Mate against mate, state against state': a case study of media constructions of hegemonic masculinity in Australian sport, *Masculinities*, 3:3, pp. 28–45.

McKay, J., Messner, M. A. and Sabo, D. (eds) (2000) *Masculinities, Gender Relations, and Sport*. Thousand Oaks, Calif.: Sage.

MacKinnon, C. A. (1982) Feminism, Marxism, method and the state: an agenda for theory, *Signs*, 7:3, pp. 515–44.

McLennon, G. (1995) Feminism, epistemology and postmodernism: reflections on current ambivalence, *Sociology*, 29:3, pp. 391–410.

McMahon, A. (1999) *Taking Care of Men: Sexual Politics in the Public Mind*. Cambridge: Cambridge University Press.

McNay, L. (1992) *Foucault and Feminism*. Cambridge: Polity.

McNay, L. (1994) *Foucault: A Critical Introduction*. Cambridge: Polity.

McNay, L. (2000) *Gender and Agency*. Cambridge: Polity.

Maddock, S. (1999) *Challenging Women: Gender, Culture and Organization*. London: Sage.

Maile, S. (1999) Intermanagerial rivalries, organizational restructuring and the transformation of management masculinities, in: S. Whitehead and R. Moodley (eds), *Transforming Managers*. London: UCL Press.

Majors, R. (1986) Cool pose: the proud signature of black survival, *Changing Men*, 17 (Winter), pp. 5–6.

Majors, R. (2001) Cool Pose: Black Masculinity and Sports, in: S. M. Whitehead and F. J. Barrett (eds), *The Masculinities Reader*. Cambridge: Polity.

Majors, R. and Mancini, J. (1992) *Cool Pose: The Dilemmas of Black Manhood*. Lexington, Ky: Lexington Books.

Makino, C. (2001) The battle for men's liberation, *South China Sunday Morning Post (Sunday Review)*, 6 May, p. 2.

Makori, G. (1999) Men and violence in Kenya, *Men in Research, IASOM Newsletter*, 6:3, pp. 30–2.

Mangan, J. A. (1981) *Athleticism in the Victorian and Edwardian Public School: The Emergence and Consolidation of an Educational Ideology*. Cambridge: Cambridge University Press.

Mangan, J. A. and Walvin J. (1987) *Manliness and Morality: Middle Class Masculinity in Britain and America.* Manchester: Manchester University Press.

Mann, K. (1992) *The Making of an English 'Underclass'? The Social Divisions of Welfare and Labour.* Milton Keynes: Open University Press.

Mapplethorpe, R. (1996) *Black Book.* Cambridge, Mass.: Bulfinch Press.

Marmor, J., Sanders, D. and Nardi, P. (eds) (1994) *Growing Up Before Stonewall: Stories of Some Gay Men.* New York: Routledge.

Marriott, D. (1996) Reading black masculinities, in: M. Mac an Ghaill (ed.), *Understanding Masculinities.* Buckingham: Open University Press.

Marshall, J. (1995) *Women Managers Moving On: Exploring Career and Life Choices.* London: Routledge.

Marsiglio, W. (1998) *Procreative Man.* New York: New York University Press.

Matthews, J. J. (1984) *Good and Mad Women: The Historical Construction of Femininity in Twentieth-Century Australia.* Sydney: Allen & Unwin.

May, L. (1998) *Masculinity and Morality.* New York: Cornell University Press.

Mead, G. H. (1934) *Mind, Self and Society.* Chicago: University of Chicago Press.

Meehan, D. (1999) The under-representation of women managers in higher education: are there issues other than style?, in: S. Whitehead and R. Moodley (eds), *Transforming Managers.* London: UCL Press.

Mercer, K. (1991) Looking for trouble, *Transition*, 51, pp. 184–97.

Mercer, K. (1992) Skin head sex thing: racial difference and the homoerotic imaginary, *New Formations*, 16, pp. 1–23.

Mercer, K. (ed.) (1994) *Welcome to the Jungle.* London: Routledge.

Mercer, K. and Julien, I. (1988) Race, sexual politics and black masculinity: a dossier, in: R. Chapman and J. Rutherford (eds), *Male Order: Unwrapping Masculinity.* London: Lawrence and Wishart.

Mercer, K. and Julien, I. (1994) Black masculinity and the politics of race, in: K. Mercer (ed.), *Welcome to the Jungle.* London: Routledge.

Merleau-Ponty, M. (1962) *The Phenomenology of Perception.* Trans. C. Smith. New York: Humanities Press.

Merrick, J. (1999) Sodomitical scandals and subcultures in the 1720s, *Men and Masculinities*, 1:4, pp. 365–84.

Messerschmidt, J. W. (1996) Managing to kill: masculinities and the space shuttle *Challenger* explosion, in: C. Cheng (ed.), *Masculinities in Organizations.* Thousand Oaks, Calif.: Sage.

Messner, M. A. (1992a) *Power At Play: Sports and the Problem of Masculinity.* Boston, Mass.: Beacon Press.

Messner, M. A. (1992b) Like family: power, intimacy, and sexuality in male athletes' friendships, in: P. M. Nardi (ed.), *Men's Friendships*. Thousand Oaks, Calif.: Sage.

Messner, M. A. (1997) *Politics of Masculinities: Men in Movements*. Thousand Oaks, Calif.: Sage.

Messner, M. A. and Sabo, D. F. (eds) (1990) *Sport, Men, and the Gender Order*. Champaign, Ill.: Human Kinetics.

Middleton, P. (1992) *The Inward Gaze: Masculinity and Subjectivity in Modern Culture*. London: Routledge.

Miles, R. (1992) *The Rites of Man: Love, Sex and Death in the Making of the Male*. London: Paladin.

Miliband, R. (1989) *Divided Societies: Class Struggle in Contemporary Capitalism*. Oxford: Oxford University Press.

Mill, J. S. (1996) [1859] *On Liberty and The Subjection of Women*. Ware: Wordsworth.

Miller, J. B. (ed.) (1978) *Psychoanalysis and Women*. Baltimore, Md: Penguin Books.

Miller, S. (1983) *Men and Friendship*. London: Gateway Books.

Millett, K. (1970) *Sexual Politics*. Garden City, NY: Doubleday.

Mills, A. J. and Tancred, P. (eds) (1992) *Gendering Organizational Analysis*. London: Sage.

Mirande, A. (1988) Chicano fathers: traditional perceptions and current realities, in: P. Bronstein and C. P. Cowan (eds), *Fatherhood Today: Men's Changing Role in the Family*. New York: John Wiley.

Mirande, A. (1997) *Hombres Machos: Masculinity and Latino Culture*. Boulder, Colo.: Westview Press.

Misztal, B. A. (1998) *Trust in Modern Societies*. Cambridge: Polity.

Misztal, B. A. (2001) Trusting the professional: a managerial discourse for uncertain times, in: M. Dent and S. Whitehead (eds), *Managing Professional Identities*. London: Routledge.

Mitchell, J. (1976) *Psychoanalysis and Feminism*. Harmondsworth: Penguin.

Mohanty, C. T., Russo, A. and Lourdes, T. (eds) (1991) *Third World Women and the Politics of Feminism*. Bloomington: Indiana University Press.

Moi, T. (1985) Power, sex and subjectivity: feminist reflections on Foucault, *Paragraph*, 5, pp. 95–102.

Moir, A. and Jessell, D. (1989) *Brain Sex: The Real Difference Between Men and Women*. London: Mandarin.

Monaghan, E. P. and Glickman, S. E. (1992) Hormones and aggressive behaviour, in: J. B. Becker, S. M. Breedlove and D. Crews (eds), *Behavioural Endocrinology*. Cambridge, Mass.: MIT Press.

Moodley, R. (1999) Masculine/managerial mask and the 'other' subject, in: S. Whitehead and R. Moodley (eds), *Transforming Managers: Gendering Change in the Public Sector*. London: UCL Press.

Moodley, R. (2000) Representation of subjective distress in black and ethnic minority patients: constructing a research agenda, *Counselling Psychology Quarterly*, 13:2, pp. 159–74.

Moore, R. and Gillette, D. (1991) *King, Warrior, Magician, Lover: Rediscovering the Archetypes of the Mature Masculine*. New York: HarperCollins.

Moore, R. and Gillette, D. (1992) *The King Within: Accessing the King in the Male Psyche*. New York: William Morrow.

More, K. and Whittle, S. (1999) *Reclaiming Gender*. London: Continuum Publishing.

Morgan, D. H. J. (1990) Issues of critical sociological theory: men in families, in: J. Sprey (ed.), *Fashioning Family Theory*. London: Sage.

Morgan, D. (1992) *Discovering Men*. London: Routledge.

Morgan, D. (1993) You too can have a Body like Mine: reflections on the male body and masculinities, in: S. Scott and D. Morgan (eds), *Body Matters*. London: The Falmer Press.

Morgan, D. (1994) Theater of war: combat, the military, and masculinities, in: H. Brod and M. Kaufman (eds), *Theorizing Masculinities*. Thousand Oaks, Calif.: Sage.

Morgan, D. H. J. (1996a) *Family Connections*. Cambridge: Polity.

Morgan, D. (1996b) The gender of bureaucracy, in: Collinson, D. L. and Hearn, J. (eds), *Men as Managers, Managers as Men*. London: Sage.

Morgan, D. H. J. (2001) Family, gender and masculinities, in: S. M. Whitehead and F. J. Barrett (eds), *The Masculinities Reader*. Cambridge: Polity.

Morris, L. (1990) *The Workings of the Household*. Cambridge: Polity.

Morris, L. (1999) The household and the labour market, in: G. Allan (ed.), *The Sociology of the Family: A Reader*. Oxford: Blackwell.

Mosse, G. L. (1996) *The Image of Man: The Creation of Modern Masculinity*. New York: Oxford University Press.

Mouffe, C. (1992) Feminism, citizenship and radical democratic politics, in: J. Butler and J. W. Scott (eds), *Feminists Theorize the Political*. New York: Routledge.

Mouffe, C. (ed.) (1996) *Deconstruction and Pragmatism*. London: Routledge.

Mudde, C. (2000) *The Ideology of the Extreme Right*. Manchester: Manchester University Press.

Mulvey, L. (1989) *Visual and Other Pleasures*. Basingstoke: Macmillan.

Munoz, J. E. (1997) Photographies of mourning, in: H. Stecopoulos and M. Uebel (eds), *Race and the Subject of Masculinities*. Durham, NC: Duke University Press.

Murphy, R. (1988) *Social Closure: The Theory of Monopolization and Exclusion*. Oxford: Clarendon Press.

Murray, C. (1990) *The Emerging British Underclass*. London: Institute of Economic Affairs Health & Welfare Unit.

Nardi, P. M. (ed.) (1992a) *Men's Friendships*. Thousand Oaks, Calif.: Sage.

Nardi, P. M. (1992b) Seamless souls: an introduction to men's friendships, in: P. M. Nardi (ed.), *Men's Friendships*. Thousand Oaks, Calif.: Sage.

Nardi, P. M. (1999) *Gay Men's Friendships: Invincible Communities*. Chicago, Ill.: University of Chicago Press.

Nardi, P. M. (ed.) (2000) *Gay Masculinities*. Thousand Oaks, Calif.: Sage.

National Centre for Social Research (NCSR) (2000) *British Social Attitudes Survey: Who Shares New Labour Values? (16th Report 1999/00)*. London: Ashgate Press.

National Family and Parenting Institute (NFPI) (2000) *Is Britain Family Friendly?* London: NFPI.

Nature (2001) The human genome, 409: 6822 (15 February).

Nead, L. (1990) *Myths of Sexuality: Representation of Women in Victorian Britain*. Oxford: Basil Blackwell.

Nelson, D. D. (1998) *National Manhood: Capitalist Citizenship and the Imagined Fraternity of White Men*. London: Duke University Press.

Newburn, T. and Stanko, E. A. (eds) (1994) *Just Boys Doing Business? Men, Masculinities and Crime*. London: Routledge.

Newsome, D. (1961) *Godliness and Good Learning*. London: Routledge.

Nicholson, L. J. (ed.) (1990) *Feminism/Postmodernism*. New York: Routledge.

Nicholson, L. and Seidman, S. (eds) (1996) *Social Postmodernism: Beyond Identity Politics*. Cambridge: Cambridge University Press.

Nietzsche, F. (1973) *Beyond Good and Evil*. Harmondsworth: Penguin.

Nixon, S. (1997) Exhibiting masculinity, in: S. Hall (ed.), *Representation: Cultural Representations and Signifying Practices*. London: Sage.

Nowatzki, R. (1999) 'Sublime patriots': black masculinity in three African-American novels, *The Journal of Men's Studies*, 8:1 (Fall), pp. 59–72.

Oakley, A. (1974) *Housewife*. London: Allen Lane.

Oakley, A. (1974) *Women's Work: The Housewife, Past and Present*. New York: Pantheon Books.

Oakley, A. (1998) Strange familiar territory, *The Times Higher Education Supplement*, 8 May, p. 22.

O'Brien, M. (1983) *The Politics of Reproduction*. London: Routledge & Kegan Paul.

O'Connell Davidson, J. and Layder, D. (1994) *Methods, Sex and Madness*. London: Routledge.

O'Doherty, D. and Willmott, H. (2001) Debating labour process theory: the issue of subjectivity and the relevance of poststructuralism, *Sociology*, 35:2, pp. 457–76.

Office of National Statistics (ONS) (1997) *Living in Britain: Results from the 1995 General Household Survey*. London: HMSO.

Office of National Statistics (1998) *National Earnings Survey*. London: The Stationery Office.

Office of National Statistics (1999) *Social Focus on Older People*. London: The Stationery Office.

Office of National Statistics (2000) *Social Trends 30*. London: The Stationery Office.

Office of National Statistics (2001) *Marriages in 1999 – England and Wales*. London: The Stationery Office.

O'Neill, J. (1985) *Five Bodies*. Ithaca, NY: Cornell University Press.

O'Neill, M. (2000) *Prostitution and Feminism: Towards a Politics of Feeling*. Cambridge: Polity.

Ortner, S. B. and Whitehead, H. (eds) (1981) *Sexual Meanings: The Cultural Construction of Gender and Sexuality*. Cambridge: Cambridge University Press.

Ozga, J. and Deem, R. (2000) Carrying the burden of transformation: the experiences of women managers in UK higher and further education, *Discourse: Studies in the Cultural Politics of Education*, 21:2, pp. 141–53.

Pahl, R. (1995) *After Success: Fin-de-Siècle Anxiety and Identity*. Cambridge: Polity.

Pahl, R. (2000) *On Friendship*. Cambridge: Polity.

Palmer, C. T. and Thornhill, R. (2000) *A Natural History of Rape: The Biological Bases of Sexual Coercion*. Cambridge, Mass.: MIT Press.

Parker, S. (1983) *Leisure and Work*. London: Unwin Hyman.

Parsons, T. (1951) *The Social System*. New York: The Free Press.

Parsons, T. (1969) *Politics and Social Structure*. New York: The Free Press.

Parsons, T. and Bales, R. F. (1955) *Family, Socialization and Interaction Process*. New York: The Free Press.

Pateman, C. (1983) Feminist critiques of the public/private dichotomy, in: S. I. Benn and F. Gauss (ed.), *Public and Private in Social Life*. London: Croom Helm.

Pateman, C. (1988) *The Sexual Contract*. Cambridge: Polity.

Paxman, J. (1999) *The English: A Portrait of a People*. London: Penguin.

Paya, M. (2000) *Women, Work and Islamism*. London: Zed Books.

Pease, B. (2000) *Recreating Men: Postmodern Masculinity Politics*. London: Sage.

Pecora, N. (1992) Superman/superboys/supermen: the comic book hero as socializing agent, in: S. Craig (ed.), *Men, Masculinity, and the Media*. Thousand Oaks, Calif.: Sage.

Petersen, A. (1998) *Unmasking the Masculine: 'Men' and 'Identity' in a Sceptical Age*. London: Sage.

Phelan, P. (1993) *Unmarked: The Politics of Performance*. London: Routledge.

Phillips, A. (1993) *The Trouble With Boys: Parenting the Men of the Future*. London: Pandora.

Phillips, M. (1999) *The Sex-Change Society: Feminised Britain and the Neutered Male*. London: The Social Market Foundation.

Pilcher, J. (1999) *Women in Contemporary Britain: An Introduction*. London: Routledge.

Pinker, S. (1998) *How the Mind Works*. London: Penguin.

Pleck, J. H. (1976) The male sex role: problems, definitions, and sources of change, *Journal of Social Issues*, 32, pp. 155–64.

Pleck, J. H. (1981) *The Myth of Masculinity*. Cambridge, Mass.: MIT Press.

Pleck, J. H. (1995) The gender role strain paradigm: an update, in: R. F. Levant and W. S. Pollack (eds), *A New Psychology of Men*. New York: BasicBooks.

Pleck, J. H. and Sawyer, J. (eds) (1974) *Men and Masculinity*. Englewood Cliffs, NJ: Prentice-Hall.

Pollert, A. (1996) Gender and class revisited; or, the poverty of 'patriarchy', *Sociology*, 30:4, pp. 639–60.

Pope, G. H., Phillips, K. A. and Olivardia, R. (eds) (2000) *The Adonis Complex: The Secret Crisis of Male Body Obsession*. New York: Free Press.

Porta, D. D. and Diani, M. (1999) *Social Movements: An Introduction*. Oxford: Blackwell.

Price, J. and Shildrick, M. (eds) (1999) *Feminist Theory and the Body: A Reader*. Edinburgh: Edinburgh University Press.

Prichard, C. (2000) *Making Managers in Universities and Colleges*. Buckingham: Open University Press.

Prosser, J. (1998) *Second Skins: The Body Narratives of Transsexuality*. New York: Columbia University Press.

Purvis, T. and Hunt, A. (1993) Discourse, ideology, discourse, ideology, discourse, ideology . . . , *Sociology*, 44:3, pp. 473–99.

Quam-Wickham, N. (1999) Rereading man's conquest of nature: skill, myths, and the historical construction of masculinity in Western extractive industries, *Men and Masculinities*, 2:2, pp. 135–51.

Rabinow, P. (ed.) (1991) *The Foucault Reader*. London: Penguin Books.

Rajchman, J. (ed.) (1995) *The Identity in Question*. New York: Routledge.

Ramazanoglu, C. (1992) On feminist methodology: male reason versus female empowerment, *Sociology*, 26:2, pp. 202–12.

Ramazanoglu, C. (ed.) (1993) *Up Against Foucault: Explorations of Some Tensions Between Foucault and Feminism*. London: Routledge.

Rankin, A. (2000) 'PC', sexual orientation, identity; e-mail correspondence received 25 February.

Redstockings Manifesto (1970) in: L. B. Tanner (ed.), *Voices from Women's Liberation*. New York: Signet, NAL.

Rendall, J. (1985) *The Origins of Modern Feminism: Women in Britain, France and the United States, 1780–1860.* London: Macmillan.

Renzetti, C. M. and Curran, D. J. (1999) *Women, Men, and Society.* Boston, Mass.: Allyn and Bacon.

Reskin, B. and Padavic, I. (1994) *Women and Men at Work.* Thousand Oaks, Calif.: Pine Forge Press.

Rich, A. (1976) *Of Woman Born: Motherhood as Experience and Institution.* New York: W.W. Norton.

Rich, A. (1980) Compulsory heterosexuality and lesbian existence, *Signs*, 5, pp. 631–60.

Ricoeur, P. (1980) Narrative time, *Critical Enquiry*, 7:1, pp. 160–80.

Ricoeur, P. (1992) *Oneself as Another.* Chicago, Ill.: Chicago University Press.

Rifkin, J. (1996) *The End of Work.* New York: Putnam.

Robinson, S. (2000) *Marked Men: White Masculinity in Crisis.* New York: Columbia University Press.

Rodman, S. (2000) Hip-hop homophobia: in a genre known for its misogynistic lyrics, big name artists also are giving gays a bad rap, *www.bostonherald.com/entertainment/music*, 27 July.

Rogers, L. (2000) *Sexing the Brain*, London: Weidenfeld and Nicolson.

Rojek, C. (1985) *Capitalism and Leisure Theory.* London: Tavistock.

Rojek, C. (1995) *Decentring Leisure: Rethinking Leisure Theory.* London: Sage.

Roper, M. (1994) *Masculinity and the British Organization Man since 1945.* Oxford: Oxford University Press.

Roper, M. and Tosh, J. (eds) (1991) *Manful Assertions: Masculinities in Britain since 1800.* London: Routledge.

Rose, H. (2000) Colonising the social sciences?, in: H. Rose and S. Rose (eds), *Alas, Poor Darwin.* London: Jonathan Cape.

Rose, H. and Rose, S. (2000a) *Alas, Poor Darwin: Arguments Against Evolutionary Psychology.* London: Jonathan Cape.

Rose, H. and Rose, S. (2000b) All-inclusive intellectual myth, *The Times Higher Educational Supplement*, 14 July.

Rosener, J. B. (1990) Ways women lead, *Harvard Business Review*, November/December, pp. 119–25.

Rossi, A. S. (1977) A biosocial perspective on parenting, *Daedalus*, 106:2, pp. 1–32.

Rowan, J. (1987) *The Horned God.* New York: Routledge & Kegan Paul.

Rowley, H. and Grosz, E. (1990) Psychoanalysis and feminism, in: S. Gunew (ed.), *Feminist Knowledge: Critique and Construct.* London: Routledge.

Rubery, J. (1998) *Women and European Employment.* London: Routledge.

Rubin, G. (1984) Thinking sex: notes for a radical theory of the politics of sexuality, in: C. S. Vance (ed.), *Pleasure and Danger: Exploring Female Sexuality*. London: Routledge.

Rubin, L. (1985) *Just Friends: The Role of Friendship in Our Lives*. New York: Harper & Row.

Rutherford, J. (1992) *Men's Silences: Predicaments in Masculinity*. London: Routledge.

Rutherford, J. (1997) *Forever England: Reflections on Masculinity and Empire*. London: Lawrence & Wishart.

Rutherford, J. (1999) *I Am No Longer Myself Without You: An Anatomy of Love*. London: Flamingo.

Sabo, D. and Gordon, D. F. (eds) (1995) *Men's Health and Illness*. Thousand Oaks, Calif.: Sage.

Saco, D. (1992) Masculinity as signs: poststructuralist feminist approaches to the study of gender, in: S. Craig (ed.), *Men, Masculinity, and the Media*. Thousand Oaks, Calif.: Sage.

Sage, G. H. (1998) *Power and Ideology in American Sport*. Champaign, Ill.: Human Kinetics.

Salisbury, J. and Jackson, D. (1996) *Challenging Macho Values: Practical Ways of Working with Adolescent Boys*. London: The Falmer Press.

Sarup, M. (1993) *Post-Structuralism and Postmodernism*, 2nd Edn. New York: Harvester Wheatsheaf.

Sawicki, J. (1991) *Disciplining Foucault: Feminism, Power, and the Body*. New York: Routledge.

Scase, R. (1999) *Britain Towards 2010*. Swindon: Economic Social Research Council.

Schwalbe, M. (1996) *Unlocking the Iron Cage: The Men's Movement, Gender Politics, and American Culture*. Oxford: Oxford University Press.

Science Magazine (2001) The human genome, 291:5507 (16 February).

Scott, S. and Morgan, D. (eds) (1993) *Body Matters*. London: The Falmer Press.

Scraton, S. (ed.) (1999) The big ghetto: gender, sexuality and leisure, *Leisure Studies* (special issue), 18, pp. 157–265.

Scraton, S. and Talbot, M. (1989) A response to 'Leisure, lifestyle and status: a pluralist framework for analysis', *Leisure Studies*, 9, pp. 249–61.

Scully, D. (1990) *Understanding Sexual Violence*. Boston: Unwin Hyman.

Sedgwick, E. K. (1994) *Epistemology of the Closet*. London: Penguin.

Segal, L. (1997) *Slow Motion: Changing Masculinities, Changing Men*. London: Virago.

Segal, L. (1999) *Why Feminism? Gender, Psychology, Politics*. Cambridge: Polity.

Seidler, V. J. (ed.) (1992a) *Men, Sex and Relationships: Writings from Achilles Heel*. London: Routledge.

Seidler, V. J. (1992b) Rejection, vulnerability and friendship, in: P. M. Nardi (ed.), *Men's Friendships*. Thousand Oaks, Calif.: Sage.

Seidler, V. J. (1994a) *Unreasonable Men: Masculinity and Social Theory*. London: Routledge.

Seidler, V. J. (1994b) *Recovering the Self: Morality and Social Theory*. London: Routledge.

Seidler, V. J. (1997) *Man Enough: Embodying Masculinities*. London: Sage.

Seidman, S. (1996) *Contested Knowledge: Social Theory in the Postmodern Era*. Cambridge, Mass.: Blackwell.

Seltzer, M. (1998) *Serial Killers: Death and Life in America's Wound Culture*. New York: Routledge.

Sennett, R. (1998) *The Corrosion of Character: The Personal Consequences of Work in the New Capitalism*. New York: W.W. Norton.

Sewell, T. (1997) *Black Masculinities and Schooling: How Black Boys Survive Modern Schooling*. Stoke-on-Trent: Trentham Books.

Sexualities (1998) Transgender in Latin America (special issue), 1:3, pp. 259–384.

Shain, F. (2000) Culture, survival and resistance: theorising young Asian women's experiences and strategies in contemporary British schooling and society, *Discourse: Studies in the Cultural Politics of Education*, 21:2, pp. 155–74.

Shaw, S. M. (1985) Gender and leisure: an examination of women's and men's everyday experience and perceptions of family time, *Journal of Leisure Research*, 17:4, pp. 266–82.

Sheldon, S. (1999) Reconceiving masculinity: imagining men's reproductive bodies in law, *Journal of Law and Society*, 26:2, pp. 129–49.

Sheldon, S. (2000) 'Sperm bandits': birth control fraud and the battle of the sexes. Paper presented to the Social Science Research Seminar on Gender, Keele University, 15 November.

Shelton, B. A. (1992) *Women, Men and Time*. New York: Greenwood.

Shelton, B. A. and John, D. (1993) Ethnicity, race, and difference: a comparison of white, black, and Hispanic men's household labor time, in: J. C. Hood (ed.), *Men, Work, and Family*. Thousand Oaks, Calif.: Sage.

Shildrick, M. and Price, J. (1999) Breaking the boundaries of the broken body, in: J. Price and M. Shildrick (eds), *Feminist Theory and the Body: A Reader*. Edinburgh: Edinburgh University Press.

Shilling, C. (1993) *The Body and Social Theory*. London: Sage.

Shorter, E. (1984) *A History of Women's Bodies*. Harmondsworth: Pelican.

Silva, E. B. and Smart, C. (eds) (1999) *The New Family?* London: Sage.

Silverman, K. (1992) *Male Subjectivity at the Margins*. New York: Routledge.

Simon, W. (1996) *Postmodern Sexualities*. London: Routledge.

Sinclair, A. (2000) Teaching managers about masculinities: are you kidding?, *Management Learning*, 31:1, pp. 83–101.

Sinfield, A. (1998) *Gay and After*. London: Serpent's Tail.

Singh, R. (1998) *Gender Autonomy in Western Europe: An Imprecise Revolution*. London: Macmillan.

Singh, V. and Vinnicombe, S. (2000) Gender meanings of commitment from high technology engineering managers in the United Kingdom and Sweden, *Gender, Work and Organization*, 7:1, pp. 1–19.

Sinha, I. (1999) Giving masculinity a history: some contributions for the historiography of Colonial India, *Gender and History*, 11:3, pp. 445–60.

Skelton, C. (1998) Feminism and research into masculinities and schooling, *Gender and Education*, 10:2, pp. 217–27.

Smith, C. D. (1998) 'Men don't do this sort of thing': a case study of the social isolation of househusbands, *Men and Masculinities*, 1:2, pp. 138–72.

Smith, D. E. (1988) *The Everyday World as Problematic: A Feminist Sociology*. Milton Keynes: Open University Press.

Smith, J. (2000) So the British have become atheists: thank God for that, *The Guardian*, 30 October, p. 20.

Social Trends (1999) 29, London: Government Statistical Service.

Solomon, K. and Szwabo, P. A. (1994) The work-orientated culture: success and power in elderly men, in: E. H. Thompson, Jr (ed.), *Older Men's Lives*. Thousand Oaks, Calif.: Sage.

Stanko, E. A. (2000) The day to count: a snapshot of the impact of domestic violence in the UK, *www.domesticviolencedata.org*, October.

Stanley, L. (1982) 'Male needs': the problems and pitfalls of working with gay men, in: S. Friedman and E. Sarah (eds), *On the Problem of Men: Two Feminist Conferences*. London: Women's Press.

Stanley, L. (ed.) (1997) *Knowing Feminisms*. London: Sage.

Stanley, L. and Wise, S. (1993) *Breaking Out Again: Feminist Ontology and Epistemology*. London: Routledge.

Staples, R. (1982) *Black Masculinity: The Black Man's Role in American Society*. San Francisco, Calif.: Black Scholar Press.

Staples, R. (1986) Black male sexuality, *Changing Men*, 17 (Winter): 3–4, p. 46.

Staples, R. (1995) Health among Afro-American males, in: D. Sabo and D. F. Gordon (eds), *Men's Health and Illness*. Thousand Oaks, Calif.: Sage.

Staples, R. (1989) Stereotypes of black male sexuality: the facts behind the myths, in: M. S. Kimmel and M. A. Messner (eds), *Men's Lives*. Boston, Mass.: Allyn and Bacon.

Stecopoulos, H. and Uebel, M. (eds) (1997) *Race and the Subject of Masculinities*. Durham, NC: Duke University Press.

Stoltenberg, J. (1977) Toward gender justice, in: J. Snodgrass (ed.), *A Book of Readings for Men Against Sexism*. Albion, Calif.: Times Change Press.

Stoltenberg, J. (1990) *Refusing to be a Man*. Glasgow: Fontana/Collins.

Stoltenberg, J. (2000) *The End of Manhood: Parables on Sex and Selfhood*. Revised edn. London: UCL Press.

Sullivan, O. (1997) Time waits for no (wo)man: an investigation of the gendered experience of domestic time, *Sociology*, 31:2, pp. 221–39.

Sullivan, O. (2000) The division of domestic labour: twenty years of change?, *Sociology*, 34:3, pp. 437–56.

Summerskill, B. (2000) Daddy's home . . . , *The Observer (Focus)*, 1 October, p. 19.

Suzik, J. R. (1999) 'Building better men': the CCC boy and the changing social ideal of manliness, *Men and Masculinities*, 2:2, pp. 152–79.

Swain, S. (1989) Covert intimacy: closeness in men's friendships, in: B. Risman and P. Schwartz (eds), *Gender and Intimate Relationships*, Belmont, Calif.: Wadsworth.

Swain, S. O. (1992) Men's friendships with women: intimacy, sexual boundaries, and the informant rule, in: P. M. Nardi (ed.), *Men's Friendships*. Thousand Oaks, Calif.: Sage.

Swedin, G. (1996) Modern Swedish fatherhood: the challenges and the opportunities, *Reproductive Health Matters*, 7.

Sweetman, C. (ed.) (1997) *Men and Masculinity*. Oxford: Oxfam.

Tacey, D. (1997) *Remaking Men: Jung, Spirituality and Social Change*. New York: Routledge.

Talbot, M. and Wimbush, E. (eds) (1989) *Relative Freedoms*. Milton Keynes: Open University Press.

The Guardian (1999) Brave new age dawns for single women, 18 October, p. 6.

The Observer (1999) Ditch your man and be happy, 17 October, p. 13.

The Times Higher Education Supplement (THES) (2000) V. Hammersley in Letters and Opinon, 24 November, p. 19.

Thom, L. (1999) Rhetoric versus reality: why women tend not to apply for senior positions in secondary education, in: S. Whitehead and R. Moodley (eds), *Transforming Managers*. London: UCL Press.

Thomas, C. (1999) Last laughs: Batman, masculinity, and the technology of abjection, *Men and Masculinities*, 2:1, pp. 26–46.

Thomas, J. L. (1994) Older men as fathers and grandfathers, in: E. H. Thompson, Jr (ed.), *Older Men's Lives*. Thousand Oaks, Calif.: Sage.

Thomas, R. (1996) Gendered cultures of performance appraisal: the experience of women academics, *Gender, Work and Organization*, 3:3, pp. 143–55.

Thomas, S. (1999) Reconfiguring the [+]net[+] of desire, in: S. Brewster and

J. Joughin (eds), *Inhuman Reflections: Thinking the Limits of the Human*. Manchester: Manchester University Press.

Thompson, Jr, E. H. (1994) *Older Men's Lives*. Thousand Oaks, Calif.: Sage.

Thompson, E. P. (1967) Time, work discipline and industrial capitalism, *Past and Present*, 38, pp. 615–33.

Thompson, P. (1983) *The Nature of Work*. London: Macmillan.

Thornton, M. (1999) Reducing wastage among men student teachers in primary courses: a male club approach, *Journal of Education for Training*, 25:1, pp. 41–53.

Thrasher, F. (1936) *The Gang*. 2nd edn. Chicago, Ill.: University of Chicago Press.

Threadgold, T. and Cranny-Francis, A. (eds) (1990) *Feminine, Masculine and Representation*. London: Allen & Unwin.

Toch, H. (1998) Hypermasculinity and prison violence, in L. H. Bowker (ed.), *Masculinities and Violence*. Thousand Oaks, Calif.: Sage.

Tolson, A. (1977) *The Limits of Masculinity*. London: Tavistock.

Tong, R. (1993) *Feminist Thought*. London: Routledge.

Tooby, J. and Cosmides, L. (1992) The psychological foundations of culture, in: J. Barkow, L. Cosmides and J. Tooby (eds), *The Adapted Mind: Evolutionary Psychology and the Generation of Culture*. New York: Oxford University Press.

Tosh, J. (1991) Domesticity and manliness in the Victorian middle class, in: M. Roper and J. Tosh (eds), *Manful Assertions: Masculinities in Britain since 1800*. London: Routledge.

Touraine, A. (1988) Modernity and cultural specificities, *International Social Science Journal*, 40, pp. 533–42.

Turner, B. S. (1984) *The Body and Society: Explorations in Social Theory*. Oxford: Basil Blackwell.

Turner, B. S. (1992) *Regulating Bodies: Essays in Medical Sociology*. London: Routledge.

Usher, R. (1998) The story of the self: education, experience and autobiography, in: M. Erben (ed.), *Biography and Education: A Reader*. London: The Falmer Press.

Usher, R. and Edwards, R. (1994) *Postmodernism and Education*. London: Routledge.

Veal, A. J. (1987) *Leisure and the Future*. London: Allen & Unwin.

Wajcman, J. (1998) *Managing Like a Man*. Cambridge: Polity.

Walby, S. (1986) *Patriarchy at Work*. Cambridge: Polity.

Walby, S. (ed.) (1988) *Gender Segregation at Work*. Milton Keynes: Open University Press.

Walker, A. (1976) *Meridian*. New York: Pocket Books.

Walker, K. (1994) 'I'm not friends the way she's friends': ideological constructions and behavioural constructions of masculinity in men's friend-ships, *Masculinities*, 2:2, pp. 38–55.

Walker, P. J. (1991) 'I live but yet not I for Christ liveth in me': men, mas-culinity and the Salvation Army, 1865–90, in: M. Roper and J. Tosh (eds), *Manful Assertions: Masculinites in Britain since 1800*. London: Routledge.

Wallace, M. (1979) *Black Macho*. London: Calder.

Walter, J. A. (1979) *A Long Way from Home*. Exeter: Paternoster Press.

Warin, J., Solomon, Y., Lewis, C. and Langford, W. (1999) *Fathers, Work and Family Life*. London: Joseph Rowntree Foundation and Family Policy Studies Centre.

Waterhouse, R. (1993) The inverted gaze, in: S. Scott and D. Morgan (eds), *Body Matters*. London: The Falmer Press.

Watt, N. (2000) Labour slipping in the equality race, *The Guardian*, 16 October, pp. 10–11.

Wearing, B. (1995) Leisure and resistance in an ageing society, *Leisure Studies*, 14:4, pp. 263–79.

Wearing, B. (1998) *Leisure and Feminist Theory*. London: Sage.

Weber, M. (1930) *The Protestant Ethic and the Spirit of Capitalism*. London: Allen Unwin.

Weedon, C. (1991) *Feminist Practice and Poststructuralist Theory*. Oxford: Blackwell.

Weeks, J. (1991) *Sexuality and its Discontents: Meanings, Myths and Modern Sexualities*. London: Routledge.

Weeks, J. (1995) *Invented Moralities: Sexual Values in an Age of Uncer-tainty*. Cambridge: Polity.

Weeks, J. (2000) *Making Sexual History*. Cambridge: Polity.

Weeks, J. and Porter, K. (eds) (1998) *Between the Acts: Lives of Homosexual Men 1885–1967*. London: Rivers Oram Press.

West, C. (1993) *Race Matters*. Boston: Beacon Press.

West, L. (1996) *Beyond Fragments*. London: Taylor & Francis.

Westwood, S. (1990) Racism, black masculinity and the politics of space, in: J. Hearn and D. H. J. Morgan (eds), *Men, Masculinities and Social Theory*. London: Unwin and Hyman.

Wheaton, B. (2000) 'New Lads'? Masculinities and the 'new sport' partici-pant, *Men and Masculinities*, 2:4, pp. 434–56.

Whitehead, J. (1998) Masculinity, motivation and academic success: a paradox. Paper presented at the *Gendering the Millennium Conference*, University of Dundee, 11–13 September.

Whitehead, S. (1999a) Hegemonic masculinity revisited, *Gender, Work and Organization*, 6:1, pp. 58–62.

Whitehead, S. (1999b) New women, New Labour? Gendered transforma-tions in the House, in: S. Whitehead and R. Moodley (eds), *Transforming Managers*. London: UCL Press.

Whitehead, S. (1999c) From paternalism to entrepreneuralism: the experience of men managers in UK postcompulsory education, *Discourse: Studies in the Cultural Politics of Education*, 20:1, pp. 57–72.

Whitehead, S. (2000) Masculinity: shutting out the nasty bits, *Gender, Work and Organization*, 7:2, pp. 133–7.

Whitehead, S. (2001a) Woman as manager: a seductive ontology, *Gender, Work and Organization*, 8:1, pp. 84–107.

Whitehead, S. (2001b) Man – the invisible gendered subject, in: S. M. Whitehead and F. J. Barrett (eds), *The Masculinities Reader*. Cambridge: Polity.

Whitehead, S. (2002) Identifying the professional 'man'ager: masculinity, professionalism and the search for legitimacy, in: J. Barry, M. Dent and M. O'Neill (eds), *Gender, Professionalism and Managerial Change: An International Perspective*. London: Macmillan.

Whitehead, S. M. and Barrett, F. J. (eds) (2001) *The Masculinities Reader*. Cambridge: Polity.

Whitehead, S. and Moodley, R. (eds) (1999) *Transforming Managers: Gendering Change in the Public Sector*. London: UCL Press.

Whitson, D. (1990) Sport in the social construction of masculinity, in: M. A. Messner and D. Sabo (eds), *Sport, Men, and the Gender Order*. Champaign, Ill.: Human Kinetics.

Whyte, W. F. (1943) *Street Corner Society: The Social Structure of an Italian Slum*. Chicago, Ill.: Chicago University Press.

Williams, R. (1973) *The Country and the City*. London: Hogarth Press.

Williams, W. L. (1992) The relationship between male–male friendship and male–female marriage: American Indian and Asian comparisons, in: P. M. Nardi (ed.), *Men's Friendships*. Thousand Oaks, Calif.: Sage.

Willis, P. (1977) *Learning to Labour*. Farnborough: Saxon House.

Winnicott, D. W. (1974) *Playing and Reality*. Harmondsworth: Penguin.

Winnicott, D. W. (1986) *Home is Where We Start From*. Harmondsworth: Penguin.

Wittig, M. (1992) *The Straight Mind and Other Essays*. New York: Harvester Wheatsheaf.

Witz, A. (1992) *Professions and Patriarchy*. London: Routledge.

Wolfe, T. (1987) *The Bonfire of the Vanities*. New York: Picador.

Wolmark, J. (ed.) (1999) *Cybersexualities: A Reader on Feminist Theory, Cyborgs and Cyberspace*. Edinburgh: Edinburgh University Press.

Woodward, A. E. (1996) Multinational masculinities and European bureaucracies, in: D. L. Collinson and J. Hearn (eds), *Men as Managers, Managers as Men*. London: Sage.

Wright, R. (1995) *The Moral Animal: Why We are the Way We are: The New Science of Evolutionary Psychology*. New York: Little, Brown & Company.

Wright, R. (1996) The occupational masculinity of computing, in: C. Cheng (ed.), *Masculinities in Organizations*. Thousand Oaks, Calif.: Sage.

Yen, H. (1999) Fight Club. *http://reviews.imdb.com/Reviews/212/21222.*

Young, I. M. (1990) *Throwing Like a Girl and Other Essays in Feminist Philosophy and Social Theory*. Bloomington and Indianapolis: Indiana University Press.

Young, M. (1988) *The Metronome Society: Natural Rhythms and Human Timetables*. London: Thames and Hudson.

Zinberg, D. (2000) E-sisters cast tradition aside, *The Times Higher Education Supplement*, 7 April, p. 9.

Index

Index compiled by Mary Madden